SOMETHIN'S COOKIN' in the MOUNTAINS

discover
the northeast
GEORGIA
MOUNTAINS

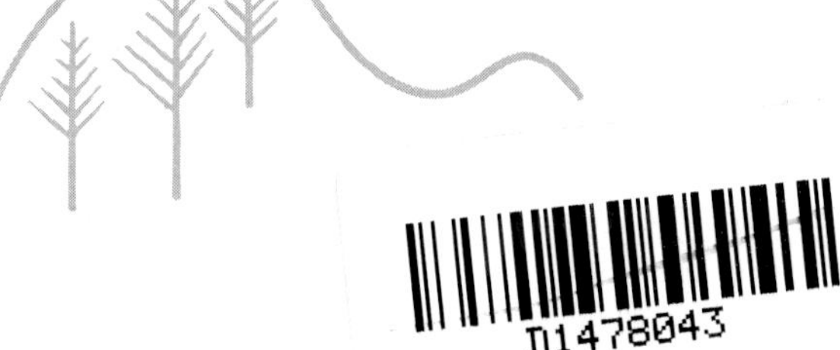

a COOKBOOK GUIDEBOOK
to NORTHEAST GEORGIA

PUBLISHED BY
SOQUE PUBLISHERS
RT. 3, CLARKESVILLE, GEORGIA 30523
(404) 947-3440

SOMETHIN'S COOKIN' in the MOUNTAINS

ORDER BLANKS INCLUDED FOLLOWING INDEX

You may order additional copies or direct inquiries to the publisher:

Soque Publishers
Rt. 3, Clarkesville, GA 30523
(404) 947-3440

First Printing	February 1982
Second Printing	June 1982
Third Printing	March 1983
Fourth Printing	October 1984
Fifth Printing	October 1985
Sixth Printing	September 1986

International Standard Book Number 0-9608770-4-5 Hardcover
International Standard Book Number 0-9608770-5-3 Spiral Bound

Cover photograph of *mark of the potter* by John E. LaRowe

Executive Editors: Cathy and Jay Bucek

Editor: John E. LaRowe

Associate Editors: Sue Williams Keith
Graham Hollis Dellinger
Glendale P. LaRowe
John Kollock

Special Contributors: Herb Rau
Carroll Proctor Scruggs
Robert Coram
Kay Blackwelder
Bruce Galphin
Mary Mac's, Ltd.
The Peasant, Inc.
The Mansion, Inc.

Illustrated by: John Kollock

Staff: Ann Head
Linda Banks Overby
Joanne Greer

ABOUT OUR CONTRIBUTORS

Over 85 local businesses and points of interest have been chosen for this publication. We have covered the area from Dahlonega through Helen and from Cornelia through Dillard with sketches by John Kollock and interesting facts about each one of them. We offer you their favorite recipes; recipes of dishes that they serve in their own homes. We hope that through this cookbook you will get to know us a little better, you will come to know a little more about our beautiful mountains, and you will want to visit us a little more often—or come to live here in our gentle hills. We love our land, our rivers, our lakes, our mountains, our people and we know that you will, too! Visit us often.

Refer to our cookbook guide and find new places to explore, new roads to travel, new and different places to eat, to stay, or shop, or camp.

Seek them out the next time you plan a visit to the beautiful Northeast Georgia mountains. Bring your copy of this cookbook guide with you when you visit us and really use it as a guide for road numbers, locations of restaurants, shops or motels or telephone numbers to call for reservations. They are all here—here in SOMETHIN'S COOKIN' in the MOUNTAINS.

Herb Rau, is a freelance travel writer, cook and gourmet columnist for dozens of newspapers, magazines and the *Atlanta Magazine.* The Raus have lived in the Sautee-Nacooche Valley since his retirement from the Miami News and his articles about his new home and about his travels when away from it have appeared in publications throughout the free world. You will learn why he chose northeast Georgia as his retirement home.

Carroll Proctor "Scoop" Scruggs, who has semiretired to the Helen area, has written for print all of his life. He wrote and took the photographs for *From Plum Orchard to Plum Nelly.* He also wrote *Georgia Historical Markers* and his latest, *History of Helen,* is a best seller in our area. Scoop tells us why he chose Helen as his place to live.

Robert Coram is a feature writer of in depth, investigative articles for *The Atlanta Journal, Atlanta Constitution, the Atlanta Magazine, The New York Times* and many more. Learn why he loves and visits our beautiful Northeast Georgia mountains.

Kay Blackwelder is a veteran science teacher who has made environmental education exciting and real to thousands of children of the Atlanta Public Schools. Kay has served several years as a member of the board of directors and officer of the Outdoor Activity Center in Atlanta, Georgia. This organization is dedicated to promoting the love of and respect for the out-of-doors. It serves the people of Atlanta but especially the inner-city youth. The Blackwelder's spend much of their leisure time in their travel trailer in the beautiful Northeast Georgia mountains.

TABLE OF CONTENTS

ALPHABETICAL LISTING OF CONTRIBUTORS

ADAMS' RIB—US 441 South, Clarkesville, Georgia 30523 (404) 754-4568. Page 16

ANDY'S TROUT FARMS—Betty's Creek Road, P.O. Box 129, Dillard, Georgia 30537 (404) 746-2550. Page 80

ANTIQUES OF DAHLONEGA, LTD.—116 North Park, Box 2046, Dahlonega, Georgia 30533 (404) 864-3637. Page 168

APPLEGATE GIFTS—US 441 By-Pass, P.O. Box 249, Cornelia, Georgia 30531 (404) 778-2220. Page 20

BABYLAND GENERAL™ HOSPITAL—19 Underwood Street, Cleveland, Georgia 30528 (404) 865-5164. Page 150

BANK OF CLAYTON—Savannah Street, P.O. Box 406, Clayton, Georgia 30525 (404) 782-4555. Page 82

BAVARIAN BROOK LODGE—1 Brook Lane, P.O. Box 333, Helen, Georgia 30545 (404) 878-2840. Page 214

BETTY'S COUNTRY STORE—Main Street, Helen, Georgia 30545 (404) 878-2943. Page 176

BOAT HOUSE STUDIO—Lake Rabun Road, Box A-81, Route 1, Lakemont, Georgia 30552 (404) 782-5622. Page 86

CASTLE, THE—Main Street at the river, Helen, Georgia 30545 (404) 878-3140. Page 216

CHATTAHOOCHEE MOTEL—Main Street, Helen, Georgia 30545 (404) 878-2184. Page 178

CHEESE HOOP—Old Street, P.O. Box 123, Helen, Georgia 30545 (404) 878-2924. Page 180

CHEROKEE LANDING, INC.—Route 1, Lake Burton, Clarkesville, Georgia 30523 (404) 947-3411. Page 24

CHIK'N COOP—US 441 South, P.O. Box 1156, Clayton, Georgia 30525 (404) 782-3437. Page 90

CLOTHES CONNECTION I and II—Horsey Ducky Plaza and White Horse Square, Helen, Georgia 30545 (404) 878-2734. Page 192

CO-OP CRAFT STORE—P.O. Box 67, Tallulah Falls, Georgia 30573 (404) 754-6810. Page 92

COPE-CREST—Betty's Creek Road, P.O. Box 129, Dillard, Georgia 30537 (404) 746-2134. Page 118

CORNELIA BANK—400 North Main Street, Cornelia, Georgia 30531 (404) 778-2264. Page 28

CRAFTS BY CHANCE—US 441, Farmers Market, P.O. Box 99, Dillard, Georgia 30537 (404) 746-5754. Page 94

FASHION HAUS—Main Street, Helen, Georgia 30545 (404) 878-3321. Page 198

FRED'S FAMOUS PEANUTS—Hwy. 356, Robertstown, Georgia 30545 (404) 878-3124. Page 230

FORREST HILLS MOUNTAIN RESORT—Route 3, GA 52, P.O. Box 510, Dahlonega, Georgia 30533 (404) 864-6456. Page 154

GOURDCRAFT ORIGINALS—Blue Creek, P.O. Box 412, Cleveland, Georgia 30528 (404) 865-4048. Page 158

GRANDPA WATTS' MILL—GA 197, Route 3, Clarkesville, Georgia 30523 (404) 947-3440. Page 98

HABERSHAM ANTIQUE SHOP—Grant Street, P.O. Box 643, Clarkesville, Georgia 30523 (404) 754-6138. Page 36

HABERSHAM CHAMBER OF COMMERCE—Railroad Depot, P.O. Box 366, Cornelia, Georgia 30531 (404) 778-4654. Page 38

HABERSHAM HARDWARE—214 Front Street, Cornelia, Georgia 30531 (404) 778-2224. Page 40

HABERSHAM PLANTATION MARKETPLACE—Beaver Dam Road, P.O. Box 786, Clarkesville, Georgia 30523 (404) 754-6225. Page 42

HALLS BOAT HOUSE—Lake Rabun Road, P.O. Box 36, Lakemont, Georgia 30552 (404) 782-4981. Page 102

HAMPTON'S FORGE—US 19 North, 105 Trahlyta Trail, Dahlonega, Georgia 30533 (404) 864-7393. Page 160

HANSEL & GRETEL CANDY KITCHEN—Main Street, Helen, Georgia 30545 (404) 878-2443. Page 182

HELEN AREA CHAMBER OF COMMERCE, GREATER—Main Street, Helen, Georgia 30545 (404) 878-2521. Page 218

HELENDORF INN—Main Street, Helen, Georgia 30545 (404) 878-2271. Page 220

HITCHING POST—Route 1, Lake Burton, Clarkesville, Georgia 30523 (404) 947-3612. Page 48

HOFBRAUHAUS INN—North Main Street, Helen, Georgia 30545 (404) 878-2248. Page 184

HOME FEDERAL SAVINGS & LOAN—102 South Washington Street, Clarkesville, Georgia 30523 (404) 754-2189. Page 50

HOUSE OF TYROL—Main Street, P.O. Box 180, Helen, Georgia 30545 (404) 878-2264. Page 188

LAKE RABUN HOTEL—Route 1, Lake Rabun Road, Box 101-A, Lakemont, Georgia 30552 (404) 782-4946. Page 106

LaPRADE'S CAMP, INC.—GA 197 North, Lake Burton, Route 1, Clarkesville, Georgia 30523 (404) 947-3312. Page 52

LAWREL SPECIALTIES—Route 3, Box 80-B, Clarkesville, Georgia 30523 (404) 754-9451. Page 53

MARK OF THE POTTER—GA 197, Route 3, Clarkesville, Georgia 30523 (404) 947-3440. Page 56

MOON VALLEY—Betty's Creek Road, Route 1, Box 680, Rabun Gap, Georgia 30568 (404) 746-2466. Page 108

MOUNTAIN SHADOWS JELLYSTONE PARK—GA 356, P.O. Box 443, Cleveland, Georgia 30528 (404) 865-4742. Page 166

LANDMARKS

John Kollock's family were among the "summer people" who were the early visitors and became settlers of our northeast Georgia mountains. He knows his history "first hand" because it has been handed down by his family and friends. He has preserved a bit of our past in his book *These Gentle Hills* and it is "required reading" for anyone who is deeply interested in our area.

John Kollock, artist, writer and historian has illustrated *SOMETHIN'S COOKIN' in the MOUNTAINS* with delightful sketches of each business and point of interest.

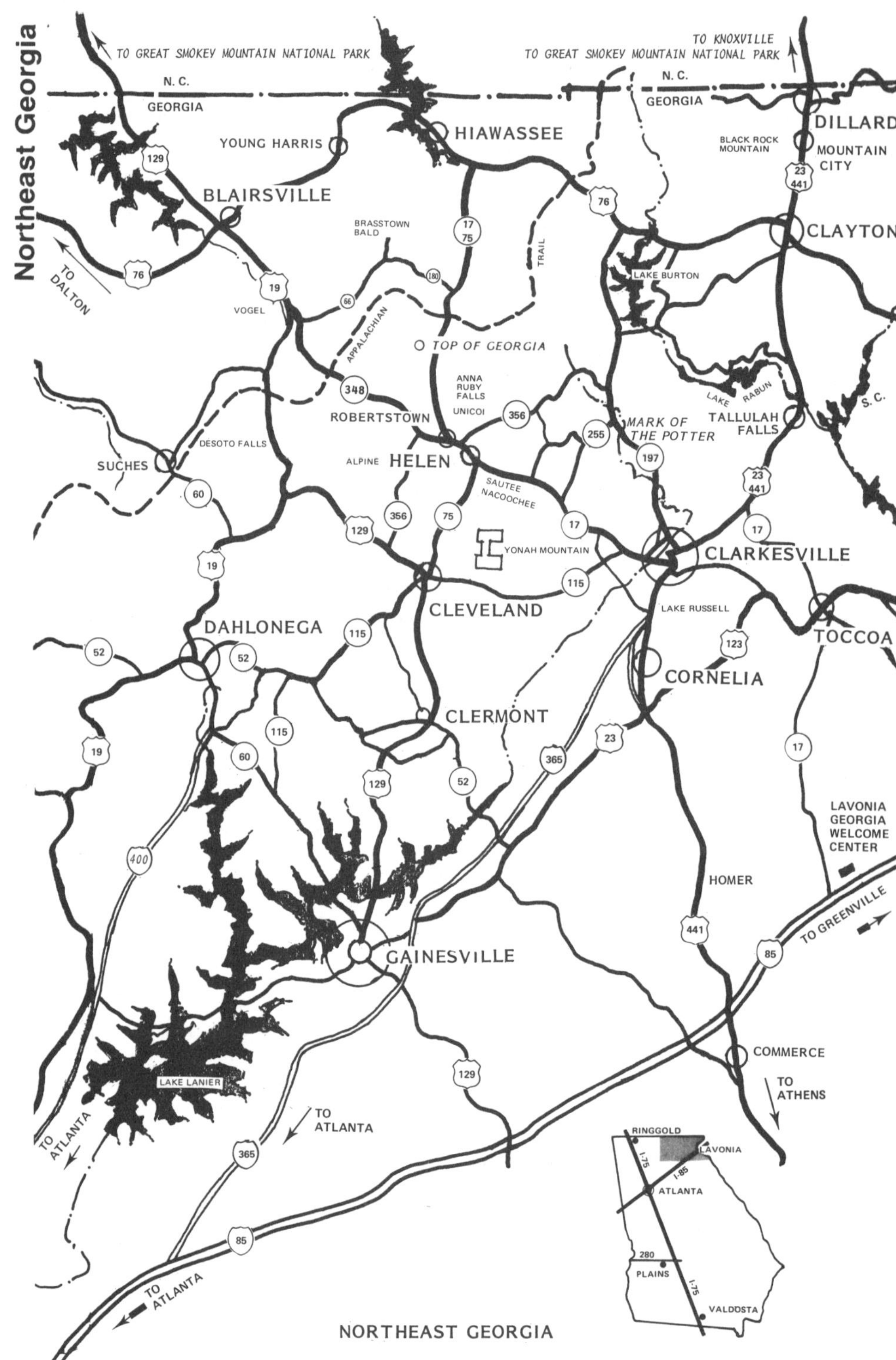
Northeast Georgia
TO GREAT SMOKEY MOUNTAIN NATIONAL PARK
TO KNOXVILLE
TO GREAT SMOKEY MOUNTAIN NATIONAL PARK
N. C.
GEORGIA
N. C.
GEORGIA
YOUNG HARRIS
HIAWASSEE
DILLARD
BLACK ROCK MOUNTAIN
MOUNTAIN CITY
BLAIRSVILLE
CLAYTON
BRASSTOWN BALD
TRAIL
TO DALTON
LAKE BURTON
VOGEL
APPALACHIAN
TOP OF GEORGIA
ANNA RUBY FALLS
UNICOI
ROBERTSTOWN
LAKE RABUN
S. C.
MARK OF THE POTTER
TALLULAH FALLS
DESOTO FALLS
SUCHES
ALPINE
HELEN
SAUTEE NACOOCHEE
YONAH MOUNTAIN
CLARKESVILLE
CLEVELAND
LAKE RUSSELL
DAHLONEGA
TOCCOA
CORNELIA
CLERMONT
LAVONIA GEORGIA WELCOME CENTER
HOMER
TO GREENVILLE
GAINESVILLE
COMMERCE
TO ATHENS
LAKE LANIER
TO ATLANTA
TO ATLANTA
TO ATLANTA
RINGGOLD
LAVONIA
ATLANTA
PLAINS
VALDOSTA
NORTHEAST GEORGIA

RENEWAL

All of us need places where we can go to fill our buckets; places to regain our strength so we can come back into the world and perform our tasks with renewed vigor; safe and secure places we can use as a refuge when the storms of life blow and beat about us.

For me, that place is the Northeast Georgia mountains.
These are old mountains. They are molded and softened and eroded by the eons; much different from the young impetuous mountains out west. The North Georgia mountains are like old shoes, old clothes, or old friends.

The moods of these mountains are many. The lush flower-strewn slopes of spring are far different from the sere woods of winter. But each season has something to offer.

Winter is my favorite. The stark leaf-shorn trees; empty valleys and lonely lakes to me show endurance, perseverance and the sure and certain knowledge that, after a while, spring must come.

I find many qualities in the mountains that can be taken back into the world. For instance, in these time-worn mountains I see great strength, permanence and solidarity. It seems here that the more storms a mountain has known, the softer and rounder and more serene it becomes. Few other places show the healing processes of nature as clearly as do the mountains.

If we are receptive to what the mountains offer, we will absorb whatever it is we need. We will find, as have these gentle hills, that the terrible storms and the lightning and the winds will pass away. And behind them is cleanness and freshness and sharpness and another beginning.

That is why I go to the mountains.

ROBERT CORAM

discover
the northeast
GEORGIA
MOUNTAINS

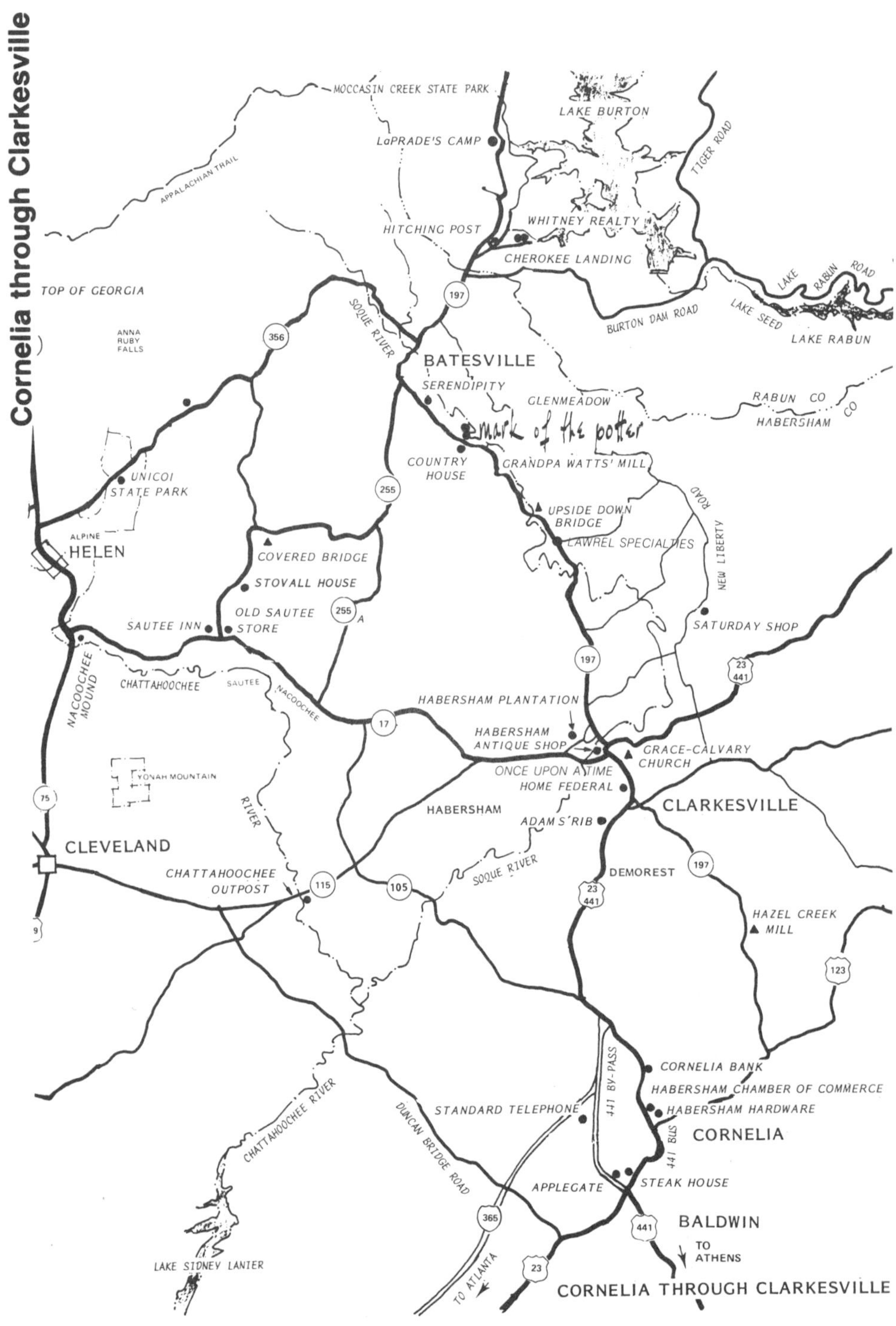
MOCCASIN CREEK STATE PARK
LAKE BURTON
LaPRADE'S CAMP
TIGER ROAD
APPALACHIAN TRAIL
WHITNEY REALTY
HITCHING POST
CHEROKEE LANDING
LAKE RABUN ROAD
TOP OF GEORGIA
197
BURTON DAM ROAD
LAKE SEED
LAKE RABUN
ANNA RUBY FALLS
356
SOQUE RIVER
BATESVILLE
SERENDIPITY
GLENMEADOW
RABUN CO
HABERSHAM CO
mark of the potter
COUNTRY HOUSE
GRANDPA WATTS' MILL
UNICOI STATE PARK
255
ROAD
UPSIDE DOWN BRIDGE
ALPINE
HELEN
COVERED BRIDGE
LAWREL SPECIALTIES
NEW LIBERTY
STOVALL HOUSE
OLD SAUTEE STORE
255 A
SAUTEE INN
SATURDAY SHOP
197
23 441
NACOOCHEE MOUND
CHATTAHOOCHEE
SAUTEE
NACOOCHEE
HABERSHAM PLANTATION
17
HABERSHAM ANTIQUE SHOP
GRACE-CALVARY CHURCH
YONAH MOUNTAIN
ONCE UPON A TIME
HOME FEDERAL
CLARKESVILLE
75
HABERSHAM
ADAM'S RIB
RIVER
CLEVELAND
SOQUE RIVER
197
CHATTAHOOCHEE OUTPOST
115
105
DEMOREST
23 441
HAZEL CREEK MILL
123
CORNELIA BANK
HABERSHAM CHAMBER OF COMMERCE
CHATTAHOOCHEE RIVER
DUNCAN BRIDGE ROAD
STANDARD TELEPHONE
441 BY-PASS
HABERSHAM HARDWARE
441 BUS
CORNELIA
APPLEGATE
STEAK HOUSE
365
441
BALDWIN
TO ATHENS
LAKE SIDNEY LANIER
TO ATLANTA
23
CORNELIA THROUGH CLARKESVILLE

CORNELIA THROUGH CLARKESVILLE

WHERE TO SLEEP

Appletree Inn 778-7678
Baldwin Mountain 778-4061
Charm House 754-9347
Cornelia Motel 778-2186
Fountain Motel 754-2402
Kimsey's Motel 754-2431
Lakeside Motel 754-6022
LaPRADE'S CAMP—Page 52 GA 197 18 MILES NORTH OF CLARKESVILLE. LAKE BURTON 947-3312
Nacoochee Valley Motel 754-6550
Skyland Motel 778-7134
Star Motel 754-4471
UNICOI STATE PARK—Page 266 GA 356 878-2201

WHERE TO EAT

ADAMS' RIB—Page 16 US 441S CLARKESVILLE 754-4568
Bob's Fish & BBQ 778-8383
CHEROKEE LANDING—Page 24 LAKE BURTON, CLARKESVILLE 947-3411
Coffee Shop & Grill 778-4041
Country Inn 778-4293
Dairy Queen & Brazier 778-2233
Dairy Queen Brazier 754-4060
Family Diner, The 754-6677
Fish House 754-6909
Flavor Crisp Chicken 754-2351
Forge, The
Grandma's 778-8322
Grant Kountry Kitchen 754-4373
Gusben's 778-2909
Hardee's 778-0633
Hickory Mountain 754-6012
HITCHING POST—Page 48 LAKE BURTON, CLARKESVILLE 947-3612
Hollywood Diner 754-6598
Huddle House 754-3128
Jimbo's Fine Food 778-8195
Juanita's Cafe 754-9500
Judy's Drive-In 754-9658
Kentucky Fried Chicken 778-8324
LaPRADE'S CAMP—Page 52 GA 197 18 MILES NORTH of CLARKESVILLE, LAKE BURTON 947-3312
Maryland's 754-3114
McDonald's 778-7002
Mountain Inn 754-2415
One Step Beyond 754-6969
P J's Sub Station 778-9898
Pickin Parlor 754-3494
Pic-a-Deli 778-3354
Pizza Hutt 778-3730
Presto Pizza 778-8424
Sandwich Shop, The 754-9050
SAUTEE INN—Page 258 GA 17 at GA 255 SAUTEE 878-2940
Shore's Stew & Que 778-6419
Snack Shack 778-5285
STEAK HOUSE—Page 68, US 441 S BUSINESS NORTH of 23, BALDWIN 778-4351
Tammy's Restaurant
Tastee-Freez 778-7440
Tastee-Freez 754-4328
UNICOI STATE PARK—Page 266 GA 356 878-2201
Western Steer 778-5214

WHERE TO SHOP

ADAMS' RIB—BEVERAGES & CHEESE—Page 16 US 441 S CLARKESVILLE 754-4568
Alexander's 754-6310
Allen's Antiques 754-4484
APPLEGATE—Page 20 US 441 BY-PASS CORNELIA 778-2220
Barn, The 778-7712
Burke's Habersham Homestead . 754-4414
Charm House 754-9347
CHEROKEE LANDING—Page 24 LAKE BURTON, CLARKESVILLE 947-3411
Co-Op Craft Shop 754-2244
Dandelion Craft Shoppe, The 778-1818
Dogwood Antiques 754-9545
Fry's Antiques 754-6976
Glass Barn, The 778-6540
HABERSHAM ANTIQUE SHOP—Page 36 CLARKESVILLE 754-6138
HABERSHAM HARDWARE—Page 40 FRONT ST. CORNELIA 778-2224

WHERE TO SHOP

Habersham Mountain Graphics . . . 754-3059
HABERSHAM PLANTATION MARKETPLACE—Page 42 BEAVER DAM RD. CLARKESVILLE 754-6225
Habersham Vintners 778-5845
Hawkins Bookstore 778-4563
HITCHING POST—Page 48 LAKE BURTON, CLARKESVILLE 947-3612
John Jones Photography 778-9000
LAWREL SPECIALTIES 754-9451
Leather, Etc., Inc.
MARK OF THE POTTER—Page 56 GA 197 10 Miles North of CLARKESVILLE 947-3440
Mountain Photo and Frame 754-2224
OLD SAUTEE STORE—Page 254 GA 17 at GA 255 SAUTEE 878-2281
ONCE UPON A TIME COMPANY 754-5789
One Stop Arts & Crafts Store 778-6344
Owl's Nest 778-5655
Parker Place, The Book Cellar 754-5057
Pine Cone Antiques 754-4304
SATURDAY SHOP—Page 114 P.O. Box 315, CLARKESVILLE, GEORGIA
SERENDIPITY—Page 64 GA 197 North of CLARKESVILLE 947-3643
Station, The 754-6430
Steffi's Store 778-9128
Steppin' Back Antiques 778-1946
Twin Rivers Orchard
UNICOI STATE PARK CRAFT SHOP—Page 266 GA 356 878-2201
WHITNEY REALTY—Page 74 LAKE BURTON, CLARKESVILLE 947-3532
Wind Vane, The—GA 255A 754-9225
Wood Barn 778-3414

SERVICES

CORNELIA BANK—Page 28 N MAIN STREET, CORNELIA 778-2264
HABERSHAM CHAMBER OF COMMERCE—Page 38 RAILROAD DEPOT CORNELIA 778-4654
HOME FEDERAL SAVINGS & LOAN—Page 50 SOUTH WASHINGON ST. CLARKESVILLE 754-2189
STANDARD TELEPHONE—Page 66 INDUSTRIAL BLVD. CORNELIA 778-2201
WHITNEY REALTY—Page 74 LAKE BURTON, CLARKESVILLE 947-3532

WHERE TO CAMP

Appalachian 754-9319
Brooks Campground 947-3773
Lake Russell Camping Area—Open May through August
Moccasin Creek State Park 947-3194
Raymond's Campground 947-3420
Tallulah Falls Resort 754-3242
TERRORA PARK—Page 132 US 441 & 23 TALLULAH FALLS 754-6036
UNICOI STATE PARK—Page 266 GA 356 878-2201
Yahoo Campground 754-6131

WHAT TO DO & SEE

BIG RED APPLE—At Railroad Depot Cornelia, Georgia—Page 38
COVERED BRIDGE—GA 255, Sautee—Page 262
Fish Hatchery—GA 197, 19 miles north of Clarkesville
GRACE CALVARY CHURCH—Corner Green & Wilson, Clarkesville—Page 32
GRANDPA WATT'S MILL—10 miles north of Clarkesville on GA 197—Page 98
HAZEL CREEK MILL—GA 197 South of Clarkesville—Page 46
LAKE BURTON—16 miles north of Clarkesville on GA 197—Page 15
Moccasin Creek State Park—19 miles north of Clarkesville on GA 197
UPSIDE-DOWN BRIDGE—GA 197 8 miles north of Clarkesville—Page 72

LAKE BURTON

Lake Burton is the largest of the six lakes created by the damming of the Tallulah River. It is also the most northern body of water in the group with its headwaters reaching back into the mountain coves to the source of the flow. Of all of the six, Burton still retains the best feeling of isolation and remoteness, in spite of the over 1000 homes that line its many coves. There are several good public boat landings and some outstanding restaurants on the lake shore. To get a real feeling of the spirit of Burton, take an evening trip up the main body of the lake and pause to watch the sunset over the mountain range that forms Tray Mountain to the west.

NOTICE: For your convenience we have listed all of the places to eat and all of the places to sleep in the area covered by this list. Quality is a personal concept and, although we have listed every place to eat or sleep known at the time of printing, some restaurants and some motels we recommend highly, while others do not quite meet our high standards of quality and we assume no responsibility for them. We would suggest that you inquire locally of any of the businesses in bold type listed above for their recommendations.

ADAMS' RIB

You will find an extensive variety of foods delicately prepared for your dining enjoyment at Adams' Rib. At breakfast we feature hot homemade biscuits and gravy, country ham, steak and eggs with hotcakes. Lunchtime brings a buffet of fine meats and vegetables, a salad bar of 25 or more delectable items, and hot homemade soups on those cold wintery days. The menu, which is available at all times, offers steaks cut to order, seafood, barbecue pork and beef ribs, chicken, and a wide variety of other short orders. Banquet rooms are available for private parties and meetings.

Adams' Rib Restaurant, US 441 South,
Clarkesville, Georgia 30523 (404) 754-4568.

COOKED MARINADE FOR GAME

This is used when there is no time for long marinating. When poured hot over the meat, the marinade hastens the flavoring and tenderizing process.

4 bay leaves
½ teaspoon thyme
4 whole cloves
6 whole allspice
1 clove garlic
6 whole peppercorns
1 onion, sliced
2 sprigs parsley, chopped
2 cups dry red wine
1½ ounces brandy

In a mortar, bruise bay leaves, thyme, cloves, allspice, garlic and peppercorns. Place in saucepan. Add remaining ingredients. Bring to a boil and pour over meat. Marinate from 4 to 24 hours, turning occasionally. Yield: 1 pint of marinade.

Harvey Adams
Adams' Rib Restaurant

RAW MARINADE FOR GAME

One ⅘-quart bottle dry red wine
¼ cup red wine vinegar
2 large carrots, sliced
2 large onions, sliced
6 shallots or green onions, chopped
½ teaspoon whole peppercorns
½ teaspoon whole cloves
½ teaspoon juniper berries
½ teaspoon thyme
1 tablespoon salt
4 sprigs parsley
1 bay leaf

Combine all ingredients. Pour over the meat; cover with foil and keep cool. Turn meat several times. Small pieces of meat are usually marinated for 24 hours, larger pieces for 2 to 3 days. If marinade completely covers the meat, turning is not necessary. Some cooks pour a little oil on top of the marinade to seal out the air. Yield: 1 quart marinade.

Harvey Adams
Adams' Rib Restaurant

BAKED SQUASH WITH BLUEBERRIES

4 acorn squash
1 pint frozen blueberries, partially thawed
½ apple, finely diced
6 tablespoons brown sugar
8 teaspoons butter
½ cup water

Cut squash in half lengthwise and remove seeds. Place in a baking pan that has a cover. Spoon partially thawed blueberries into each squash half. Add a few pieces of apple. Sprinkle the brown sugar over the blueberries and squash and place 1 teaspoon of butter in the center. Pour ½ cup water into the pan, cover, and bake in moderately hot oven, 375 degrees, for 45 minutes; remove cover and bake 15 minutes longer. Yield: 8 servings.

Harvey Adams
Adams' Rib Restaurant

FAMOUS SWEET POTATO PUDDING OF 1828

1 pound sweet potatoes, cooked, peeled
1 cup sugar
½ cup margarine, melted
6 egg yolks, well beaten
1 tablespoon lemon rind, grated
¼ teaspoon mace
1 cup orange juice
6 egg whites, stiffly beaten
¼ cup sugar
1 tablespoon slivered citron

Rub the sweet potatoes through the sieve. Add sugar and margarine. Combine with beaten egg yolks, lemon rind, mace and orange juice. Beat the egg whites until stiff and fold carefully into the sweet potato mixture. Pour the pudding into a well-greased three-quart baking dish. Sprinkle with sugar and citron. Bake in a 350-degree oven for one hour.

Harvey Adams
Adams' Rib Restaurant

BLEU CHEESE DRESSING

4 ounces bleu cheese, crumbled
1 cup sour cream
1 cup mayonnaise
⅓ cup dill pickle vinegar (liquid from jar of dill pickles)
1 garlic clove, crushed
½ teaspoon Worcestershire sauce
¾ teaspoon monosodium glutamate (optional; omit if low sodium diet is a factor)
White pepper to taste

Combine all ingredients and beat with whisk. If desired, a blender or food processor may be used, but in that case reserve about ¼ of the crumbled bleu cheese to add at the end (the lumps are desirable). This dressing is improved by standing an hour or so. It will keep for 3 to 4 days in refrigerator. *A really good bleu cheese salad dressing, but when well chilled it may be used as a dip!*

Kay Blackwelder
Mark of the Potter

PEANUT BUTTER POTATOES

Two 16-ounce cans sweet potatoes
½ cup butter
One 8-ounce can crushed pineapple, including juice
3 eggs
1 cup brown sugar
¼ cup milk
1 large jar crunchy peanut butter

Combine first six ingredients in mixing bowl and beat until fluffy. Heat peanut butter until it will spread. Put ¾ of potato mixture in a 13 x 9-inch casserole; spread all peanut butter over mixture and top with remainder of potato mixture. Bake at 375 degrees for 30 minutes or until center is firm.

Frances Mathis
Home Federal Savings & Loan Association

APPLEGATE

APPLEGATE

Applegate is a unique gift shop offering a wide variety of items and prices for its customers. Owned by Beth Eldridge Cathey, you will find not only unusual and distinctive gifts and accessories, but a relaxed and cheerful atmosphere for both the shopper and browser.

Presently located on the US 441 By-pass, Applegate is the "gift store for all reasons," not only for Habersham countians, but for people from many parts of Georgia, and a growing number of travelers from around the United States. Each purchase, whether "a dime or a diamond," is gift wrapped free of charge, and shipping is available daily. Open Monday through Saturday 9:00 to 5:00.

Applegate, US 441 Cornelia, By-pass,
Cornelia, Georgia 30531, (404) 778-2200.

FOOLPROOF ROAST BEEF

3- to 5-pound eye of round roast
Salad oil

Preheat oven to 300 degrees. Oil roast all over with salad oil. Place unsalted roast on rack in shallow pan. Cook 1 hour at 300 degrees, then lower temperature to lowest setting (usually 150 degrees) and leave meat in oven 12 to 14 hours. It will not hurt the roast to cut part way through to check for doneness. Meat will be pink all the way through. If it is too pink, continue cooking and check in an hour. After meat is completely cool, have it sliced paper thin.

Linda H. Wingate
Applegate

APPLEGATE POTATO SALAD

1 pound bacon
1 pound fresh green beans
3 pounds red new potatoes, unpeeled

Cook bacon, drain and reserve. Cook beans in ½″ boiling salted water 8 to 10 minutes until tender but crisp. Slice potatoes ¼″ thick. Put into another pan of boiling salted water. Heat to second boil; cover; lower heat. Cook 8 to 10 minutes. Drain and combine gently with beans. Make following dressing:

½ cup olive or salad oil
¼ cup tarragon vinegar
¼ cup beef consommé, undiluted
½ cup green onions, chopped
¼ cup fresh parsley, chopped
1 garlic clove, crushed
1 teaspoon salt
1 teaspoon dry mustard
½ teaspoon basil
½ teaspoon tarragon

Mix together. Pour over beans and potatoes, tossing gently. Potatoes will absorb liquid. Let stand at room temperature. Better after 2 to 3 hours or overnight. Before serving, add reserved bacon that has been broken into bite-sized pieces.

Linda H. Wingate
Applegate

ZUCCHINI GOODIES

4 small zucchini, unpeeled and sliced thinly (about 3 cups)
1 cup biscuit mix
½ cup onion, finely chopped
½ cup Parmesan cheese, grated
2 tablespoons parsley, minced
½ teaspoon salt
½ teaspoon seasoned salt
½ teaspoon oregano, dried
½ teaspoon marjoram, dried
Dash of pepper
2 to 5 garlic cloves, finely chopped (depending on your tolerance to garlic!)
½ cup vegetable oil
4 eggs, slightly beaten

Heat oven to 350 degrees. Grease 13 x 9 x 2 oblong pan. Mix all ingredients; spread in pan. Bake about 25 minutes, or until golden brown. Cut into 2 x 1-inch pieces. Yield: 4 dozen.

Beth E. Cathey
Applegate

TOMATO DEMITASSE

This is different and fun when served in demitasse cups with demitasse spoons. It will dress up any meal (even hamburgers) and works well if served before people are seated for dinner.

6 large ripe tomatoes
1 small onion
Salt and pepper to taste

Mix in a blender until smooth. (If fresh tomatoes are unavailable, use drained canned tomatoes.) Refrigerate. When ready to serve, pour into demitasse cups. Add a dollop of the following topping.

1 cup mayonnaise
½ cup sour cream
2 to 3 drops lemon juice
½ to 1 cup crabmeat, picked clean
1 tablespoon chopped chives (or tops of green onions)
½ to 1 teaspoon curry powder
Dash of dill
Capers (optional)

Mix ingredients thoroughly. The flavor improves if it sits 2 to 3 hours. Garnish with capers, if desired.

Linda H. Wingate
Applegate

ASPARAGUS CONGEALED SALAD

1 can asparagus, drained, save juice
1 jar pimentos, diced
1 white onion, grated
1 avocado, diced
1 cup celery, diced
1 cup green pepper, diced
½ cup pecans, chopped
Juice of ½ lemon
¾ cup sugar
1 cup asparagus juice (if you don't have quite one cup, add water to juice to make 1 cup)
½ cup white vinegar
½ teaspoon salt
1 package dry Italian salad dressing
2 tablespoons unflavored gelatin softened in ½ cup water

Mix all ingredients except asparagus juice and gelatin. Heat asparagus juice and gelatin just enough to dissolve gelatin. Add dissolved gelatin mixture to other ingredients, and put into a large ring mold, or a square or oblong dish. Refrigerate until set, and serve with mayonnaise mixed with a little lemon juice.

Beth E. Cathey
Applegate

LAYERED POTATO SALAD

Must be prepared the day before.

8 medium new potatoes
1½ cups mayonnaise
1 cup sour cream
1½ teaspoons horseradish
1 teaspoon celery seed
½ teaspoon salt
1 cup fresh parsley, chopped
2 medium onions, finely minced

Cut potatoes in ⅛-inch slices, and boil in lightly salted water 8 to 10 minutes or until they stick tender. Drain thoroughly. Combine mayonnaise, sour cream, horseradish, celery seed, and salt; set aside. In another bowl mix parsley and onion. In large serving bowl arrange layer of potatoes; salt lightly; cover with layer of mayonnaise-sour cream mixture, then layer of onion mixture. Continue layering, ending with parsley and onion. *Do not stir!* Cover and refrigerate at least 8 hours before serving; 24 hours is even better. Yield: 8 to 10 servings.

VARIATION: You can add layers of chopped sweet pickle, and hard-boiled eggs, if desired . . . a little crumbled bacon is good too. Just be sure anything you add is drained well, and make some extra mayonnaise-sour cream mixture if you add many extras.

Beth E. Cathey
Applegate

CHEROKEE LANDING

Cherokee Landing is Lake Burton's only full-service marina and is located just off GA 197 at the head of Cherokee Cove. The Marina offers both wet and dry boat storage and a complete shop for year-round boat repair and major overhauls. The store offers sandwiches, groceries, sundries, picnic supplies and your favorite beverages for all occasions, plus the only laundromat open 24 hours a day all year. Come and enjoy the most beautiful mountain lake in the world!

Cherokee Landing, Incorporated, Route 1, Lake Burton, Clarkesville, Georgia 30523, (404) 947-3411.

HATTIE'S PIDGEON PEAS AND RICE

1 can Pidgeon peas, or Blackeyed peas
Diced bacon (regular or smoked)
1 small onion, diced
1 tablespoon tomato paste
4 cups water
Salt to taste
2 cups rice, raw

Drain peas, reserving juice. Brown onion with bacon; add tomato paste and peas; stir. Add water, juice from peas and salt. Stir in washed, raw rice and mix well. Place in casserole dish and cook for 1 hour in 300-degree oven. Stir occasionally. Holds well for groups and late meals.

Cynthia Whitney
Cherokee Landing

FISH SOUP

6 strips bacon, cut in pieces
3 onions, diced
4 potatoes, diced
3 stalks celery, diced
1 large can tomatoes
1 cup milk, room temperature
2 cucumbers, sliced, blended with a little milk
Salt and pepper to taste
3 medium-sized whole fish (snapper is great)
2 cups water

Brown bacon in heavy Dutch oven. Remove bacon from pot and add onions, potatoes, celery; heat on medium until onions and celery are clear. Return bacon to pot and add tomatoes and milk. Cook on medium heat until thoroughly heated. Add cucumbers, salt and pepper. Cook slowly for approximately 3 hours. When mixture thickens, add whole fish and water to desired consistency. Cook fish about 20 minutes. Remove whole fish, bone and return fish pieces to soup.

Cynthia Whitney
Cherokee Landing

"LEFTOVER HAM" CASSEROLE

½ small bottle extra dry vermouth or chablis
Mushrooms and juice
2 cloves garlic, minced
2 tablespoons chives or finely chopped onions
1 pint half and half
Salt and pepper to taste
Butter
Leftover ham, cut in chunks
6 hard-cooked eggs, sliced
Seasoned croutons
Parmesan cheese, grated

In heavy skillet place ½ cup vermouth, mushrooms with juice, garlic, chives, half and half. Heat to gentle boil and reduce heat. Add salt and pepper to taste. If needed, thicken with white sauce. Butter casserole; add ham chunks and ½ to ¾ cup vermouth. Place sliced eggs over ham and pour sauce over all. Top with seasoned croutons and Parmesan cheese. Bake in 350-degree oven for 45 minutes.

Cynthia Whitney
Cherokee Landing

AUNT JOHNNIE'S BEEF STEW

½ pound thick bacon, sliced
Stew beef
Potatoes
Carrots
Onions
Celery
Salt and pepper to taste
½ cup water
Parmesan cheese, grated

Line heavy Dutch oven with bacon. Layer cut potatoes, carrots, beef, celery, onions; add salt and pepper. Turn to high heat until bacon smells good. Add water, turn to low heat and simmer for 1 hour. Turn out in large casserole, top with lots of Parmesan cheese and heat until cheese softens. Serve with crusty French bread, a crunchy green salad and a hearty red wine.

Cynthia Whitney
Cherokee Landing

TUNA AND CHAMPAGNE CASSEROLE

¾ cup celery, chopped
¾ cup onions, chopped
½ cup butter
Garlic salt
Salt and pepper to taste
2 cans white tuna in water, drained
1 teaspoon curry powder
1 egg
½ cup champagne or white wine
1 cup sour cream
Potato chips
Spaghetti, cooked, drained

Cook celery and onions in butter with garlic salt, salt and pepper. Remove celery and onion, reserving butter in pan, and mix with tuna. Add curry, egg and wine to sour cream and blend by hand. Pour over tuna and mix. Cook and drain spaghetti; place in casserole and mix with seasoned butter from pan. Pour tuna mixture on spaghetti and toss lightly. Crumble chips on top and bake 30 minutes in 375-degree oven.

Cynthia Whitney
Cherokee Landing

THE MANSION

The grand old mansion built in 1885, in the then popular "high Victorian" style, is now more beautiful than ever. You can still enjoy the splendor of this fine old home by dining in the elegance of yesteryear.

"The Ornaments of a Home are the Friends Who Frequent It" reads the inscription on the stone hearth. In this spirit we invite you to join us at The Mansion.

The Mansion, 179 Ponce de Leon,
Atlanta, Georgia 30308 (404) 876-0727

CREAM OF BROCCOLI SOUP

8 ounces fresh broccoli, finely chopped
1 quart water
1 quart half and half
Pinch of white pepper
¼ teaspoon baking soda
4 cubes of chicken bouillon
12 tablespoons butter
10 tablespoons flour

In a large saucepan combine broccoli, water, half and half, white pepper, baking soda and chicken bouillon; bring to a boil. While waiting for soup to boil, in a small skillet slowly melt butter, adding flour. Stir slowly with a wire whisk making sure there are no lumps. After soup comes to a boil, reduce heat and add butter and flour mixture, stirring in slowly with wire whisk. When soup has reached desired thickness, return to light boil for 5 to 8 minutes. Yield: 12 one-cup servings.

Elizabeth Swearingen
The Mansion

SAUTÉED FILET OF SOLE

Seasoning salt
3 to 4-ounce filet of sole
Flour (for dusting)
1 tablespoon butter
½ teaspoon chopped parsley
Juice from ½ lemon

Sprinkle seasoning salt on the filet and flour on both sides. Put a skillet on a low flame and melt butter. Brown the sole on both sides. Be sure to let the skillet get hot enough so that the sole will brown quickly. When the sole has browned, remove it from the skillet and place on serving plate. To the skillet, add chopped parsley and the lemon juice. Leave on flame about 30 seconds, then pour over sole for additional flavor.

Bill Swearingen
The Mansion

CORNELIA BANK

WE BELIEVE IN PEOPLE . . . . .
Chartered on July 3, 1900, Cornelia Bank is the oldest bank in Habersham County. Cornelia Bank has been a "pioneer" in many respects. We were the first, and to date only, bank in the area to introduce 24-hour banking. In order to strengthen our position in the highly competitive decade ahead, and to better serve the citizens of all the communities in which we are located, we were the first bank in Northeast Georgia to form a bank holding company. Formed in 1981, Community Bankshares, Inc., will enable us to continue to grow, to expand our services and to prosper.

We provide five convenient locations to serve you . . . Cornelia, Demorest, Alto, and our new Clarkesville location. We are extremely proud of the confidence that the people of our area have shown in us over the past 81 years.

WE BELIEVE IN PEOPLE LIKE YOU!

Cornelia Bank, 400 North Main Street,
Cornelia, Georgia 30531 (404) 778-BANK

GOLD BRICKS or "CONGO BARS"

2/3 cup shortening
One 1-pound package brown sugar
3 eggs
3 cups plain flour, sifted
1 1/2 teaspoons baking powder
1 teaspoon salt
1/2 package semi-sweet chocolate morsels (12 ounce package)

Cream shortening and brown sugar. Add all other ingredients and mix. Pour into greased 9 x 13-inch pan. Bake 30 minutes at 350 degrees. Let cool for 10 minutes, then cut into little squares.

Daisy Rickett
Cornelia Bank

BIG MAMA'S POUND CAKE

3 cups sugar
2 cups shortening
4 cups plain flour
10 eggs
1/2 cup butter
1/2 cup sweet milk
1 tablespoon flavoring (your favorite)

Mix sugar and shortening together until creamy. Add 4 cups flour, 1 cup at a time, the eggs 2 at a time. Add butter, milk and flavoring and mix until creamy. Pour into greased and floured tube pan. Beat side of pan with hand to remove bubbles. Bake at 350 degrees for 1 1/2 hours; do not open oven while baking.

Woodie Reems
Cornelia Bank

PEANUT BUTTER COOKIES

1 cup margarine
1 cup crunchy peanut butter
1 cup sugar
1 cup light brown sugar
2 eggs
1 teaspoon vanilla
2 1/2 cups plain flour, sifted
1 1/2 teaspoons soda
1/2 teaspoon salt
Additional sugar

Cream margarine, peanut butter, sugars, eggs, and vanilla. Sift dry ingredients. Add to creamed mixture, mixing well. Form into balls. Roll in sugar. Place on cookie sheet and crisscross with fork. Bake at 350 degrees for 10 minutes. Yield: Approximately 6 dozen.

Linda Smart
Cornelia Bank

FRENCH FRIED FRESH VEGETABLES

Fresh vegetables such as okra, yellow summer squash, zucchini
Vegetable oil
1 cup pancake mix
1 egg, beaten

Wash and cut vegetables into slices, ¼" thick for squash and ¾" long for okra. Heat oil to 375 degrees, preferably in deep fat fryer. Place dry pancake mix in brown paper bag. Dip vegetable slices in beaten egg; drop a few pieces at a time into pancake mix and shake. Place on sheet of waxed paper until you have enough pieces to fry a batch in the oil. Fry until golden brown, remove from oil, place on paper towel; salt, and serve hot!

Phoebe Martin
Cornelia Bank

PEANUT BUTTER CUP FUDGE

Melt together:
1½ cups peanut butter
½ cup margarine

Stir in:
2 cups powdered sugar
1 teaspoon vanilla

Pour mixture into 9-inch square pan.

Spread on top:
6 ounces chocolate chips, melted

Do not refrigerate.

Barbara Holcomb
Cornelia Bank

MOM CARVER'S 24-HOUR SLAW

Large head of cabbage, shredded extremely fine
1 large onion, shredded
1 cup sugar
1 cup cider vinegar
1 teaspoon celery salt
2 teaspoons celery seed
1 tablespoon prepared mustard
Caraway seed, if desired
½ cup salad oil

Cover shredded cabbage and onion with 1 cup sugar; stir well, cover and let stand while making dressing. Bring vinegar, celery salt, celery seed and mustard to boil. Add ½ cup salad oil and bring to boil again. Cool and toss with cabbage mixture. Slaw is better the second day and will keep indefinitely in refrigerator.

Cecil Carver
The Hitching Post

SHRIMP CURRY DIP

1 can frozen cream of shrimp soup
1 small can cocktail shrimp
One 8-ounce package cream cheese
1 clove garlic, crushed (or small amount of garlic powder)
1 can mushrooms, drained, sliced
1 can black olives, pitted, sliced
2 tablespoons sherry
Salt to taste
Curry powder to taste

Combine all ingredients in small covered pan on lowest heat. Stir well. Serve in chafing dish, as dip is much better served quite warm. Yield: 6 to 8 servings.

Suggested additions: ground peanuts, chutney, or shredded boiled eggs.

Minnie Carver
The Hitching Post

GRACE-CALVARY CHURCH

Grace-Calvary Episcopal Church, located in Clarkesville on GA 23-441, is a short side trip well worth the visit by anyone who wants to touch the living past of this area. Clarkesville was the first of the major resort towns in Northeast Georgia. At one time the square and much of Washington Street were taken up with hotels and accommodations for the summer visitor. In 1838 a group of coastal families from Savannah and Charleston organized Grace Church and acquired a lot two blocks off the square. In 1840 the first Bishop of Georgia, Rt. Rev. Stephen Elliott, was elected at a convention in Clarkesville. He returned in 1842 to consecrate the little white frame church which still stands as it was originally built and remains the oldest unaltered Episcopal church building in the state. It was completely restored in 1975 and is now on the National Register of Historic Places.

Grace-Calvary Episcopal Church, Corner Green & Wilson Streets, Clarkesville, GA 30523 (404) 754-2451

ZUCCHINI HORS D'OEUVRES

1 cup biscuit mix
½ cup onion, finely chopped
½ cup Parmesan cheese, grated
2 tablespoons parsley, chopped
½ teaspoon salt
½ teaspoon seasoned salt
½ teaspoon oregano
Pepper and garlic to taste
¼ cup oil
4 eggs, beaten
3 cups zucchini, thinly sliced

Combine ingredients, adding zucchini last. Pour into greased 8 x 11-inch baking dish. Bake for 30 minutes at 350 degrees. Cut into 1-inch squares.

Nancy Irish
Grace-Calvary Episcopal Church

VEAL AND PORK PIE

Pastry:
2 cups flour
Pinch of salt
½ cup butter
3 tablespoons lard
1 egg
Milk

Cut into flour the salt, butter and lard with a pastry blender. Blend in beaten egg and enough milk for firm dough. Chill 1 hour in refrigerator.

Filling:
1 pound lean pork, ground
1 pound lean veal, ground
3 ounces salt pork, ground
1 large onion, chopped
1 clove garlic, chopped fine
2 whole cloves
2 tablespoons parsley, chopped
1 tablespoon celery leaves, chopped
¼ cup boiling water
Salt and pepper

Filling: Grind pork and veal together, add salt pork and grind in. Brown mixture with onion and garlic clove for 3 minutes, stirring occasionally. Add cloves, parsley, celery leaves, boiling water, salt and pepper. Simmer 25 minutes, stirring occasionally. Roll ½ of pastry into 10-inch slope-sided pottery baking dish, add filling and cover with remaining pastry. Cut slits into top. Bake in 450 to 475 degree oven for 15 minutes, then reduce to 350 degrees and bake for another 30 minutes.

Glen LaRowe

APPLE CRISPIE

4 cups apples, sliced
1 teaspoon cinnamon
1 teaspoon salt
¼ cup water
1 tablespoon lemon juice
¾ cup regular flour, sifted
1 cup sugar
⅓ cup butter

Place sliced apples in buttered 10 x 6 x 2-inch baking dish. Sprinkle with cinnamon, salt, water, lemon juice. With fingertips, rub together flour, sugar and butter. Drop mixture over apples. Bake at 350 degrees for 40 minutes. Serve warm with cream or ice cream. Yield: 6 servings.

Alice Driver
Grace-Calvary Episcopal Church

VEGETABLE ASPIC

2 packages lemon gelatin
2 cups boiling water
½ cup cold water
½ cup white vinegar
One 14- to 16-ounce can tiny green peas, drained
One 14- to 16-ounce can French green beans, drained
One 14- to 16-ounce can artichokes, drained, halved or quartered
2 tablespoons onion, chopped
2 tablespoons celery, chopped
2 tablespoons olives, chopped
Salt and pepper to taste

Dissolve gelatin in boiling water; add cold water and vinegar. Chill until partially congealed, then add all other ingredients and pour into mold or 9 x 13 pan. Chill until set. Serve with Vegetable Aspic Dressing.

Dressing:
¾ cup mayonnaise
¾ cup sour cream
1 tablespoon horseradish

Mix well. Yield: 8 to 12 servings.

Mollie Pollitt
Grace-Calvary Episcopal Church

HONEY OF A LAMB

1 lamb shoulder, 5 to 6 pounds
1 cup honey
1 clove garlic, finely chopped
½ teaspoon kelp (sold in health food stores)
½ teaspoon cayenne pepper

Place lamb on broiler rack and broil in preheated 350 to 400 degree oven, turning meat often until it is half done, or meat can be roasted in 325 degree oven. Combine remaining ingredients and brush over both sides of the meat and continue to broil, basting every 10 minutes until meat is tender, a total of about 1¼ hours. Serve any leftover basting sauce separately. Yield: 4 servings.

Berry Wright
Glenmeadow

APPLE FRITTERS

1 cup plain flour
Pinch of salt
2 egg yolks, plus 1 egg white
1 tablespoon cooking oil
5 fluid ounces milk
1 pound cooking apples (North Georgia)
Juice from 1 lemon
Sugar
½ cup butter or cooking oil

Sift flour and salt into medium sized mixing bowl. Make a well in the center and add eggs and oil. With wooden spoon, mix eggs and oil slowly into flour, gradually adding milk. Beat well, then cover and keep in cool place for 30 minutes.

Peel and core apples; slice into rings ¼" thick. Sprinkle with lemon juice and sugar. Dip apples into batter and fry in the hot butter. Drain and serve immediately.

Sue Tharpe
Glenmeadow

HABERSHAM ANTIQUE SHOP

Habersham Antique Shop, doing business since 1974, carries a general line of antique furniture and glassware, along with a varied line of new brass ware and copper at very reasonable prices. Wicker furniture is a special item in the shop with wicker restoration one of the services offered by the shop. Owned and operated by Jan Muggy, it has established a reputation for good prices and honest dealing with the public.

Habersham Antique Shop, Highway 441, Grant Street, P.O. Box 643, Clarkesville, Georgia 30523, (404) 754-6138.

OLD FASHIONED HUSH PUPPIES

1 cup corn meal
$\frac{1}{2}$ cup flour
1 tablespoon sugar
$2\frac{1}{3}$ teaspoons baking powder
$1\frac{1}{2}$ teaspoons salt
1 egg
1 medium onion, chopped fine
$\frac{2}{3}$ cup buttermilk

Sift dry ingredients together; add egg, onion and milk. Mix and add just enough water to bring mixture to a stiff batter. Immediately after mix is made, spoon into 375-degree grease used for frying fish. Brown, turn and brown underside. Drain on paper towel. Yield: 6 servings.

Suwannee Watson
Habersham Antique Shop

BREAD AND BUTTER PICKLES

1 gallon cucumbers, sliced thin
8 small onions, sliced
2 green peppers, cut into strips
½ cup salt
5 cups sugar
1½ teaspoons turmeric
2 tablespoons mustard seed
1 teaspoon cloves, ground
1 teaspoon celery seed
5 cups vinegar (not too strong)

Mix all vegetables together in large container. Sprinkle over with salt and pack about a quart of ice around. Cover and let stand 3 hours. Meanwhile prepare pickling syrup: bring to a boil mixture of sugar, turmeric, mustard seed, cloves, celery seed, and vinegar. Drain vegetables thoroughly and pour syrup over. Heat over slow fire, paddle occasionally and bring to a simmer. Do not boil. Pack into sterilized jars and seal.

Suwannee Watson
Habersham Antique Shop

HOMEMADE YEAST BREAD

2 small potatoes
2 packages yeast
½ cup sugar
3 teaspoons salt
3 tablespoons shortening, softened
2 cups plain flour
Water
Melted butter

Boil potatoes in water enough to cover well. Drain, reserving potato water. Mash potatoes (about 1 cup); add enough water to potato water to make 2½ cups. Dissolve yeast in ½ cup warm water. In large bowl put potatoes, water and yeast; add sugar, salt and soft shortening and flour. Beat well (I use hand mixer). Cover and let stand in warm place for about 1 hour, until bubbly. Gradually add flour to form a stiff dough. Turn on a floured board, knead about 10 minutes until it has an elastic feel. Put in greased bowl, greased side up and cover, letting rise until double. Punch down, divide into equal amounts, shape into loaves and let rise in greased loaf pan until double. Bake at 375 degrees until brown. Loaves will be done if, when thumped, they sound hollow. Turn out on rack and brush with butter.

Suwannee Watson
Habersham Antique Shop

HABERSHAM COUNTY CHAMBER OF COMMERCE

Habersham County apples are widely known for extra high quality flavor. In downtown Cornelia the mammoth steel and concrete monument, a natural-color replica of a big red apple, proclaims the superb quality of fruit grown in Habersham. The apple gives the county its widely recognized legend: "Habersham County, Georgia, HOME OF THE BIG RED APPLE."

Erected and dedicated in 1926, the Big Red Apple has been a Habersham County landmark and a tribute to one of the county's primary industries. Due in part to the monument, countless thousands of Georgians and visitors from all over the United States associate our area with the apple-growing industry.

Visitors stop daily to view, sketch, paint and photograph the Habersham County landmark located adjacent to the Habersham County Chamber of Commerce in the Depot.

Habersham County Chamber of Commerce, Main Street at the Railroad Depot, P.O. Box 366, Cornelia, Georgia 30531 (404) 778-4654.

HOT APPLE SOUP

4 cups apple juice
1 small stick cinnamon, broken
4 cloves
1 small red apple

About 10 minutes before serving, in a 2-quart saucepan over high heat, heat apple juice, cinnamon stick pieces and cloves to boiling. Boil 5 minutes to blend flavors. Strain to remove cinnamon and cloves. Meanwhile, core and quarter apple; cut each quarter into thin slices. Add apple pieces to juice mixture and heat through. Yield: 4 servings.

Susan Adams
Habersham County Chamber of Commerce

APPLE SALAD DELUXE

4 cups red apples, thinly sliced, unpared
One 20-ounce can pineapple chunks, drained
½ to ¾ cup pecans or walnuts, chopped
One 3½-ounce can coconut, flaked
Salad dressing (Below)
Salad greens

Combine apples, pineapple chunks, nuts and coconut with enough salad dressing to moisten. Serve on salad greens with additional dressing. Yield: 8 servings.

Salad Dressing:
2 tablespoons flour
⅔ cup sugar
2 eggs, well beaten
1 cup of pineapple juice (no syrup)
Juice of 1 lemon
Juice of 1 orange
1 cup whipping cream

Combine flour and sugar; stir in eggs. Strain fruit juices and stir in. Cook over hot water, stirring constantly until thick. Cool. Whip cream; fold in.

This salad makes a delightful final course for dinner.

Susan Adams
Habersham County Chamber of Commerce

HABERSHAM HARDWARE

Habersham Hardware and Home Center is North Georgia's most complete shopping center for all home fixings, repairs, decorating and building. In addition to the tools and materials for any size job, we also have a complete Lawn and Garden Center, Gift and Housewares Shop, everything in Sports and outdoor living merchandise, and a full service Appliance and Television Department. We strive to offer the best in selection and quality brand names at the lowest possible price while still providing friendly and helpful sales people in each department.

Habersham Hardware and Home Center, 214 Front Street, Cornelia, GA 30531 (404) 778-2224.

FROZEN DESSERT

1 graham cracker crust
1 medium or small container whipped topping
1 package frozen strawberries

Partially thaw strawberries. Mix whipped topping and strawberries; pour in crust. Chill until firm.

Habersham Hardware and Home Center

GROUND BEEF CASSEROLE

1 pound ground beef or ground chuck
Salt
Pepper
Worcestershire sauce
Garlic salt
1 medium onion, cut up
1 medium bell pepper, cut
One 16-ounce can tomatoes
3 pieces loaf bread, toasted
½ block Cheddar cheese, shredded

Preheat oven to 425 degrees. Crumble and brown ground beef, add salt and pepper, Worcestershire sauce, garlic salt. Cut up onion and bell pepper, drain grease off beef, add onion and bell pepper and tomatoes; let simmer until onions and peppers are done. Place in casserole dish, put crumbled bread on top, top with Cheddar cheese. Put in oven briefly, letting cheese melt.

Patsy Rice
Habersham Hardware and Home Center

TOMATO-ZUCCHINI CASSEROLE

2 medium zucchini, cut in ½-inch slices
½ cup onion, minced
1½ teaspoons salt, or 1 teaspoon salt and ½ teaspoon garlic salt
1 teaspoon Italian seasoning
½ teaspoon black pepper
4 medium tomatoes, cut in ¼-inch slices
1 cup Cheddar cheese, shredded
1 cup Italian herb-flavored bread crumbs

Place zucchini in a medium-sized casserole. Combine onion, salt, Italian seasoning and pepper; sprinkle *half* over zucchini. Arrange tomatoes over seasoning. Sprinkle with remaining seasoning. Cover and bake 20 minutes at 300 degrees. Remove cover and bake 10 minutes longer or until vegetables are tender and almost all liquid has evaporated. Combine cheese with crumbs; sprinkle over all. Bake 5 minutes more or until cheese is melted.

Habersham Hardware and Home Center

HABERSHAM PLANTATION MARKETPLACE

Certainly one of the most symbolic and timeless forms of art, from any period of civilization, is furniture. Classic examples of this art form are still sought out and admired around the world. At Habersham Plantation's Marketplace, we, too, appreciate the heritage and value associated with "old world" craftsmanship. In fact, we feel there is no other period in the history of our country that has influenced furniture and interior design like the early days of the American Colonies. We are proud to offer a sophisticated collection of expertly crafted reproductions from this historical period. All items are rich in tradition, as attitudes and methods of construction parallel those from centuries ago. Handmade, mellow and functional are key words here, and each and every piece has the ability to extend this great tradition of quality for centuries to come. There are more than 20 independent artisans in our Southern Appalachian Mountain region who also craft furniture for us; and they, like us, are so proud of their work that each piece is initialed by its craftsman. This is truly a mark of integrity. While our works are displayed most prominently at our Marketplace, they are not the only products you will find there. To further enrich the atmosphere of this early American environment, we have searched out over 200 other sources of similar period articles and accessories. Quilts, pottery, braided rugs and baskets . . . all reflecting the quality of dedicated craftsmen . . . all available to you. So why not enjoy your own piece of history in the making from Habersham Plantation's Marketplace?

Habersham Plantation Marketplace, Beaver Dam Road, Clarkesville, Georgia 30523, (404) 754-6225

MEXI-CHICKEN

1 can cream of chicken soup
1 can mushroom soup
1 medium onion, grated
1 large can of mushrooms
1 pint sour cream
4 chicken breasts, cooked, cut up
6 corn or flour tortillas, torn into pieces
1 can green chili salsa, drained
1 can green chilies
1 package Cheddar cheese, shredded
(Taco sauce with green chilies may be used)

Combine soups, onion, mushrooms and sour cream. Arrange layers in this order, using half of each ingredient: soup mixture, then chicken, tortillas, salsa, chilies, cheese. Repeat. Bake uncovered for 1 hour at 350 degrees.

Joyce Eddy
Habersham Plantation Marketplace

CHICKEN STROGANOFF

4 cups chicken, cooked, diced
One 8-ounce carton sour cream
½ package onion soup mix
1 can mushroom soup, undiluted
One 4-ounce can sliced mushrooms, drained
Hot rice, cooked

Combine all ingredients except rice, mixing well. Spoon into a lightly greased 2-quart casserole. Bake at 350 degrees for 45 minutes. Serve over rice. Yield: 6 to 8 servings.

Melba Caudell
Habersham Plantation Marketplace

STRAWBERRY BREAD

Two 10-ounce packages frozen strawberries, thawed
1¼ cups oil
4 eggs
3 cups all-purpose flour
2 cups sugar
2 teaspoons cinnamon
1 teaspoon salt
1 teaspoon soda
1 cup nuts, chopped

Grease and flour two 9 x 5-inch loaf pans. Set aside. In a medium bowl, combine strawberries, oil and eggs. Set aside. In a large bowl, combine flour, sugar, cinnamon, salt, soda, and nuts. Add the strawberry mixture to dry ingredients, mixing just until blended. Bake at 375 degrees for 1 hour. Yield: 2 loaves.

Charlene Garrett
Habersham Plantation Marketplace

ASPARAGUS SALAD

1 cup sugar
½ cup vinegar
½ teaspoon salt
1 cup water
1 small can asparagus
¼ cup onion, chopped
2 packages gelatin, dissolved in ½ cup cold water
Juice of ½ lemon
1 cup celery, chopped
1 small can pimento
½ cup pecans
Green food coloring

Mix together sugar, vinegar, salt and water and bring almost to a boil. Add remaining ingredients, plus a little green coloring. Pour into mold and allow to congeal.

Jeannette Crowder
Habersham Plantation Marketplace

VEGETABLE CASSEROLE

One 16-ounce can shoepeg corn
One 16-ounce can French green beans
1 package frozen lima beans, cooked
¼ cup onion, diced
¼ cup bell pepper, diced
¼ cup celery, diced
⅛ cup pimento, chopped

Drain all vegetables in a colander.

Sauce:
1 can cream of celery soup
1 cup sour cream
1 cup cheese, shredded

Mix all these ingredients together and fold in vegetables and salt and pepper.

Topping:
½ box cheese tidbits, crushed
¼ cup slivered almonds, toasted
¼ cup margarine, melted

Mix all ingredients together. Sprinkle over top of casserole. Bake at 300 degrees for 1 hour.

Habersham Hardware and Home Center

BLENDER BERNAISE SAUCE

4 egg yolks
1 cup butter, melted
½ teaspoon salt
½ teaspoon cayenne powder
2 teaspoons onion, minced
2 teaspoons lemon juice
2 teaspoons dry parsley
1 teaspoon tarragon

Beat egg yolks in blender at a high speed until thick. Melt butter and add ¼ cup of it, a teaspoon at a time, to the egg yolks, beating constantly. Add salt to mixture, then slowly add the remaining butter and spices to the mixture. Serve immediately.

Jane Blackmon
Habersham County Chamber of Commerce

APPLE CAKE

2 cups sugar
1 cup oil
2 eggs
3 cups flour
1 teaspoon soda
2 teaspoons vanilla
1 cup nuts
1 teaspoon salt
3 cups apples, finely chopped

Combine sugar, oil and eggs. Add other ingredients and bake in 325-degree oven for 45 minutes. Serve with whipped cream or ice cream.

Lois Shortt
Habersham County Chamber of Commerce

BROWNIE LA CREAM LOG

Two 16-ounce packages brownie mix
Eggs as directed for mix
½ cup chopped walnut meats
1 quart brick ice cream

Prepare brownies as directed for cake brownies. Line well-oiled and lightly-floured 15 x 1 x 10½-inch jelly roll pan with waxed paper. Pour mixture into pan and spread evenly. Sprinkle with chopped nuts. Bake at 350 degrees for 25 minutes. Remove from oven and cool on rack for 10 minutes. Cut cake into three layers. Alternate cake sections with slices of ice cream, using three layers of cake and 2 layers of cream. Wrap and place in freezer until needed. Slice to serve. Yield: 16 servings.

Suwannee Watson
Habersham Antique Shop

HAZEL CREEK MILL

This mill on Hazel Creek can easily be seen from GA 197 between Clarkesville and the intersection with GA 123. It is typical of the medium-sized mill used to serve the immediate community in which it is located. When you realize that most grinding was done for people who brought their raw material by wagon or on foot, it is easy to understand that at one time this countryside was filled with mills. Hazel Creek contained a number of such operations in its flow to the Chattahoochee River. Around Demorest it powered an assortment of small factories, each of which returned its source of energy to the stream for reuse by the next mill downstream. If no one contaminated the flow, this same water could generate energy, water fields, provide breeding ground for fish and water for wildlife, give recreation to communities and transportation for goods—all the way to the Gulf. And the same principle works today—if we are considerate of our neighbor downstream.

CHERRY BOUNCE LIQUEUR

8 cups (2 pounds) fresh, unpitted tart red cherries
2 cups sugar
1½ teaspoons whole allspice
1½ teaspoons whole cloves
2 inches stick cinnamon, broken
4 cups bourbon (or vodka, if you prefer)

Wash and stem cherries. Place alternate layers of cherries, sugar and spices in a 2-quart jar. Pour in bourbon and cover. Stir daily until sugar is dissolved. Screw on top and place in cool, dark place for at least 2 months. Strain before serving. Serve in liqueur glasses. Yield: 1 quart liqueur.

Minnie Carver
The Hitching Post

GREEN BEAN CASSEROLE

4 tablespoons butter
2 tablespoons flour
1 teaspoon salt
¼ teaspoon pepper
½ cup onion, grated
1 cup sour cream
4 cans green beans
¼ pound Swiss cheese, shredded
1 cup cornflake crumbs

Melt 2 tablespoons of the butter; add flour, salt, pepper, and grated onion. Stir in sour cream. Fold in beans; heat slightly and pour into oiled baking dish or casserole. Sauté cornflakes in 2 tablespoons butter. Sprinkle Swiss cheese and cornflakes on top of casserole. Bake 30 minutes in 400-degree oven.

Minnie Carver
The Hitching Post

FANCY CHOCOLATE CANDY

1 cup butter, softened
2 boxes powdered sugar
1 small can condensed milk
1 box or can flaked coconut
3 cups pecans, chopped
Two 6-ounce packages chocolate chips
1 block paraffin

Cream butter and sugar well; mix next 3 ingredients. Make into balls on a cookie sheet and put in refrigerator to cool. Mix in double boiler chocolate chips and paraffin. Use toothpick and dip balls in the chocolate mixture. Keeps well, stored in covered container. Yield: 80 balls.

Habersham Hardware and Home Center

THE HITCHING POST

The Hitching Post, located just off GA 197, on Laurel Lodge Road at Lake Burton, is a store for your convenience shopping while en route or visiting the North Georgia Mountains.

Our take-out liquid refreshments include most popular brands of beer, all wines available in this area, and soft drinks. We stock lots of fishing tackle and bait for your fishing pleasure, and we have seriously tried to stock all the snacks and edibles you forgot to bring along. People keep returning for our special quarter-pound, all meat, hot and delicious Hot Dogs.

We're Open All Year 'Round, Too!

The Hitching Post, off GA 197, Laurel Lodge Road, Lake Burton; Route 1, Clarkesville, Georgia 30523, (404) 947-3612.

GOURMET ASPARAGUS

Olive oil
1 large can asparagus
1½ cups American cheese, shredded
½ cup Romano cheese, grated
1 cup shrimp boiled with salt, lemon, onion, cayenne sauce, wine and garlic to taste
2 eggs
1 cup sauterne
1 tablespoon Worcestershire sauce
1 teaspoon cayenne sauce
1½ teaspoons salt
1 can cream of mushroom soup, undiluted
¾ cup bread crumbs

Coat casserole with olive oil and line with asparagus. Layer with half of required cheeses. Add the prepared shrimp and layer the remainder of cheeses. Beat well the 2 eggs and add the sauterne a little at a time. Blend in Worcestershire sauce, cayenne sauce and salt. Beat again. Pour over the casserole. Spread undiluted soup over all, and sprinkle bread crumbs on top. Bake at 350 degrees for 1 hour, or until bubbly and brown.

Minnie Carver
The Hitching Post

LIME MIST SALAD

Heat over low heat until gelatin dissolves:

Two 3-ounce packages lime gelatin
2 cups applesauce

Cool gelatin and stir in:

1 cup celery, chopped
½ cup pecans, chopped
¼ cup maraschino cherries, drained, chopped
2 cups lemon-lime carbonated beverage
2 tablespoons lemon juice
1 heaping cup whipped topping
Green food coloring

Chill until syrupy. Fold in whipped topping and add a little green coloring if desired. Pour into mold and chill until firm.

Minnie Carver
The Hitching Post

HOME FEDERAL SAVINGS AND LOAN ASSOCIATION

Home Federal Savings & Loan of Clarkesville opened its doors on February 7, 1972. They have been serving the savings needs of North Georgians for the past 8 years and have helped many of their friends and neighbors get home loans. Times have been changing and Home Federal has stayed abreast of the needs of North Georgians by now offering interest-bearing checking accounts (NOW) and consumer loans. Hours: Monday, Tuesday and Thursday, 9:00 a.m. until 4:00 p.m.; Wednesday, closed; Friday, 9:00 a.m. until 6:00 p.m.; Saturday, 9:00 a.m. until 1:00 p.m.

The following recipes, favorites of guests at Home Federal functions, were submitted by Frances Mathis, wife of James E. Mathis, Sr., President of Home Federal.

Home Federal Savings and Loan Association, 102 South Washington Street, Clarkesville, Georgia 30523 (404) 754-2189

CHAMPIGNONS GRILLÉS (BROILED MUSHROOMS)

18 large brown mushrooms
5 tablespoons butter
1 teaspoon shallots, finely chopped
½ teaspoon seasoned salt
¼ teaspoon pepper, freshly ground

Scrub mushrooms lightly. Remove stems. In a large iron skillet, melt 2 tablespoons butter; place mushroom caps, tops down, in the butter. Blend 3 tablespoons butter with shallots, salt and pepper. Fill mushroom caps with the butter mixture. Broil about 6 inches from heat for about 5 minutes, watching carefully. Turn off broiler and allow mushrooms to sizzle for 5 more minutes. Baste mushrooms with any juice in pan and serve with juice.

Note: We like these with hamburgers, steaks, or as an appetizer. But one of my favorite treats is broiled mushrooms with heated canned hominy that has had a well dented into the center, filled with melted butter and sprinkled with white pepper.

Frances Mathis
Home Federal Savings & Loan Association

BAKED BEANS

Note that this recipe, the earliest I have found, leaves out what would have been considered an essential ingredient—the sweetening. Bostonians would have used ¼ cup of molasses, for which Vermonters would have substituted ½ cup of maple syrup, while in New Hampshire they might well have needed ¾ cup of brown sugar.

Baked beans are a very simple dish, yet few cook them well. The night before they are baked, they should be put in cold water, and hung over the fire. In the morning, they should be put in a colander, rinsed two or three times, then again placed in a kettle, with pork, covered with water, and kept scalding hot, an hour or more. A pound of pork is quite enough for a quart of beans, and that is a large dinner for a common family. The rind of the pork should be slashed. Pieces of pork alternately fat and lean are the most suitable; the "cheeks" are the best. A little pepper sprinkled among the beans, when they are placed in the bean-pot, will render them less unhealthy. They should be just covered with water, when put into the oven; and the pork should be sunk a little below the surface of the beans. Bake three or four hours.

Frances Mathis
Home Federal Savings & Loan Association

LaPRADE'S

Mr. LaPrade built his camp in 1916 to house and feed engineers and workmen who were harnessing the Tallulah River as a power supply. As a recreational area, Lake Burton was completed in 1925. Mr. LaPrade then turned his camp into a fishing retreat, which has evolved into a rustic Georgia mountain camp near the Appalachian Trail. Its heart is the dining room, where people come from far and wide to enjoy the truly fresh, family-style Southern dinners. The owners operate several farms which provide most of the meat and vegetables served; and the meals are noteworthy. At breakfast, country ham, sausage, red gravy, grits, eggs, hot biscuits, sorghum syrup, honey, and homemade jellies; for lunch, chicken and dumplings, and other meat, hot biscuits, corn bread, several vegetables, and peach or apple or berry cobbler; dinners begin with onion relishes and coleslaw, the specialty—fried chicken—or country ham, hot biscuits, vegetables, and end with dessert.

Guests are reminded that this is essentially a fishing retreat, and the lodgings with their casual, rustic-Georgia-mountains furnishings and atmosphere, sleep up to twelve people each. Some of the cabins on the property have fireplaces, and two others are at lakeside. The simple, locally-handcrafted beds are covered with hand-sewn quilts and comforters. Cabins have front porches with rockers and have gas heat and indoor facilities. The game room has pinball machines, ice and beverage machines. The marina has rentals of fishing boats, canoes, rowboats and motors. They also sell all necessary bait and marine gas.

The accommodations include 21 cabins with private baths. No pets are allowed. LaPrade's is open from the first day of trout season (approximately April 1st) until the last day of deer season (approximately December 1st). The dining room is closed on Wednesdays. LaPrade's is located 18 miles north of Clarkesville on GA 197.

*LaPrade's, GA 197 N, Lake Burton, Route 1,
Clarkesville, Georgia 30523 (404) 947-3312.*

PLEASE CALL 947-3312 FOR MEAL RESERVATIONS

RAW CRANBERRY RELISH

1 pound fresh cranberries
2 oranges
2 lemons
2 apples
1½ cups sugar

Wash and sort cranberries. Wash and quarter all fruit, coring the apples and removing seeds and hard ends of oranges and lemons. Do not peel any of the fruit. Grind all in food chopper. Blend in sugar and allow to marinate 24 hours before serving. This will make a quart or more of relish and may be stored in the refrigerator for at least a month. Serve as is or add to gelatin for molded salads.

Rachel Nichols
LaPrade's

MARINATED SLAW

Will keep in refrigerator for weeks.

1 head of cabbage
2 onions, sliced
⅞ cup sugar
1 cup vinegar
¾ cup oil
2 tablespoons sugar
1 teaspoon dry mustard
1 teaspoon celery seeds
1 tablespoon salt

Arrange cabbage and onions in layers and top with sugar. Bring vinegar, oil, 2 tablespoons sugar, mustard, celery seeds, and salt to a boil and pour over cabbage and onions. Store for 3 days in refrigerator.

Rachel Nichols
LaPrade's

LaPRADE'S CARROT CAKE

3 cups self-rising flour
2 cups sugar
1 teaspoon cinnamon
1 cup oil
2 teaspoons vanilla
2 cups carrots, grated
½ cup fresh crushed pineapple
1½ cups chopped pecans
3 eggs

Sift together flour, sugar, and cinnamon. Mix remaining ingredients, then add flour mixture, mixing well. Pour into a greased and floured 13 x 9 x 1½-inch pan. Bake for 30 minutes at 325 degrees.

Topping:
1 cup evaporated milk
1 cup sugar
3 egg yolks
½ pound margarine
1 teaspoon vanilla
1 cup coconut
1 cup chopped pecans

Combine ingredients and cook for 8 minutes over medium heat. Cool and spread on cake.

Rachel Nichols
LaPrade's

MACARONI AND STRING BEANS

½ cup macaroni
3 tablespoons butter
3 tablespoons flour
¼ teaspoon dry mustard
¾ teaspoon salt
⅛ teaspoon pepper
½ teaspoon Worcestershire sauce
1 cup evaporated milk
1 cup water
1 tablespoon minced onion
1¾ cups American Cheddar cheese, shredded
2 cups string beans, cooked

Cook and drain macaroni. Place in a greased 1½-quart casserole. Melt butter in double boiler; blend in flour, mustard, salt, pepper, and Worcestershire sauce. Add milk, water and cook, stirring until thickened. Add onion and 1½ cups of the cheese and stir until cheese is melted. Add string beans; then pour sauce over macaroni and toss with fork. Sprinkle with the remaining ¼ cup cheese. Bake in moderately hot oven of 375 degrees for 30 minutes. Yield: 6 servings.

Rachel Nichols
LaPrade's

LaPRADE'S SWEET POTATO SOUFFLÉ

3 tablespoons butter or margarine
3 cups fresh sweet potatoes, mashed
1 cup sugar
½ teaspoon salt
½ cup sweet milk
1 tablespoon orange flavoring
2 eggs

Melt the butter and mix with potatoes. Add sugar, salt, milk, and flavoring. Beat eggs and fold into potato mixture. Pour into greased baking dish; cover with topping.

Topping:
1 cup brown sugar
⅓ cup flour
3 tablespoons butter or margarine, melted
1 cup pecan halves

Mix sugar and flour, sprinkle on soufflé; pour butter over top. Cover with pecan halves and bake at 350 degrees for 35 minutes.

Rachel Nichols
LaPrade's

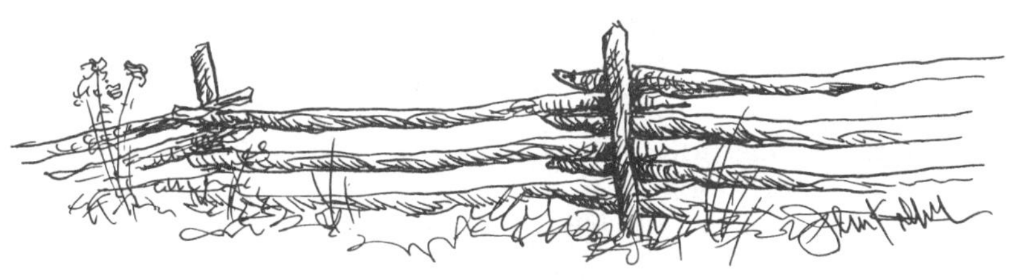

VANILLA WAFER POUND CAKE

2 sticks butter
2 cups sugar
6 eggs
12 ounces vanilla wafers
½ cup sweet milk
2 cups chopped pecans
1¾ cups coconut

Cream butter and sugar, add eggs one at a time mixing well after each addition. Add vanilla wafers, milk, pecans, and coconut, mixing well. Pour in a greased and floured tube pan. Bake 1½ hours at 300 degrees.

Rachel Nichols
LaPrade's

MARK OF THE POTTER

Mark of the Potter is an interesting shop of contemporary crafts. Located in the converted Grandpa Watts grist mill on the Soque River, Jay and Cathy Bucek make and sell their own pottery as well as the works of over 40 other Southeastern craftsmen. On a porch overlooking the river, visitors can feed the trout—rainbows, brooks, and browns—that inhabit the pool below. Although no fishing is allowed, throwing trout food and watching the trout churn the water is a pleasure to young and old alike. The studio is open to the sales shop and you can watch craftsmen who are usually working at some phase of their craft. Come to Mark of the Potter, 10 miles north of Clarkesville on GA 197, and visit the most picturesque craft shop in the southeast.

Open everyday 10:00 to 6:00
Closed Christmas

Mark of the Potter, GA 197, Route 3, Box 83
Clarkesville, Georgia 30523, (404) 947-3440.

GRANDMA RAWSON'S APPLESAUCE CAKE

2 cups white sugar
3/4 cup butter
3 cups plain flour
2 cups raisins
2 cups pecans
1 or 2 teaspoons allspice and cloves
2 cups apples cooked low without sugar

Cream butter and sugar. Add apples to which 2 teaspoons soda has been added. Add the rest of the ingredients. Cook at 325 degrees for 1 1/2 hours.

Cathy Bucek
Mark of the Potter

POP'S ONION SOUP

2 cans beef boullion
2 medium white onions sliced
Parmesan cheese
dash of celery salt
pepper
optional garlic salt

Combine beef broth, onions and seasonings. Bring to a boil. Reduce heat and simmer approximately 40 minutes. Sprinkle Parmesan cheese lightly and stir frequently. Serve with croutons and mild cheese on top.

Cathy Bucek
Mark of the Potter

SAUTEED MUSHROOMS

1 pound mushrooms, cleaned and sliced
butter
1/4 cup white wine (more to taste)
1 to 2 cloves garlic, minced
pepper
flour (optional)

Sautee garlic in butter. Use approximately 1/2 to 1 stick of butter. Add a dash of pepper. Add mushrooms cook until done, stirring frequently. When almost done, push mushrooms to sides of pan. Combine wine and a tablespoon of flour in a small cup or bowl. Pour in the center of the pan. Turn up heat and stir until it is the desired thickness. Combine with mushrooms. Heat on a lower temperature for about 3 to 4 minutes.

Cathy Bucek
Mark of the Potter

LAWREL SPECIALTIES

Located 3 miles south of Mark of the Potter on GA 197, Lawrel Specialties offers a broad line of hand-crafted pine furniture.

Come and visit Bonnie and Tom Lawrence and see the many finely made items on display and ready for sale in their log cabin style showroom. If you do not find the special piece you want, you may place an order for any of the items they offer or design a custom-made piece of your own.

Open 10:00 to 6:00 Friday and Saturday, weekdays by appointment or chance.
Closed Sundays.

Lawrel Specialties, Route 3, Box 80-B,
Clarkesville, Georgia 30523, (404) 754-9451.

PEAS WITH A FLAIR

2 pkgs. frozen peas or
2 cans green peas (drained)
2 cans sliced water chestnuts
1 can mushroom soup
1 medium onion, diced
½ green pepper, diced
1 cup diced celery
2 jars pimentos

Sautee pepper, onion and celery in butter, combine all ingredients in baking dish and bake 350 degrees for 30 to 40 minutes. This is a delicious casserole served either hot or cold.

Bonnie Lawrence
Lawrel Specialties

GRANDMOTHER'S WHISKEY CAKE

1 cup butter
2 cups sugar
5 eggs, separated
3½ cups flour, sifted
2 teaspoons baking powder
½ teaspoon cinnamon
¼ teaspoon cloves
½ teaspoon nutmeg
1 cup milk
½ cup whiskey
½ cup flour to dredge fruit and nuts
1 cup raisins
1 cup nuts, chopped
½ cup citron, chopped

Cream butter and sugar. Add egg yolks, one at a time, beating after each one. Sift dry ingredients. Add alternately with combined liquids until all ingredients are blended. Fold in beaten egg whites. Dredge fruit and nuts; add to mixture. Pour into greased and well-floured tube pan. Cook at 325 degrees for 1¼ hours or until cake tests done with a toothpick.

Glen LaRowe
Mark of the Potter

MOTHER'S FUDGE BAR CAKE

2 ounces unsweetened chocolate squares, cut up
½ cup boiling water
1 cup cake flour, sifted
1 cup sugar
½ teaspoon salt
½ teaspoon soda
¼ cup vegetable shortening
¼ cup sour milk
½ teaspoon vanilla
1 egg, unbeaten

Place chocolate in large mixing bowl. Pour boiling water over chocolate and stir until melted. Cool. Sift flour, sugar, salt, and soda into chocolate mixture. Add shortening and beat 200 strokes. Add milk, vanilla and egg. Beat 160 strokes. Bake in greased 8 x 8 x 2-inch pan at 350 degrees for 35 to 40 minutes.

Fudge Frosting:
1 ounce unsweetened chocolate, finely cut
1 cup sugar
⅓ cup milk
¼ cup vegetable shortening
¼ teaspoon salt
1 teaspoon vanilla
¼ cup nuts, chopped (optional)

Place all ingredients except vanilla in skillet and slowly bring to a full rolling boil, stirring constantly. Boil 1 minute. Add vanilla. Cool to lukewarm, beating until thick and creamy. Add chopped nuts if desired.

Doris Lake
Glenmeadow

ONCE UPON A TIME COMPANY

Described by its owners as a "majestic emporium of the old, odd and unusual", the Once Upon A Time Company is actually an interesting antique and gift store located in the village of Clarkesville, GA. Owned by a partnership of an Englishman and an American, the shop imports most of its merchandise directly from Europe.

Because of the direct connection with England, Once Upon A Time Company offers some outstanding bargains on antiques, imported brass, porcelains, and fine prints. You will also find a fascinating collection of old books and fine English teas and preserves.

While the company offers a vast amount of gifts and antiques to purchase, they also offer refinishing services and repairs on most types of antiques. If you do not find the antique you desire, they custom make and design furniture in various types of old or new wood. Delivery services are available.

Open Monday thru Saturday 10:00 to 6:00
Sunday 12:30 to 5:30

Once Upon A Time Company, Box 978 N. Washington Street, Clarkesville, Georgia 30523, (404) 754-5789.

CHOW MEIN FOR SIX A LA CHARLIE LEONARD'S DAD

- 2 pounds beef, cut in bite-size chunks
- 1 pound pork, cut in bite-size chunks
- 1 medium-sized bunch celery, diced
- 1 large-sized onion or equivalent, sliced
- 5 tablespoons soy sauce
- 1 can bamboo shoots
- 1 can water chestnuts, sliced
- 2 cans chop suey or chow mein vegetables
- 1 large or 2 small cans mushrooms
- 2 cans chow mein noodles
- 2 bouillon cubes
- Sugar
- 2 tablespoons cornstarch
- Salt and pepper to taste
- 2½ cups rice, uncooked
- Cooking oil for onions

Now here's where the fun begins. There isn't much to it—but there are certain end points that should be observed. And you want to stop just when it's over. (It's like surgery: if all you want is an appendix—why make a midline incision when a 2″ incision will do.) Anyhow you slice your onions and dice your celery and shove 'em aside in separate bowls so you can stop crying. Then put your bite-sized beef and pork in separate bowls and add 2 tablespoons soy sauce to each consignment of meat and mix it all up in each bowl—then shove these bowls aside. Now you can take your time because this meat wants to soak for at least 30 minutes but not over an hour. When your cans are all open, drain the juice off of everything but the mushrooms and the "noodles." Put two bouillon cubes and the juice from the mushrooms in a pint of good hot water and shove that aside to dissolve. Next put your rice on, but be sure you don't forget it. Just cook it your favorite way, but let it end up dry and fluffy.

In a pretty big metal pot put in some cooking oil and start to frying onions. You can add a little water to keep them from burning. When they are nice and soft, add celery, a little bouillon mixture and some pepper. Then cover your pot and let 'er cook until the whole business is good and soft and juicy—stirring the while.

Now add your beef. If it's tough you had better pressurize it first. It's better tho' if you can add it raw. Stir it all up good and then cover your pot. Cook the mess for about 15 minutes or until meat is tender but don't let it get too done or it will be hard when you eat it.

continued . . .

Put pork in hot skillet with a little grease and fry until good and brown. Stir while frying and add salt and pepper to it. Turn off pork and check beef. If tender, add pork and stir up good and let the two meats cook together about 2 minutes. Pour canned ingredients into pot, add rest of bouillon, cover and let boil about 3 minutes. Stir. Pour a cup of cold water in bowl, add to it 2 tablespoons of cornstarch, 1 tablespoon soy sauce, and a sugar shell of sugar. Stir this up. Check pot. Salt and pepper to taste, then thicken with cornstarch solution. Serve with rice and noodles. *Charlie's Dad says you may want to throw this whole thing in the garbage and go out to eat.*

Charlie Leonard's Dad
Pierian Studios

CUBAN BLACK BEAN SOUP
(for pressure cooker)

1 pound dried black beans
1 tablespoon vinegar
½ pound cured slab bacon, diced
10 to 12 garlic cloves, minced
1 large Spanish onion, diced
1 bell pepper, diced
2 tablespoons oregano, ground
1 tablespoon vinegar
1 tablespoon cumin, ground
1 tablespoon sugar
1 tablespoon salt
1 teaspoon Tabasco
1 teaspoon ground pepper
1 bay leaf, not the California variety

On the day before cooking, wash the beans in cold running water. Place beans in pot and add water to cover, plus two inches. Add vinegar; stir (this will draw color from beans.) Let stand overnight. If beans rise over water, add more water.

In pressure cooker, sauté diced bacon until it renders approximately 4 ounces fat and is brown. Set bacon aside. In rendered fat, sauté garlic, onion and bell pepper until brown. Add oregano, vinegar, cumin, sugar, salt, Tabasco, pepper, bay leaf, diced bacon; stir. Add black beans and water in which they soaked overnight (water should be about 1½ to 2 inches above beans.) Stir well. Cook at 15 pounds pressure for 25 minutes. Reduce pressure, open lid and continue simmering until desired thickness is obtained. Stir frequently to avoid sticking.

Flavor improves if made one day ahead, refrigerated overnight and re-heated over a low flame, stirring frequently to avoid sticking.

Manuel P. Anton, M.D.
Glenmeadow

MOTHER'S CARAMEL BARS

2 cups brown sugar
1 cup butter
2 eggs
2 cups flour, sifted
2 teaspoons baking powder
2 cups nuts, chopped
Powdered sugar

Cream sugar and butter. Add eggs, beating well. Stir in flour and baking powder. Add nuts. Pour in greased 8 x 12-inch pan. Bake 30 minutes in a 350-degree oven; cool, cut in squares. Sprinkle with powdered sugar.

Glen LaRowe
Mark of the Potter

CRANBERRY SALAD (OHIO RECIPE)

2 cups raw cranberries, ground
1 orange, ground
2 cups sugar
1 cup celery, diced
1 cup nuts, chopped
1 cup pineapple, crushed
1 large package lemon gelatin
3 cups water

Grind cranberries and orange; add sugar and let stand until sugar dissolves. Add next 3 ingredients. Make gelatin. When chilled add mixture and let set. Better if made the day before using.

Suwannee Watson
Habersham Antique Shop

SOUR CREAM ROLLS

¾ cup margarine
1 cup sour cream
2 cups self-rising flour, sifted

Mix all ingredients; put in ungreased muffin pan. Bake at 350 degrees for 20 minutes. Dough will keep in refrigerator for about a week. Yield: 12 rolls.

Frances Mathis
Home Federal Savings & Loan Association

SERENDIPITY

J. P. and Gladys Bell are stained glass artists. Their work is handcrafted of unique glass of many textures, hues and densities. The leaded stained glass lamps, window panels and suncatchers are made so that they can become cherished heirlooms handed down from generation to generation. J. P. and Gladys live and work in Habersham County. Their combination home and stained glass shop, called Serendipity, is located in Batesville, one of the most beautiful areas in the county.

Serendipity, GA 197, 11 miles north of Clarkesville, Route 1, Clarkesville, Georgia 30523. (404) 947-3643.

CREAM OF ONION SOUP

1 onion, chopped
2 tablespoons butter
2 tablespoons flour
3 cups of chicken stock or 6 bouillon cubes to make 3 cups stock
Salt and pepper to taste
6 tablespoons Parmesan cheese, grated
1 cup cream

Sauté onion in butter. Add flour and mix. Add stock and bring to a boil. Add salt, pepper, cheese and cream. Heat, but do not boil.

Gladys Bell
Serendipity

CABBAGE-APPLE SALAD

2 cups cabbage, shredded
1 cup apple with peel, diced
½ cup salted peanuts, chopped

Toss ingredients with dressing. Yield: 4 servings.

Sure-to-Please Dressing:
½ cup creamy peanut butter
¼ cup honey
½ cup mayonnaise

Blend ingredients together. Yield: 1 cup.

Gladys Bell
Serendipity

J.P.'s PECAN PIE

1 cup white corn syrup
1 cup dark brown sugar
⅓ teaspoon salt
⅓ cup butter or margarine, melted
1 teaspoon vanilla
3 eggs, slightly beaten
One 9-inch unbaked pie shell
1 heaping cup pecans, whole

Combine syrup, sugar, salt, butter, vanilla and mix well. Add slightly beaten eggs. Pour into pie shell and sprinkle pecans over all. Bake in preheated 350-degree oven for approximately 45 minutes. Cool. Top with whipped cream or ice cream.

J. P. Bell
Serendipity

POPPY SEED DRESSING

½ cup sugar
1 teaspoon salt
1 teaspoon dry mustard
1 tablespoon onion, grated
2 tablespoons vinegar
1 cup salad oil, chilled
3 tablespoons vinegar
1 tablespoon poppy seed

Place sugar, salt, mustard, onion and 2 tablespoons vinegar in mixing bowl. Add salad oil very slowly while beating. Add the 3 tablespoons vinegar and poppy seed and continue beating until thick. Store in the refrigerator. Use on tossed or fruit salad.

Gladys Bell
Serendipity

STANDARD TELEPHONE COMPANY

Standard Telephone Company employees with 5 to 15 years of telephone-related service are eligible for membership in the Bruce Williams Future Pioneer Club. The club's purpose is to give members the opportunity to volunteer their time and talent for community service. Employees with 15 years of service are eligible for membership in the H. M. Stewart, Sr., Pioneer Club.

As a fund-raising project, the Future Pioneer Club published the "Kitchen Directory," a collection of recipes from Standard Telephone Company employees and friends. These recipes are from their cookbook which is still being sold to provide funds for community service projects.

If you know of someone for whom the Club could provide assistance or if you are interested in buying a "Kitchen Directory," please contact any Standard Telephone Company employee and they can direct your inquiries to the Club.

Standard Telephone Company, 2000 Industrial Blvd.,
Cornelia, Georgia 30531 (404) 778-2201.

SQUASH BAKE

3 cups yellow squash, cooked, sliced and drained
2 tablespoons butter, melted
2 tablespoons pimento, diced
2 tablespoons onion, finely chopped
½ cup toasted almonds, chopped
1 can condensed cream of chicken soup, undiluted
Buttered bread crumbs
Salt and pepper to taste

Combine squash, butter, pimento, onion and almonds in buttered casserole. Cover with soup and top with crumbs. Bake at 350 degrees for about 20 minutes, or until bubbly.

Standard Telephone Company, "Kitchen Directory"

CAULIFLOWER SALAD

½ head lettuce
1 head cauliflower, without leaves
Small amount fresh broccoli flowerettes
Several green onions
4 tablespoons mayonnaise
Bacon bits
Parmesan cheese, grated
Mushrooms (optional)
Black olives (optional)

In large bowl, chop lettuce, cauliflower, broccoli, and green onions. Add mayonnaise. Top with Parmesan cheese and bacon bits. Add mushrooms and black olives if desired. If you make it the night before, wait until next day to stir together.

Standard Telephone Company, "Kitchen Directory"

CHICKEN PIE

1 can cream of chicken soup
2 cups chicken, cooked, diced
1 medium onion, chopped
1¼ cups chicken broth
1 cup plain flour
2 teaspoons baking powder
Salt and pepper
½ cup butter, room temperature
1 cup milk

Place soup, chicken, onion and broth in bottom of casserole dish. Mix flour, baking powder, salt, pepper, and butter until crumbly. Add milk and spoon into casserole. Bake 30 to 40 minutes at 350 degrees.

Note: Add 2 boiled eggs, peas, and carrots if desired.

Standard Telephone Company, "Kitchen Directory"

THE STEAK HOUSE

For that good home cooking of vegetables and the pleasure of a juicy steak, there is only one stop, THE STEAK HOUSE, North Georgia's most famous restaurant, located on US 441 in Baldwin.

Start your day with a breakfast of hot homemade biscuits, country ham, bacon, sausage and eggs. Southern grits and hotcakes are always a favorite, too.

A buffet of delicious meats and vegetables is available at lunchtime. For that light meal a salad bar and a variety of fruits and congealed salads provide an excellent meal.

Fine steaks, seafoods, pork chops, and chicken are only a sample of the wide selection from the menu served each night until 10:00 p.m.

There is parking and entrance in the rear to accomodate banquets and club meetings.

The Steak House, US 441 at US 23,
Baldwin, Georgia 30511, (404) 778-4351.

CHANTILLY POTATOES

3 cups mashed potatoes
3 tablespoons butter
1 teaspoon salt
½ cup hot milk or cream
½ cup whipping cream
½ cup cheese, grated

Preheat oven to 375 degrees. Beat potatoes, butter, salt, and milk until creamy. Beat whipping cream until stiff and fold in grated cheese. Shape the potatoes into a mound in an ovenproof dish. Cover the mound with the whipped cream mixture. Bake until cheese is melted and the potatoes are lightly brown.

Bobby Joe Caudell
The Steak House

LEMON NUT BARS

1 cup shortening
½ cup brown sugar
½ cup granulated sugar
1 egg
2 tablespoons lemon juice
1 tablespoon lemon rind, grated
2 cups flour, sifted
¼ teaspoon soda
¼ teaspoon salt
½ cup nuts, chopped

Cream shortening and sugars. Add egg, lemon juice and rind, flour, soda and mix well. Blend in chopped nuts. Shape into roll and chill. Slice as needed and bake. Bake for 10 to 12 minutes at 400 degrees. Yield: 4½ dozen.

Glen LaRowe
Mark of the Potter

ZUCCHINI BREAD CAUDELL

3 cups zucchini, sliced
1 cup biscuit mix
1 small onion, chopped
½ cup Parmesan cheese, grated
¼ cup oil
3 eggs, beaten

Mix ingredients together, reserving enough cheese for topping. Bake in 7 x 11 or 9 x 13-inch pan. Top with cheese. Bake in 350-degree oven for 40 minutes. May mix and freeze to bake later.

Bobby Joe Caudell
The Steak House

THE STEAK HOUSE

DELICIOUS QUAIL

6 quail
Salt and pepper to taste
½ cup margarine
1 teaspoon Worcestershire sauce
Dash garlic salt
2 slices lemon

Salt and pepper birds and flour lightly. Brown on top of stove in margarine. Add small amount of water, Worcestershire, garlic and lemon. Cover roaster and cook in 350-degree oven 1 to 1¼ hours. Baste birds often. Water may be added if necessary while cooking, in order to have desired amount of gravy.

Bobby Joe Caudell
The Steak House

BROCCOLI CASSEROLE

2 packages broccoli, cooked, drained
½ can mushroom soup, undiluted
3 tablespoons mayonnaise
3 tablespoons onion, chopped
1 egg
½ cup sharp cheese, shredded
¼ cup margarine
Ritz cracker crumbs

Cook, drain and chop broccoli. Mix next six ingredients and pour over broccoli in a casserole. Top with Ritz crackers. Bake at 325 degrees until bubbly and firm on top. Yield: 6 servings.

Anne Gale
The Wildewood Shop

ANGEL FOOD CAKE

1 cup powdered sugar
1 cup granulated sugar
1 cup flour
12 egg whites
¼ teaspoon salt, in whites
1 teaspoon cream of tartar
1 teaspoon vanilla

Sift sugar 3 times. Sift flour 3 times. Beat salted egg whites to soft peaks; add cream of tartar. Add flour and sugar alternately to beaten egg whites. Pour into greased and floured tube pan. Place in a cold oven and bake for 1 hour at 350 degrees.

SPANISH SAUSAGE (CHORIZO)

2 parts pork, 10 to 15% fat
1 part lean beef
Salt
Oregano
Paprika, cayenne, balance to taste
Garlic, pressed
Casings, preferably pig's small intestine
Lard

Cut pork and beef into very small dice size. Do not grind. Mix well with salt, oregano, paprika, cayenne, and pressed garlic. Paprika is used rather freely. Mixture should appear deep red. Use fresh paprika as old loses color. Leave mixture in refrigerator overnight for flavoring, but do not wait more than 24 hours to fill casings. Tie casings every 6 inches. Smoke them every day until sufficiently dry.

TO KEEP: Arrange chorizos horizontally in a tin can. Pour melted lard to cover; adding rock salt will help them keep longer. Will keep several months in refrigerator.

Blanca Anton, M.D.
Glenmeadow

UPSIDE-DOWN BRIDGE

Upside-down Bridge. Eight miles north of Clarkesville and 2 miles south of Mark of the Potter on GA 197 a state highway sign says "DIP" "15 MPH." And it is a dip because this is almost the only place remaining in the country on a state highway where the motorist can ford a creek. Lovell Creek actually flows over the roadbed on its way into the Soque River. Enjoy the long-forgotten thrill of fording Lovell Creek which our neighbors in lower Batesville call "the upside-down bridge."

HOT FRUIT

1 can fruits for salad, drained well
1 can apricots, drained well
3 teaspoons curry powder
1 cup brown sugar

Heat until bubbly.

Helen Whitney
Whitney Realty

ARTICHOKE CHICKEN

¾ cup butter
1 cup onion, chopped
½ teaspoon garlic, minced
½ pound fresh mushrooms, sliced
1 teaspoon basil
¼ teaspoon rosemary, crushed
1 teaspoon salt
Dash white pepper
4 boned chicken breasts, cut into bite-sized pieces
¼ cup dry white wine
1 lemon
One 14-ounce can artichoke hearts, sliced ¼″ thick (do not use marinated artichokes)
One 7-ounce package rice mix

Melt ⅔ cup of butter. Saute onions and garlic until the onions are transparent. Add mushrooms and spices and saute 2 minutes; remove from heat. Melt remaining butter. Saute chicken until lightly browned. Add wine and the juice of one lemon. Combine chicken with onion and mushroom mixture. Add artichoke hearts and mix lightly until heated through. Serve over rice prepared according to package directions. Shrimp, veal, or firm-fleshed fish may be substituted for chicken. If fish is used, broil filets in lieu of sauteing. Yield 4 servings.

John and Kelly Byron
Upside-Down Bridge

RASPBERRY BARS

2½ cups flour, sifted
½ cup sugar
½ pound butter, room temperature
2 egg yolks
12-ounce jar red raspberry jam

Preheat oven to 350 degrees. Sift flour and sugar in medium bowl. Add soft butter and egg yolks. Use fingers or spatula to make cookie dough. Spread in jelly roll pan, 11 x 15, prick with fork and bake for 10 or 12 minutes until slightly brown around edges. Remove from oven and spread with jam.

4 egg whites
1 cup sugar
¼ teaspoon almond flavoring
1½ cup nuts, grated

Make meringue: Beat egg whites and flavoring and slowly add sugar, beating until slightly stiff. Fold in grated nuts and spread over the jam. Bake 20 to 25 minutes. Note: Grated almonds produce a whiter meringue.

Annette G. Cook
Upside-Down Bridge

WHITNEY REALTY

Whitney Realty was established in 1973 with offices located at Cherokee Landing on Lake Burton to serve the real estate needs of the public interested in lake and mountain properties in Georgia, North and South Carolina. The firm is dedicated to increased professionalism through continuing education for all of its associates and active participation in the National Association of Realtors and all of its affiliates. Come by or call for the best professional assistance in real estate available in Northeast Georgia. "GO FOR IT" in the beautiful mountains where life takes on a whole new meaning.

Whitney Realty, Route 1, Lake Burton,
Clarkesville, Georgia 30523, (404) 947-3532.

ARTICHOKE DIP

2 medium cans artichoke hearts
1 cup Parmesan cheese, grated
2 cups mayonnaise
2 teaspoons lemon juice
Sprinkle of garlic salt

Drain artichokes and squeeze or mash to small pieces. Mix all ingredients, pour in baking dish. Bake at 350 degrees for 45 minutes or until crusty on top. Serve with crackers.

Helen Whitney
Whitney Realty

TOMATO PUDDING

1 cup butter, melted
4 cups bread, cubed
2 cups tomato purée
½ cup water
1 cup brown sugar
½ teaspoon salt
1 teaspoon curry powder

Pour butter over cubed bread in flameproof baking dish. Simmer 5 minutes. Combine all other ingredients and pour over cubes and mix together. Set dish in pan of hot water. Bake at 375 degrees for 30 minutes or until brown on top. Yield: 8 servings.

Helen Whitney
Whitney Realty

MITZI'S CASSEROLE

¼ cup onions, chopped
½ cup celery, diced
¼ cup green pepper, chopped
3 tablespoons butter
1½ pounds ground beef
One 16-ounce can tomatoes
One 16-ounce can creamed corn
One 10-ounce can tomato soup
1 small can mushrooms, drained
Salt and pepper to taste
Dash Worcestershire sauce
1 medium-sized package egg noodles
Cheese, grated
Parsley (optional)

Sauté onions, celery and pepper in butter. Brown beef and drain off excess oil. Combine tomatoes, corn, tomato soup, mushrooms, salt and pepper. Cook and drain noodles. Combine all mixtures in a baking dish. Top with grated cheese. Dot with butter and sprinkle parsley flakes if desired. Bake 1 hour at 325 degrees.

Helen Whitney
Whitney Realty

DEVILED CHICKEN

4 to 6 chicken breasts, boned, skinned
4 tablespoons mayonnaise
3 tablespoons Durkee's sandwich spread
½ cup margarine, melted
Herb seasoned stuffing mix

Combine mayonnaise, spread and margarine. Dip chicken in mixture; roll in stuffing mix. Bake at 325 degrees for 1½ hours.

Robin Williams
Whitney Realty

Clarkesville through Dillard

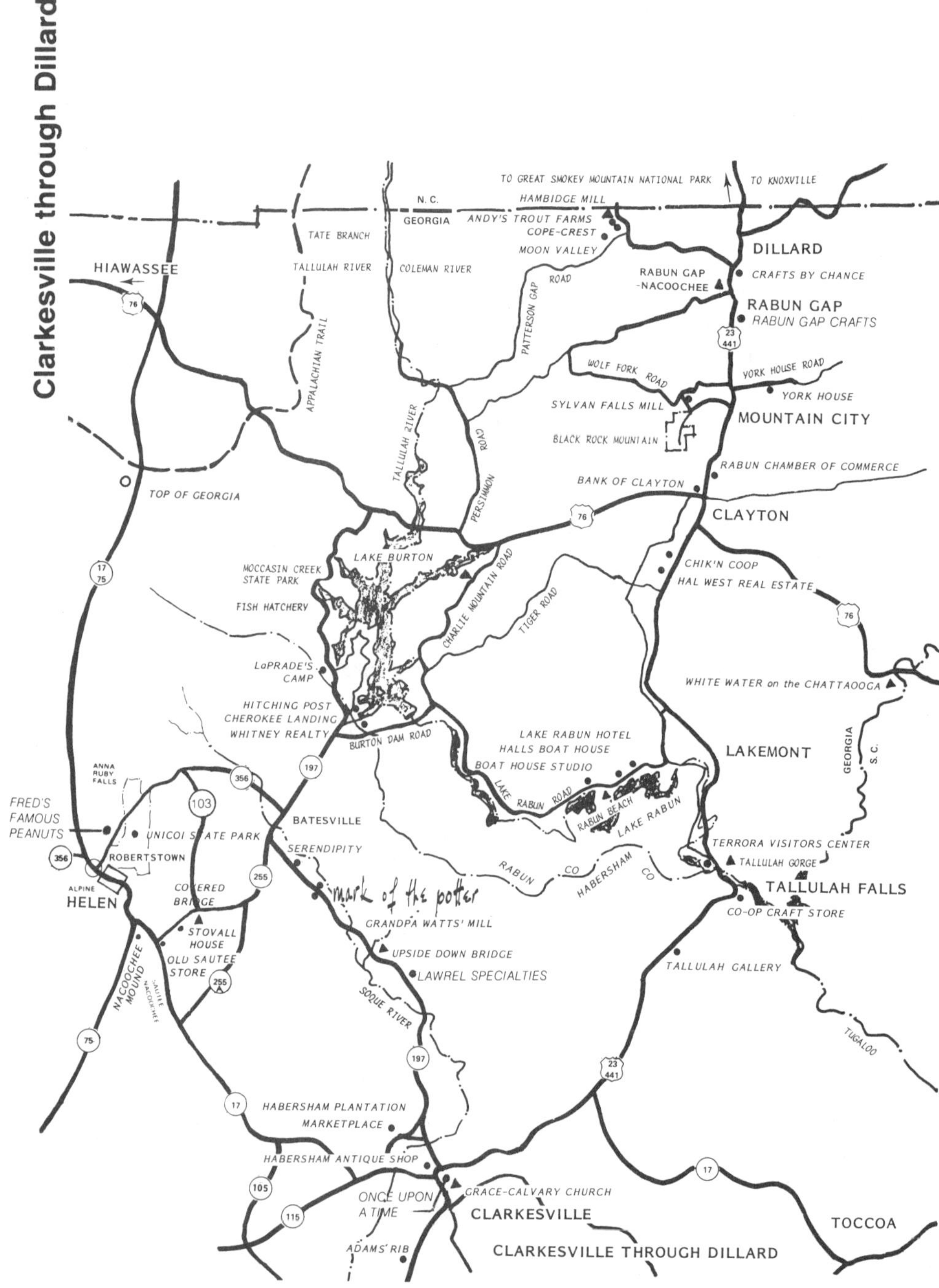

CLARKESVILLE THROUGH DILLARD

WHERE TO SLEEP

Best Western Dillard Motel 746-5321
Blue Ridge Camp & Resort 746-5491
Blue Ridge Motel 782-3415
Cannon's Cabins 782-3433
Chalet Village 746-5348
Charm House 754-9347
Commodore Motor Inn 782-4269
COPE-CREST—Page 118 BETTY'S CREEK ROAD, DILLARD 746-2550
Dillard House, The 746-5348
Dillard Motor Lodge 782-4207
Heart of Rabun 782-4258
LAKE RABUN HOTEL—Page 106 LAKE RABUN ROAD, LAKEMONT . . . 782-4946
LaPRADES CAMP—Page 52 GA 197 on LAKE BURTON 947-3312
Lakeside Lodge 754-6022
Lunsford's Motel 782-4229
MOON VALLEY—Page 108 BETTY'S CREEK ROAD, DILLARD 746-2466
Mountainaire Motel 782-3318
Mountain View Cottages
Rabun Beach Cabins 782-4887
YORK HOUSE, THE—Page 142 YORK HOUSE ROAD, MOUNTAIN CITY 746-2068

WHERE TO EAT

ANDY'S TROUT FARMS—Page 80 BETTY'S CREEK ROAD, DILLARD 746-2550
Appalachian Inn 782-2253
Barto's Bar-B-Que Shak 782-4038
CHIK 'n COOP—Page 90 US 441 SOUTH, CLAYTON 782-3437
Clayton Cafe 782-5438
COPE-CREST—Page 118 BETTY'S CREEK ROAD, DILLARD 746-2550
Countryside Kitchen 782-4258
Dairy Queen Brazier 782-5598
Dillard House, The 746-5348
Dillard, Jr. 746-5321
Dillard Motor Lodge 782-4207
HALLS BOAT HOUSE—Page 102 LAKE RABUN RD., LAKEMONT 782-4981
Heart of Rabun Restaurant 782-4258
House of Specials (sandwich) 746-5359
Jacks Cafe & Donut Shop 782-4613
Karan's 746-2726
Kentucky Fried Chicken 782-3970
LaPRADES CAMP—Page 52 GA 197 on LAKE BURTON 947-3312
Lakeside Restaurant 754-6022
MOON VALLEY—Page 108 BETTY'S CREEK ROAD, DILLARD 746-2466
Pizza Hut 782-2111
Rabun House Restaurant 782-4787
Richard's 782-3925
Sky Valley (Membership Resort) . . 746-5301
Tastee Freeze 782-3627
Village Pizza 782-2514
Wayne's Hideaway 782-5080

WHERE TO SHOP

Barker's Creek Crafts 746-5724
BOAT HOUSE STUDIO—Page 86 LAKE RABUN ROAD LAKEMONT . . . 782-5622
Burke's Habersham Homestead . . 754-4414
Carnes' "Nectars of the Wild"
CHEROKEE LANDING—Page 24 GA 197 at LAKE BURTON 947-3411
Clayton Flower Bed 782-5175
Clayton Gallery 782-5972
CO-OP CRAFT STORE—Page 92 US 441 & 23 at RAILROAD STATION, TALLULAH FALLS 754-6810
CRAFTS BY CHANCE—Page 94 US 441 FARMERS MARKET, DILLARD . 746-5754
Country Antiques 782-2229
Drug Store, Inc., The 782-4642
Fence Rail, The 782-3579
Fran's Gift Shop 782-4253
Gifts From Debbie 782-4323
GRANDPA WATTS' MILL—Page 98 GA 197, 10 MILES NORTH of CLARKESVILLE 947-3440

WHERE TO SHOP

HALLS BOAT HOUSE—Page 102 LAKE RABUN ROAD, LAKEMONT . . . 782-4981
Ham House, The 782-3152
HABERSHAM ANTIQUES—Page 36 GRANT ST., CLARKESVILLE . . . 754-6138
HABERSHAM PLANTATION MARKETPLACE—Page 42 BEAVER DAM ROAD, CLARKESVILLE 754-6225
Hambidge Center 746-5718
HITCHING POST—Page 48 GA 197 at LAKE BURTON 947-3612
Mountain City Antiques 746-2320
Pine Cone Antiques of Dillard 746-2450
Lakeview Orchards—US 441 north 754-4003
LAWREL SPECIALTIES 754-9451
Log Cabin Crafts 746-2991
MARK OF THE POTTER—Page 56 GA 197 10 Miles North of CLARKESVILLE 947-3440
RABUN GAP CRAFTS 746-5343
ONCE UPON A TIME COMPANY 754-5789
SERENDIPITY—Page 64 GA 197 11 Miles North of CLARKESVILLE 947-3643
Sheffield's Arts & Crafts 782-3565
SYLVAN FALLS MILL—Page 122 WOLF FORK ROAD, RABUN GAP 746-2762
TALLULAH FALLS GALLERY—Page 126 US 441 TALLULAH FALLS 754-6020
WEST REALTY, HAL—Page 136 US 441 SOUTH, CLAYTON 782-4504

WHERE TO CAMP

ANDY'S TROUT FARMS—Page 80 BETTY'S CREEK ROAD, DILLARD 746-2550
Appalachian Camper Park 754-9319
Best Western, Dillard R.V. 746-5321
Blue Ridge Camp & Resort 746-5491
COPE-CREST—Page 118 BETTY'S CREEK ROAD, DILLARD 746-2550
Persimmon Valley Campground . . 782-2624
Rabun Beach Campground 782-2303
Tallulah Falls—12 miles north on US 441 & 23 754-3242
Tallulah River Camping—North of US 76 on Tallulah River
Tate Branch Camping—North of US 76 on Tallulah River
TERRORA PARK—Page 132 US 441 & 23 12 MILES NORTH of CLARKESVILLE 754-3276

SERVICES

BANK OF CLAYTON—Page 82 SAVANNAH STREET, CLAYTON 782-4555
Dillard House Stables 746-5348
Hambidge Center 746-5718
Outdoor Ventures 746-2134
RABUN COUNTY CHAMBER OF COMMERCE—Page 110 US 441 NORTH, CLAYTON 782-4812
Sky Valley, skiing (Membership Resort) 746-5301
Southeastern Expeditions 782-4331
TERRORA VISITORS CENTER—Page 132 US 441 & 23 12 MILES NORTH of CLARKESVILLE 754-3276
WEST REALTY, HAL—Page 136 US 441 SOUTH, CLAYTON 782-4504

NOTICE: For your convenience we have listed all of the places to eat and all of the places to sleep in the area covered by this list. Quality is a personal concept and, although we have listed every place to eat or sleep known at the time of printing, some restaurants and some motels we recommend highly, while others do not quite meet our high standards of quality and we assume no responsibility for them. We would suggest that you inquire locally of any of the businesses in bold type listed above for their recommendations.

WHAT TO DO & SEE

Appalachian Trail
Blackrock Mountain State Park—Just off of US 441, Mountain City
Coleman River—North of US 76
Fish Hatchery—GA 197, 19 miles north of Clarkesville
GRACE CALVARY CHURCH—Page 32 Corner Green & Wilson, Clarkesville
HAMBIDGE MILL—Page 104 Betty's Creek Road, Dillard
LAKE BURTON—Page 15, 16 miles north of Clarkesville on GA 197
LAKE RABUN—Page 79 Off US 441 & 23, 6 miles south of Clayton
Moccasin Creek State Park—GA 197, 19 miles north of Clarkesville
Rabun's Lost Mine—Warwoman Road
SYLVAN FALLS MILL—Page 122 Wolf Fork Road, Mountain City
TALLULAH GORGE—Page 136 US 441 & 23, Tallulah Falls
Tallulah River—North of US 76
Tate Branch—North of US 76
TERRORA VISITORS CENTER—Page 132 US 441 & 23, 12 miles north of Clarkesville
UPSIDE-DOWN BRIDGE—Page 72, 8 miles north of Clarkesville on GA 197
Vintage Autos—Dillard
WHITEWATER ON THE CHATTOOGA—Page 140 US 76 at the Chattooga River

LAKE RABUN

Lake Rabun has the feeling of being settled for a long time. It has a bygone elegance reflected in the many walled entrances and iron gateways that lead to large estates built in the 1920's, when Rabun was the most accessible of the new lakes. The village of Lakemont, located near the dam, is a pleasant confusion of boat houses, homes, restaurants and a fantastically quaint old hotel. The upper end of Rabun becomes more remote, resembling a large river with no movement. Rabun Beach affords the visitor picnic, swimming and camping facilities in a quiet area densely covered with mountain laurel. At the very top of the lake a bridge crosses the river giving a good view of the dam for Seed Lake.

ANDY'S TROUT FARMS

Remember, the best place for a great catch is the Trout Farm that won the "Farm Family of the Year Award" as early as 1967! Come see why! Bring the family to Andy's Trout Farms, located on Betty's Creek Road, just west of Dillard, Georgia off US 441. Rainbow trout are sold by the pound. There's no license, no limit, and we dress them for you. Restaurant orders delivered.

Andy's Trout Farm, Betty's Creek Road, P.O. Box 129,
Dillard, Georgia, 30537 (404) 746-2550.

PARMESAN COATED TROUT

Two 1-pound trout filets
Salt and pepper to taste
12 saltine crackers, crushed
¼ cup Parmesan cheese, grated
Margarine

Mix crushed crackers and Parmesan cheese. Put in a bag and coat trout filets. Place in buttered baking dish, laying fish skin side down. Put margarine on fish and bake 20 minutes at 350 degrees.

Mrs. Andy Cope
Andy's Trout Farms

BEER BATTER TROUT

Four 1-pound rainbow trout filets
Vegetable oil
3 to 4 tablespoons biscuit mix
1 cup biscuit mix
½ teaspoon salt
1 egg
½ cup beer

Heat 1½ inches oil in heavy saucepan. Lightly coat trout with 3 to 4 tablespoons biscuit mix. Mix 1 cup biscuit mix, salt, egg, and beer until smooth. Dip fish into batter, letting excess drip into bowl. Fry until golden brown, about 2 minutes on each side; drain. Yield: 4 servings.

Mrs. Andy Cope
Andy's Trout Farms

SHRIMP STUFFED TROUT

½ cup butter
¼ cup onion, minced
2½ cups fresh mushrooms, chopped
1 pound shrimp, cooked, peeled and deveined
1 cup fresh bread crumbs, toasted
2 teaspoons thyme
1 teaspoon salt
6 whole rainbow trout, dressed
Melted butter

Lemon Sauce:
¼ cup butter
¼ cup flour
¾ teaspoon salt
1½ cups milk
Hot sauce
1 egg, beaten
⅓ cup fresh lemon juice

In a skillet, sauté onion and mushrooms in butter until tender. Stir in shrimp, bread crumbs, thyme, and salt. Pat trout dry and season cavity with salt and pepper. Spoon about two tablespoons stuffing into each trout. Keep remaining stuffing warm while baking fish. Place trout on baking pan and brush with melted butter. Bake in a preheated 450 degree oven 20 minutes or until fish flakes easily when tested with a fork.

Meanwhile, prepare lemon sauce. In a saucepan, melt butter. Stir in flour and salt. Gradually blend in milk and heat to boiling, stirring constantly. Boil one minute. Add a little hot sauce to the beaten egg and stir into mixture; continue heating until thickened. Stir in lemon juice. Serve lemon sauce with fish and additional stuffing.

Mrs. Andy Cope
Andy's Trout Farms

BANK OF CLAYTON

The Bank of Clayton was founded in 1904 to serve the community of Clayton, Georgia, and the county of Rabun in the Northeast Georgia Mountains. We like to feel that we have contributed to the development of our area and have been instrumental in making our region what it is today. As a full service bank, we provide a complete range of banking services from saving for a rainy day to business loans for a specific endeavor. On a regular basis we try to encourage employee camaraderie through such activities as group meals where each employee contributes his own special dish. Some of the recipes which follow are among those we judge as the best.

Bank of Clayton, P.O. Box 406,
Clayton, Georgia 30525, (404) 782-4555

RICE CASSEROLE

⅓ cup butter or margarine
1 cup rice
One 8-ounce can water chestnuts, drained and sliced
1 can onion soup
1¼ cans water

Melt butter in a large casserole dish and then combine all other ingredients. Bake at 350 degrees for approximately 1 hour.

Bank of Clayton

CHICKEN POT PIE

1 stewed chicken, boned
One 16-ounce can mixed vegetables, drained
1 can cream of chicken soup, undiluted
9 ounces chicken broth from stewed chicken
Salt and pepper to taste

Mix all ingredients and put in casserole dish.

Topping:
1 cup self-rising flour
1 stick margarine, melted
1 cup milk

Mix and pour over top of casserole. Bake 30 minutes at 350 degrees.

Bank of Clayton

SQUASH CASSEROLE

2 cups squash, cooked
1 carrot, grated
1 medium onion, grated
1 cup sour cream
1 can cream of chicken soup
Salt & pepper to taste
1 bag herb stuffing mix
Butter

Thoroughly mix all ingredients except the stuffing mix. Pour half of stuffing mix in casserole dish, then pour mixture over this. Add the remaining stuffing mix. Dot with butter and bake at 350 degrees for 45 minutes.

Bank of Clayton

SAUSAGE CASSEROLE

1 pound sausage (mild or hot to taste)
1 medium onion, chopped
2 stalks celery, chopped
1 can cream of mushroom soup
1¼ cans water
1 cup rice

Brown sausage in a frying pan and drain off grease. Combine sausage and all other ingredients in a large casserole dish and bake at 350 degrees for approximately one hour.

Bank of Clayton

QUICHE

This is a basic quiche recipe to which many other ingredients may be added to meet your own special taste.

1 pie crust, partially baked
2 tablespoons butter
3 eggs
½ pint heavy whipping cream
4 ounces Swiss cheese, grated
Seasoning to taste, depending on the type of quiche you are creating: (salt, pepper, cayenne pepper, nutmeg, garlic)

Spread the butter on the pie crust. Whip together the eggs and whipping cream until blended thoroughly. Add the spices you have chosen for the particular quiche you are making. Line the crust with the cheese, then add your flavor ingredients (some ideas follow). Pour the egg and whipping cream mixture over these ingredients and then bake in a 350-degree oven for approximately 45 minutes. The quiche will rise and turn golden brown when ready.

Flavor ideas:

Sausage Quiche:
½ pound sausage, cooked like ground beef and drained of excess fat
¼ large green pepper, chopped
1 medium onion, chopped
1 small can mushrooms dotted over the top of the quiche

Shrimp and Crab Quiche:
1 small can shrimp parts and small shrimp
1 small can crab meat, separated with all shell removed
1 small can mushrooms dotted over the top of the quiche

Use your imagination and come up with your own favorite flavors. Many people use ham or bacon.

Bank of Clayton

THE PEASANT

Ever since its opening night, in a converted drug store, *The Pleasant Peasant* has remained "the in-place to dine" in Atlanta. Whether you dine at the ever popular *Public House* in Roswell, the new *Dailey's* in downtown Atlanta or *The Country Place* in Colony Square (recently published in *Gourmet Magazine*), this group of fine restaurants continues to please. Try at home these two delicious recipes.

KAHLÚA CHEESECAKE

2 pounds cream cheese
¼ cup flour
½ teaspoon salt
6 tablespoons cocoa
1½ cups sugar
7 eggs, separated
6 fluid ounces whipping cream
2.5 fluid ounces Kahlúa
3 cups graham cracker crumbs
5½ tablespoons margarine

Blend cream cheese on low speed of electric mixer. When well blended, add flour, salt, cocoa, and half of the sugar. Separate egg whites and yolks. On low speed, blend whipping cream, egg yolks, and Kahlúa. Blend well. Mix in cream cheese mixture. On high speed in another bowl, beat egg whites with the remaining sugar until stiff. Fold into cheese mixture. Cover bottom of pan with aluminum foil. Grease sides. Make crust of graham crackers and margarine. Pat ½-inch thick into pan bottom. Carefully spoon cheese mixture into crust. Bake at 350 degrees for 1½ to 1¾ hours.

The Peasant, Inc. This cheesecake is served at The Public House, Roswell, Georgia. (404) 992-4646.

WHITE GAZPACHO

2 cups dry white wine
4 cups chicken broth
½ cup lemon juice, freshly squeezed
1 bunch scallions
1 bunch parsley
3 large cucumbers
3 medium tomatoes
Dash Tabasco
Salt to taste
½ teaspoon white pepper

Bring the wine, chicken broth and lemon juice to a boil. Chill several hours or overnight. Chop scallions and parsley. Slice cucumbers and roughly chop tomatoes. Combine all ingredients with chilled soup. Taste for seasonings. Yield: 6 servings.

The Peasant Inc. This gazpacho is served at The Country Place, Colony Square, Atlanta, Georgia. (404) 881-0144.

THE BOAT HOUSE STUDIO

The Boat House Studio is a teaching-working studio and is located on beautiful Lake Rabun where the artist, Martha Anne Oakley Pool, has spent her summers since childhood.

Commissions are accepted for works on porcelain, including portraits and handpainted, custom designed lavatories for new and older homes are a speciality. Matching bathroom accessories and lamps for other rooms are also available. Another medium in which the artist works is watercolor, and both these and the works on porcelain will be shown by appointment.

The artist is a member of the International Association of Porcelain Teachers and the Portrait Society of Atlanta. Her works are shown at the Tallulah Gallery in Tallulah Falls and at member shows at the Quinlan Gallery in Gainesville, Georgia. Classes for students are available.

*Boat House Studio, Lake Rabun Road, Box A-81, Route 1,
Lakemont, GA 30552, (404) 782-5622 or (404) 736-7973.*

HONEYWHEAT CORNBREAD

This recipe has become one of our family traditions.

1½ cups enriched corn meal
1 cup whole wheat flour
1 tablespoon baking powder
1 teaspoon salt
1½ cups milk
⅓ cup honey
2 eggs
¼ cup vegetable oil
⅔ cup carrots, shredded
¼ cup green onion, sliced

Combine dry ingredients. Add milk, honey, eggs and oil. Mix. Stir in carrots and onions. Spread into greased 9-inch square baking pan. (I use my "ole" iron skillet.) Bake in preheated, 400-degree oven about 25 minutes or until golden brown.

Martha Anne Pool
The Boat House Studio

MUSKITS
(A CROSS BETWEEN MUFFINS AND BISCUITS)

This is an original recipe by Mrs. W. H. Pool, Sr. who created it for her father who liked to do his own cookin'.

It is one of my children's favorites and is great for week-end visitors at the lake. I bake mine in those great big pottery muffin pans from Mark of the Potter.

6 cups of flour, sifted before measuring
1½ teaspoons soda
4 teaspoons baking powder
3 teaspoons salt
¾ cup shortening
Buttermilk

Sift the dry ingredients together. Cut in shortening with pastry blender. This mixture may be stored in a closed container on the shelf and used as needed or you may proceed with the remainder of the recipe.

Measure out needed amount of mix (above). Add enough buttermilk to make a soft dough. Spoon into greased muffin tins. Bake at 450 degrees until desired brownness. Caution: Do not over stir. Yield: about 2 dozen 2-inch muskits.

Martha Anne Pool
The Boat House Studio

BLUEBERRY PANCAKES
A LA MOBROSIS

An original recipe for those hungry mountain guests.

1 cup buttermilk
6 tablespoons cooking oil
2 eggs
½ cup brown sugar
1¼ cups flour, plain
¾ cup whole wheat flour
1 teaspoon cloves
1 teaspoon allspice
1 teaspoon cinnamon
2 level teaspoons baking powder
½ teaspoon soda, dissolved in ½ cup water
2 cups blueberries

Combine first 4 ingredients. Whisk with wire whisk until eggs are combined. Add next 5 ingredients. Stir. Add next 3 ingredients one at a time. Stir. Add grease to grill so your pancakes will not stick. Serve pancakes topped with cream cheese sauce and strawberry syrup. Serve a poached egg as a tip top nestled in cream cheese and sausage for those hearty souls.

Cream Cheese Topping:
8 ounces cream cheese, softened
2 tablespoons lemon juice
¼ cup sugar
¼ teaspoon almond extract

Blend. I use my food processor.

Strawberry Syrup:
Double package frozen strawberries, thawed, or fresh strawberries
½ cup brown sugar
4 tablespoons brandy
2 cups water

Simmer in an iron skillet while your pancakes cook.

Martha Ann Pool
The Boat House Studio

LEMON DELIGHT

Served by my mother, Mrs. Charlie Mae Oakley, on many occasions at our lake home.

3 cups water
1 cup sugar
Juice of 3 lemons
3 bananas, mashed
1 can crushed pineapple, drained

Boil water and sugar for 5 minutes. Cook and add fruit juice and fruit. Freeze, stirring occasionally. Run through food processor before serving. A very cooling dessert in the summer.

Martha Anne Pool
The Boat House Studio

SPINACH CASSEROLE

This recipe came to me from my sister-in-law, Trudi Oakley.

3 packages frozen spinach, chopped
½ cup butter or margarine
One 8-ounce package cream cheese
Herb seasoned stuffing mix

Cook spinach according to package directions; drain well. Squeeze in colander until dry. Return to top of stove, add butter, stir until melted. Add cream cheese in hunks until melted. Pour into deep casserole. Top with 1 cup herb seasoned stuffing mix. Bake at 375 degrees for 30 minutes.

Martha Anne Pool
The Boat House Studio

THE CHIK'N COOP

The Chik'n Coop is a family-owned and operated restaurant on US 441 South in Clayton, Georgia. Pat and Judy Marcellino established the restaurant in 1976 after moving to Clayton from Florida. They specialize in fried chicken, seafood, barbecued ribs, Italian dishes, corn fritters, and a variety of sandwiches, submarines, and salad bar items. Their popular sauces, salads, and cheesecake are their exclusive recipes and are homemade. Both take-out and dining room service are provided. There is an additional large dining room for banquets, receptions, and meetings. Special menu selections are available for buffet service on such occasions.

The Chik'n Coop, Incorporated, US 441 South, Clayton, Georgia 30525, (404) 782-3437. Open Wednesday through Sunday, 11:00 a.m. to 9:00 p.m. Closed Monday and Tuesday.

BAKED CORN CASSEROLE

2 cups cream style corn
1 cup milk
3 tablespoons flour
2 eggs, beaten
1 tablespoon sugar
Salt to taste

Mix ingredients well and pour into shallow buttered baking dish. Bake at 350 degrees until slightly brown and firm in center, approximately 45 minutes. Yield: 4 to 6 servings.

Judy Marcellino
The Chik'n Coop, Inc.

COPPER PENNIES

4 cups sliced cooked carrots, drained
1 small onion, chopped fine
1 medium bell pepper, chopped fine
1 can tomato soup
1 cup sugar
½ cup vegetable oil
¾ cup apple cider vinegar
1 tablespoon dry mustard
1 tablespoon Worcestershire sauce

Combine carrots, onion and peppers. Set aside. Bring to boil sugar, soup, oil, vinegar, mustard and Worcestershire sauce. Pour hot mixture over vegetables and refrigerate overnight. May be served hot or cold. Yield: 6 to 8 servings.

Judy Marcellino
The Chik'n Coop, Inc.

HOT SHERRIED FRUIT

1 pound can pineapple chunks
1 pound can pears
1 pound can peaches
1 pound can apricots
½ cup margarine
2 tablespoons flour or cornstarch
½ cup sugar
1 cup sherry

Drain all fruit and arrange attractively in glass casserole dish. Melt margarine in saucepan; add flour or cornstarch, sugar and sherry. Blend and heat until thickened. Pour over fruit. Bake 30 minutes in 350 degree oven. Yield: 8 servings.

Judy Marcellino
The Chik'n Coop, Inc.

FRENCH ONION SOUP AU GRATIN

4 large onions, chopped or sliced
4 tablespoons margarine or butter
Four 10½-ounce cans condensed beef broth
½ cup dry sherry
2 tablespoons Worcestershire sauce
Dash pepper
¾ cup Parmesan cheese, grated

In large pan, cook onion in margarine or butter until tender but not brown, about 20 minutes. Add beef broth, sherry, Worcestershire sauce and pepper. Bring to boil. Simmer 10 minutes. Sprinkle with Parmesan cheese when served. Yield: 6 to 8 servings.

Judy Marcellino
The Chik'n Coop, Inc.

CO-OP CRAFT STORE

Over 100 members bring together many types of hand-made items at the Co-op Craft Store. These include quilts, pillows, pottery, jewelry, wooden toys, baskets, brooms, tatting, stuffed toys and stained glass. Sale of these items adds to the economy and also encourages the preservation of traditional crafts.

The main store is at Tallulah Falls, Georgia, in the Train Station, with another retail outlet in downtown Clarkesville on US 441. In addition to the store—open 10:00 to 5:00 Monday through Saturday, 12:30 to 5:00 on Sunday—a mail order catalog is available for $1.00. Wholesale orders are offered on some items.

Co-op Craft Store, US 441-23, P.O. Box 67,
Tallulah Falls, Georgia 30573, (404) 754-6810.

VINEGAR PIE

½ cup margarine
1 cup sugar
2 eggs
3 teaspoons vinegar
1 teaspoon vanilla
½ cup pecans, chopped
1 pie shell, unbaked

Melt margarine; add ingredients as listed. Mix well. Pour into pie shell. Bake 30 minutes at 350 degrees. Yield: 8 servings.

Mildred Barron
Co-op Craft Store

HOMEMADE ROLLS

1 egg
¼ cup sugar
1 teaspoon salt
½ cup shortening
1 cup boiling water
1 package yeast
¼ cup warm water
4 or 5 cups plain flour

Put egg, sugar, salt, shortening and hot water in blender; mix well. Dissolve yeast in warm water. Combine both mixtures in large bowl; add flour to make stiff dough. Put out on floured board, knead until dough holds shape. Make into rolls and let rise until double in size. Bake at 350 degrees until brown. Can be stored in refrigerator for several days and then allowed to rise and bake. Yield: 24 rolls.

Mary Franklin
Co-op Craft Store

PEPPER JELLY

2½ cups cider vinegar
2 bell peppers, medium pods, chopped
2 or 3 pods hot pepper, depending on "how hot"
5 cups sugar
1 bottle Certo

Combine vinegar and both peppers in blender until peppers are very fine. Add mixture to sugar and cook 5 minutes. After it starts to boil, set off heat for 5 minutes. Add Certo and reheat to boiling. Pour into sterilized jars. (Add food coloring if desired.) Seal. Yield: six ½-pint jars.

This jelly, along with other pickles and jellies, is sold at our store.

Mary Franklin
Co-op Craft Store

ZUCCHINI BREAD

3 eggs
1 cup oil
2 teaspoons vanilla
2 cups grated zucchini
2 cups sugar
3 cups flour
1 teaspoon baking soda
½ teaspoon baking powder
¼ teaspoon salt
3 teaspoons cinnamon
1 cup nuts
1 cup raisins

Beat eggs until foamy. Add oil, vanilla, and zucchini. Stir well. Add dry ingredients, nuts and raisins. Mix well and put in 2 greased loaf or baking pans. Bake at 325 degrees until done, about 30 to 45 minutes. Yield: 2 loaves. Much better when frozen.

Francesca Lee Franklin
Co-op Craft Store

CRAFTS BY CHANCE

Crafts by Chance is on US 441 in the Farmers Market in Dillard, Georgia. Dozens of local people handmake fabulous crafts for the shop. Here is one of the largest and most beautiful selection of quilts found anywhere.

Here, also, are handloomed rugs, afghans and placemats, handstitched pot holders, aprons and pillows, wooden games, cars and doll houses, precious cloth or china dolls, Christmas decorations, jellies from wild berries.

Be inspired by a pattern, kit, or book or make your own craft.

Crafts by Chance is open January through March, Friday, Saturday and Sunday; April through December seven days a week from 9:30 a.m. until 6:00 p.m.

Crafts by Chance, US 441-23, Dillard Farmers Market, Box 99, Dillard, Georgia 30537 (404) 746-5754.

PRIZE-WINNING BARBECUED CHICKEN

1 cup vegetable oil
⅔ cup wine vinegar
3 tablespoons sugar
3 tablespoons catsup
1 tablespoon onion, grated
1½ teaspoons salt
1 teaspoon dry mustard
1 tablespoon Worcestershire sauce
1 clove garlic, minced
Dash liquid hot pepper seasoning
2 broiler fryers (3 pounds each), cut up

Combine all ingredients except chicken in a 2-cup measure. Place chicken in a shallow glass baking dish; pour marinade over and marinate in refrigerator 6 to 8 hours or overnight, turning occasionally, if possible. Grill chicken 5 to 6 inches from coals, 20 to 30 minutes on each side, turning and brushing often with marinade. If you have any remaining marinade, skim fat, then heat and serve hot with chicken. Yield: 6 servings.

Happy Chance
Crafts by Chance

BRANDIED PEACHES AND LIQUEUR

4 gallon churn crock
13 to 15 pounds sugar
17 to 18 pounds firm, just ripe, unbruised clingstone peaches (if you can get clingstone)

Buy about a bushel of small, firm clingstone peaches (Georgia or South Carolina peaches are best). Pick out the most perfect peaches (unbruised and as uniform in size as possible). Wash thoroughly to remove fuzz. Don't peel. Into clean churn crock, pour ½ inch layer of sugar. Place a layer of peaches on the bottom. Cover the peaches with a good layer of sugar. Repeat until churn is full. Finish with a very heavy layer of sugar on top.

Weight peaches with flexible plastic lid and heavy rock in strong plastic bag. This holds the peaches down when liquid forms. Cover with cheesecloth. A churn top can also be used because it has a hole in it. Don't seal crock. Store in dark, cool place. In 4 to 6 months you'll have delicious brandied peaches and a peach liqueur that must be tasted to be believed. This recipe is probably as old as peaches in Georgia.

Lucy Chance
Crafts by Chance

GRATED SWEET POTATO SOUFFLÉ

1½ cups sugar
½ cup milk
3 cups raw sweet potato, coarsely grated
2 eggs
½ cup butter or margarine
⅛ teaspoon soda
½ teaspoon cinnamon
¾ cup buttermilk
½ cup ground pecans

Mix sugar and milk; add potatoes, eggs and butter. Add soda, cinnamon, buttermilk and pecans. Bake at 400 degrees for 1 hour in greased casserole. Stir occasionally. Yield: 6 to 8 servings.

Lucy Chance
Crafts by Chance

PORK-RIB DINNER

4 pounds pork loin country-style ribs, cut into serving pieces
⅓ cup all-purpose flour
2 tablespoons salad oil
1½ cups apple juice
1 tablespoon salt
½ teaspoon pepper
2 pounds small red potatoes
One 16-ounce bag carrots, cut into 2-inch pieces
1 pound small whole onions
1 small head cabbage, shredded

About 2½ hours before serving: On waxed paper, coat ribs with flour; reserve leftover flour. In 8-quart Dutch oven with oven-safe handles, over medium-high heat, in hot salad oil, cook meat, a few pieces at a time, until well browned on all sides, removing pieces as they brown. Reduce heat to medium. Blend reserved flour into drippings in Dutch oven. Gradually stir in apple juice. Return meat to Dutch oven; add salt and pepper; heat to boiling. Cover Dutch oven and bake at 350 degrees for 30 minutes. Add potatoes, carrots and onions, cover; bake 30 minutes. Skim off fat from liquid in Dutch oven. Add cabbage; cover and bake 1 hour longer or until vegetables and meat are tender, stirring occasionally. Yield: 8 servings.

Happy Chance
Crafts by Chance

CHEESE CORN BREAD

1½ cups corn meal
1 cup cream corn
1½ cups mild cheddar cheese, shredded
1 onion, chopped
1 cup milk
2 eggs
½ cup oil
1 teaspoon sugar

Mix all ingredients. Pour into a greased and heated 12-inch skillet. Bake at 350 degrees for about 40 minutes.

Lucy Chance
Crafts by Chance

SUPPER ESCARGOT FOR TWO

Did you ever dream of having as much escargot as you want? Here's how! This is an easy dish to prepare and makes a delicious entree. Serve with crusty French bread and a hearty tossed salad.

1 can of 24 snails, well drained
24 fresh mushrooms with 1-inch diameter caps
⅓ cup butter, softened
1 clove garlic, finely minced
2 tablespoons parsley, finely minced
½ cup white wine
½ cup bread crumbs

Use individual baking dishes. Remove stems from caps, dice stems and place in baking dishes. Place 12 caps in each dish on top of stems. Beat minced garlic and parsley into butter. Place a snail in each cap and cover each with butter mixture. Pour ¼ cup wine over each dish. Sprinkle bread crumbs. Microwave, tightly covered, for 2 to 3 minutes at full power or bake uncovered in a hot oven for 10 minutes.

Glen and John E. LaRowe
Mark of the Potter

"GRANDPA WATTS' WATER-GROUND MEAL" MILL

This mill building was built in 1930 and it replaces 3 older buildings on this site. Mills have existed here since the early 1800's, and until the ravages of time took their toll, the site contained a small grist mill a hundred feet or so upstream, a lumber sizing and planing mill on the present mill site and—just a hundred feet downstream—a mill that turned porch posts and bed posts during the Victorian Era. All of these efficient old mills operated from the water power that flows so abundantly and beautifully here.

We often wonder what the earlier settlers thought when they first looked at the rapids beside this grand old mill, and, for that matter, what Grandpa Watts would think if he could see the pottery here now.

In September of 1985, Jay and Cathy Bucek purchased Mark of the Potter. They are both potters. The working studio is open to the sales shop and you can usually find Jay or Cathy at work at some phase of their craft. Visit Mark of the Potter, feel the history of the old mills, the present mill building and make up your own story of the past of these mills, these beautiful rapids and this beautiful Soque River.

Open everyday 10:00 to 6:00
Closed Christmas

Mark of the Potter, GA 197, 10 miles north of Clarkesville, Route 3, Box 83, Clarkesville, Georgia 30523, (404) 947-3440.

GRANDMA WATTS' POKE "SALAT"

Young, tender poke leaves, washed and drained
2 to 3 tablespoons bacon drippings
3 to 4 eggs

Gather poke leaves when young and only 3 to 4 inches tall. (Mrs. Watts said it was not good unless you had to dig it, to pick a mess.) Parboil poke for 15 minutes. Drain well, cover with fresh water, and cook until tender. Drain well. Heat bacon drippings in pan. Stir in poke. Before serving, beat eggs and "scramble" them with poke. Garnish with slices of hard cooked egg. Serve hot with cornbread.

As told to Glen LaRowe by Mrs. Leta Watts
Watts' Mill

KIFLI

6 egg yolks
1 pound sweet butter
½ pint sour cream
2 teaspoons vanilla
5 to 6 cups flour

Cream butter and egg yolks. Add cream and vanilla. Mix in flour. Work into a smooth dough. Roll into balls the size of walnuts. Cool in refrigerator overnight. The next day, roll each ball separately to the size of a saucer. Put a teaspoonful of filling straight across center. Roll toward you. Bend into half-moon shapes toward you. Bake on cookie sheets 10 to 15 minutes at 350 degrees. Roll in additional powdered sugar. Yield: 150.

Nut Filling:
6 egg whites
½ pound nut meats, ground
1½ pounds powdered sugar
½ teaspoon cinnamon
2 tablespoons orange juice (or ¼ teaspoon grated lemon rind)

Beat egg whites. Fold in sugar, nuts and flavoring.

Glen LaRowe

MARY MAC'S

Mary Mac's is one of the few remaining "tearooms" in the downtown Atlanta area. It offers 15 or more fresh vegetables, 6 or 7 meat choices, hot homemade breads, delicious old-fashioned desserts, and lots of Georgia hospitality. The restaurant is open from 11:15 a.m. until 2:00 p.m. for lunch, and 5:00 p.m. until 8:00 p.m. for dinner, closed Saturday and Sunday. There is a full bar. Reservations are not necessary unless it is a very large party.

Mary Mac's Ltd., 224 Ponce de Leon,
Atlanta, Georgia 30308, (404) 875-4337 or (404) 876-6604.

BUTTERMILK BISCUITS

2 cups plain flour
1 teaspoon salt
½ teaspoon sugar
2 teaspoons baking powder
4 tablespoons vegetable shortening or lard
1 cup buttermilk

Mix flour, salt, sugar, baking powder. Cut into this mix shortening or lard. This mix, or any multiple of it, can be stored in a jar with a tight lid, on a cool pantry shelf, for as long as a month. At any time, mix this with buttermilk, roll out, cut and cook on greased sheet at 375 degrees for 10 minutes.

Margaret Lupo
Mary Mac's Ltd.

CORNBREAD MUFFINS

2 eggs, beaten
2 cups buttermilk
3 tablespoons shortening or lard, melted
2 teaspoons salt
1 teaspoon sugar
2½ cups white waterground fine meal
3 teaspoons baking powder
1 teaspoon soda

Add buttermilk, shortening, salt and sugar to eggs. Stir well. Mix meal with baking powder and soda; slowly add to egg mixture. It should be a medium batter, not too thick with corn meal. Pour into hot greased muffin tins. Cook at 400 degrees about 15 to 20 minutes.

Margaret Lupo
Mary Mac's Ltd.

MARY MAC'S HONEY-BAKED ONION

6 medium white sweet onions, Vidalias if possible
1½ cups tomato juice
1½ cups water
6 teaspoons butter, melted
6 teaspoons honey

Peel and trim onions. Cut in half and place in buttered baking pan. Mix other ingredients; pour over onions. Bake one hour at 325 degrees, or until soft.

Margaret Lupo
Mary Mac's Ltd.

MARY MAC'S FAMOUS "CARTER CUSTARD"

One 6-ounce package cream cheese, room temperature
¾ cup milk
½ cup peanut butter
1 cup powdered sugar
1 package whipped topping
1 graham cracker crust
Peanuts, chopped

Beat cream cheese, milk, peanut butter and powdered sugar. In a separate bowl beat whipped topping. Fold whipped topping gently into cheese mix and pour into crumb crust. Top with chopped peanuts and freeze.

Margaret Lupo
Mary Mac's Ltd.

HALLS BOAT HOUSE

Located on picturesque Lake Rabun, Halls Boat House was established in the 1920's. In its early years it provided transportation for residents whose summer cottages were accessible only by water as well as scenic boat rides around the lake for tourists. Over the years residents bought their own boats and chartered rides were discontinued in lieu of boat rentals.

A first-rate marine service has developed to meet the needs of the increasing boat population. A fully equipped shop provides complete boat maintenance and repair work.

On Saturday nights during the summer, Halls features Pickin' and Grinnin', a hub of social activity with free bingo for the kids and the best live bluegrass music for the whole family. From toddlers to senior citizens, everyone joins in the dancin' and clappin'.

Halls Boat House, P.O. Box 36,
Lakemont, Georgia 30552. (404) 782-4981.

CRÊPES WITH SAUSAGE AND MUSHROOMS

3 eggs
1 teaspoon salt
1½ teaspoons sugar
1 scant cup flour
2 cups milk
4 to 5 tablespoons butter
Additional butter, to coat pan

These crêpes may be prepared the day before. Beat the eggs until light; add salt and sugar, beating constantly. Continue beating and alternately add the flour, milk and 3 tablespoons melted butter. Melt remaining butter in a small skillet. Pour in a small amount of batter and tilt the pan to cover the bottom in a thin layer. Cook over medium heat until underside of the crêpe is delicately browned. Turn and brown the other side, then transfer to a piece of waxed paper. Repeat until all the batter is used, and continue stacking crêpes between pieces of waxed paper.

Filling:
1 pound fresh mushrooms
¼ cup butter
1 tablespoon lemon juice
1 pound sausage
1 pint sour cream

Clean and slice mushrooms. Melt butter in a skillet. Sauté mushrooms in butter until all the liquid is evaporated. Add lemon juice. In another pan, brown sausage; drain excess grease. Combine mushrooms with sausage and sour cream. Spoon about ⅓ cup of filling on a crêpe; roll up and place seam side down. Continue until all crêpes are used. If any filling remains, spoon over the top. This is our traditional Christmas Day Brunch dish.

Pat White
Halls Boat House

BRAN MUFFINS

1 cup hot water
3 cups all bran or bran buds
3 cups flour
1 cup sugar
3 teaspoons baking soda
1 teaspoon salt
2 cups buttermilk
½ cup oil
2 eggs
½ cup nuts and/or ½ cup raisins

In large mixing bowl pour hot water over bran. Add flour, sugar, baking soda and salt. In another bowl combine buttermilk, oil and eggs; add to dry ingredients and mix until just blended. Stir in nuts and raisins. Spoon into greased muffin tins. Bake in 350-degree oven for 25 minutes. Yield: 3 dozen.

Pat White
Halls Boat House

HAMBIDGE MILL

One of the most exciting things about our mountains, even for a person who has lived in the area for years, is the discovery of the unexpected. Unlike the mountains of the west where you can see for miles before you reach a location, the Blue Ridge is a constant series of twists and turns that give you sudden vistas of little pastures and farms, or tumbling waterways set deep in thickets of laurel and rhododendron. Betty's Creek Road out of Dillard is one such adventure. If you watch carefully just past the entrance to Andy's Trout Farm, a tiny dirt road will drop off to the left. In a moment you are in a hidden valley surrounded by high peaks. The pastureland is dotted with sheep from the Hambidge Foundation (who maintain the property). Nearby is a lovely small meal-grinding mill which is operated on Fridays. For a moment it is as if you were in Switzerland. Then it's back in the car to seek out the next surprise the mountains hold for you.

Write the Hambidge Center for information on informal workshops, seminars, creative retreats or concerts that are held throughout the year.

The Hambidge Center, P.O. Box 33, Rabun Gap, Georgia 30568 (404) 746-5718.

BEEF STROGANOFF

1 pound boneless stew beef, cut in small pieces
3 tablespoons flour
Salt and pepper to taste
¼ cup margarine
1 large onion, coarsely chopped
1 can cream of mushroom soup
Toast or cooked rice

Salt and pepper beef pieces; dredge in flour. Brown in margarine in a heavy pan. Cook until meat is tender. Sauté the onion and add to meat. Cook briefly. Add enough water with the mushroom soup to make thick gravy; combine with meat. Serve over toast or rice.

Mary Franklin
Co-op Craft Store

ORANGE ALASKA

6 large navel oranges
¼ teaspoon salt
1¼ cups sugar
1½ cups milk
1 cup heavy cream
4 tablespoons Grand Marnier
2 egg whites, at room temperature
½ cup powdered sugar
¼ teaspoon vanilla extract

Set control of freezer at lowest setting. Cut a thick slice from the navel end of each orange (slice should be approximately ¼ of the orange). With a grapefruit knife and a teaspoon, scoop out orange pulp into a bowl; remove any seeds. Place orange cups in a shallow pan and set aside. Place orange pulp and juice in the container of an electric blender and blend until smooth, or place pulp in a bowl and with a potato masher press out the juice. Strain the juice and measure 2 cups. In a large bowl combine the 2 cups orange juice, salt, sugar, milk and heavy cream. Pour mixture into a 13 x 9 x 2-inch pan, cover with plastic wrap and place in the freezer until almost firm, stirring occasionally. Scrape mixture into a chilled bowl; add Grand Marnier. Beat with an electric or rotary beater until smooth but not melted. Fill the orange cups with the sherbet. There may be some sherbet left over; freeze it, covered in a small loaf pan. Cover orange cups and place in freezer until firm. At serving time, heat oven to 425 degrees. Beat egg whites until soft peaks form. Gradually add the powdered sugar, 1 tablespoon at a time, and beat until stiff peaks form. Stir in vanilla. Spread meringue over orange sherbet to edge of the orange cups. Bake uncovered 3 to 5 minutes, or until lightly browned. A light refreshing dessert. Yield: 6 servings.

Pat White
Halls Boat House

LAKE RABUN HOTEL

The Lake Rabun Hotel, in the heart of the Chattahoochee National Forest, is a rustic two-story lodge constructed of stone and wood. Built in 1922, it could have come straight out of a fairy tale. The furniture is handmade of mountain laurel and rhododendron branches. The focal point of the wood-paneled lobby is a marvelous stone fireplace. There are 16 guest rooms and some baths are shared. A continental breakfast is included. A restaurant, serving home style cooking, is across the street.

Boats may be rented at a nearby marina; a public beach area and spectacular waterfalls are close by.

Rates are reasonable. Dick and Barbara Gray, Innkeepers. Season: April 1st through October 31st.

Lake Rabun is about 9 miles south of Clayton off U.S. 441/23. Drive 6 miles south of Clayton, then turn right at Wiley Standard Service and the Clayton Carpet Center. Turn sharp left and proceed 4 miles to the hotel on the right.

Lake Rabun Hotel, Lake Rabun Road,
Lakemont, Georgia 30552, (404) 782-4946.

SWEET POTATO MUFFINS

½ cup butter
1¼ cups sugar
2 eggs
1¼ cups canned sweet potatoes, mashed
1½ cups all-purpose flour
2 teaspoons baking powder
¼ teaspoon salt
1 teaspoon cinnamon
¼ teaspoon nutmeg
1 cup milk
¼ cup pecans or walnuts, chopped
½ cup raisins, chopped

Preheat oven to 400 degrees. Grease 1½-inch muffin tins. Cream the butter and sugar. Add eggs and mix well. Blend in the sweet potatoes. Sift flour with baking powder, salt, cinnamon and nutmeg. Add alternately with milk. Do not over mix. Fold in nuts and raisins. Fill greased muffin tins ⅔ full. Bake at 400 degrees for 25 minutes. Can be frozen and reheated. Yield: 6 dozen.

Barbara Gray
Lake Rabun Hotel

PEPPERMINT STICKS

4 eggs
2 cups sugar
1 cup cocoa
1 cup flour
1 teaspoon peppermint extract or ¼ teaspoon oil of peppermint
1 cup butter

Beat eggs with sugar until thick. Add cocoa, flour, peppermint extract. Melt butter and add. Pour into greased, 11 x 17-inch pan, and bake at 350 degrees for 12 to 15 minutes. Recipe may be halved using smaller pan. Do not overbake. Cool, frost and coat with chocolate.

Frosting:
1 package powdered sugar
½ cup margarine
Peppermint flavoring
Milk

Beat powdered sugar and margarine until creamy. Add peppermint flavoring and enough milk to make icing. May be colored green.

Coating:
2 squares bitter chocolate
2 tablespoons margarine

Melt chocolate and margarine in shallow pan. With a pastry brush, paint the sheet of frosted cookies. Place in refrigerator about 10 minutes to harden. Cut into sticks. Yield: 96 cookies.

Barbara Gray
Lake Rabun Hotel

MOON VALLEY

Snug in the mountains of beautiful Northeast Georgia just off Betty's Creek Road, 3½ miles from Dillard, you will find peaceful Moon Valley. Trout fishing, hiking, exploring the backroads and byways for wild flowers and waterfalls are easy and fun. The quiet serenity of a private lake and streams calms the spirit. Rock on your front porch, sit by your cottage fire and eat in our gourmet dining room or in our gazebo. Small intimate parties can be arranged and gourmet dining is by reservations only. Your hosts Robert and Joan Moon invite you to Moon Valley: "The place where you belong."

Moon Valley, off Betty's Creek Road, Route 1, P.O. Box 680
Rabun Gap, Georgia 30568, (404) 746-2466.

VEAL ROBERT

1½ pounds veal
Fresh top cream
Flour
Olive oil
Butter
½ pound mushrooms
¼ cup Marsala wine

Marinate veal in fresh top cream. Flour lightly and cook 15 minutes in olive oil and butter, turn and cook another 10 minutes. Set aside veal and sauté mushrooms in drippings from veal; set aside. Pour in Marsala wine, top cream and cook down. Serve over veal and mushrooms.

Robert Moon
Moon Valley

CHEESE CAKE ROBERT

16 ounces small curd cottage cheese
16 ounces cream cheese
1½ cups sugar
4 eggs
⅓ cup cornstarch
2 tablespoons lemon juice
1 teaspoon vanilla
½ cup butter, melted
1 pint sour cream

Grease springform pan. Sieve cottage cheese and add cream cheese. Beat with high-speed electric mixer until blended and creamy. Beating at high speed, blend in sugar, then eggs. Reduce speed to low. Add cornstarch, lemon juice and vanilla. Beat until blended. Add butter and sour cream. Blend. Pour into pan and bake at 325 degrees for 1 hour and 10 minutes; turn off oven. Let cake stand in oven 2 hours. Cool and chill. Remove sides of pan.

Robert Moon
Moon Valley

HONEYED APPLES

1 cup honey
½ cup vinegar
2 cups apples

Heat honey and vinegar in a small porcelain or stainless steel pan. Pare, core, and thinly slice the apples. Drop apples a few at a time into the bubbling honey mixture. Remove them when transparent.

RABUN COUNTY CHAMBER OF COMMERCE

The Rabun County Welcome Center, headquarters for information about Rabun County and the Northeast Georgia Mountain Area, is located on US 441-23 in Clayton and operated by the Rabun County Chamber of Commerce in cooperation with the Georgia Department of Industry and Trade.

Rabun County is the home of: the *Foxfire* Books; the Wild Scenic Chattooga River of "Deliverance" fame; Sky Valley, the Southernmost ski slope in the United States; Tallulah Gorge, "the little wonder of the world"; miles of hiking trails; five beautiful lakes; and is a family mountain vacation land. It's a great place to visit, to work and to call "home."

Rabun County Chamber of Commerce, US 441-23, P.O. Box 761, Clayton, Georgia 30525, (404) 782-4812.

ROAST BEEF AND GRAVY

One 5-pound roast
4 tablespoons monosodium glutamate
4 tablespoons salt
1 medium onion, sliced
4 tablespoons cornstarch
1 cup water

Place roast in deep pan, fatty side up; sprinkle meat with salt and monosodium glutamate; place onions over meat. Pour water one inch high around meat. Cover pan with aluminum foil and bake in oven until meat thermometer registers 140 degrees for rare, 150 degrees for medium. Remove roast from oven; drain off stock and allow to cool until tallow has hardened. Remove tallow and bring liquid to a boil; thicken with cornstarch dissolved in one cup of water. Slice roast to desired thickness and ladle gravy over it. Yield: 12 to 15 servings.

Mary Ann Welch, Appalachian Inn
Rabun County Chamber of Commerce

EGGPLANT PARMESAN

1 medium to large eggplant
1 egg
¼ cup white wine
Bread crumbs
Olive oil (or olive and corn oil mixed)
One 15-ounce can tomato sauce
2 cloves garlic, finely chopped
½ teaspoon basil
½ pound Mozzarella cheese, sliced
½ cup Parmesan cheese, grated

Peel and slice eggplant ⅜-inch thick. Beat egg and wine together. Dip eggplant slices in egg mixture, then in breadcrumbs and brown in oil. Drain on paper towels. Simmer tomato sauce, garlic and basil together in saucepan 10 to 15 minutes. Layer half the eggplant, mozzarella, Parmesan and sauce in baking dish, then repeat layers. Bake at 350 degrees for 30 minutes. Yield: 6 servings.

The Dillard House
Rabun County Chamber of Commerce

CHEESE SQUASH CASSEROLE

¾ cup onion, chopped
¾ cup margarine
3 pounds squash
1½ tablespoons sugar
Salt and pepper to taste
2 eggs, separated
1 cup cheddar cheese, shredded
1½ cups bread crumbs

Sauté onion in margarine. Cook squash. Drain well. Separate eggs. Add beaten egg yolks, onion, sugar, and ½ of the cheese. Add beaten egg whites. Turn into buttered dish. Sprinkle with remaining cheese and bread crumbs. Bake at 300 degrees until firm. Yield: 6 servings.

The Dillard House
Rabun County Chamber of Commerce

MARINATED GARDEN VEGETABLES

Two 15½-ounce cans French-style green beans, drained
One 16-ounce can cut green beans, drained
One 17-ounce can English peas, drained
1 cup celery, finely cut
¼ cup onion, chopped
1 medium green pepper, finely chopped
¼ cup pimento
¼ cup water chestnuts, sliced
½ cup cider vinegar
½ cup vegetable oil
1¼ cups sugar

Combine first 8 ingredients. Set aside. Combine vinegar, oil, and sugar. Mix well and pour over vegetables, tossing gently to coat thoroughly. Refrigerate overnight. Drain well before serving. Yield: 12 to 14 servings.

Judy Marcellino
The Chik'n Coop, Inc.

THE OLD STAND-BY: FRIED RAINBOW TROUT

6 dressed rainbow trout
Salt and pepper to taste
Seasoned corn meal, add salt and pepper to meal and mix
Hot grease to cover at least ½ inch in skillet

Season trout with salt and pepper and roll in corn meal. Fry in hot grease until golden brown, turning only once. Allow about 7 minutes to each side. Serve with tartar sauce and lemon slices.

Mrs. Andy Cope
Andy's Trout Farms

BROCCOLI, RICE AND CHEESE CASSEROLE

2 tablespoons butter or margarine
½ cup celery, diced
½ cup onion, diced
1 can cream of chicken soup
1 can cream of mushroom soup
One 8-ounce jar processed cheese spread
One 10-ounce package chopped broccoli, cooked
3 cups rice, cooked
Paprika

Sauté celery and onion in butter or margarine until tender. Mix with chicken and mushroom soups, cheese, broccoli, and one cup of the rice. Grease a large casserole dish and line with remaining rice. Add broccoli mixture and sprinkle with paprika. Bake at 350 degrees for 20 minutes or until bubbly. Yield: 6 to 8 servings.

Francesca Lee Franklin
Co-op Craft Store

BLUEBERRY CREAM DESSERT

This is our family's favorite way to eat North Georgia blueberries.

1½ cups graham cracker crumbs
6 tablespoons butter or margarine, melted
½ cup sugar
1 envelope unflavored gelatin
¾ cup cold water
1 cup dairy sour cream
One 8-ounce carton blueberry yogurt
½ teaspoon vanilla
1 cup fresh blueberries

In a bowl, combine cracker crumbs and the melted butter. Reserve ¼ cup of the crumb mixture; press remaining crumbs in bottom of 10 x 6 x 2-inch dish. In saucepan, mix the ½ cup sugar and gelatin; add the water. Heat and stir until gelatin and sugar dissolve. Combine sour cream and yogurt; gradually blend in gelatin mixture. Add vanilla. Chill until partially set. Stir in blueberries. Turn into crust. Sprinkle reserved crumbs on top. Chill until set. Yield: 8 servings.

Pat White
Halls Boat House

THE SATURDAY SHOP

John Kollock, whose illustrations fill this book, is a well-known artist, writer, historian and painter of the mountain area. In addition to illustrating over 20 books for other authors, he has written three books of his own—*THESE GENTLE HILLS, THE LONG AFTERNOON, and MEG'S WORLD.*

He does several one-man shows each year throughout the Southeast. He also has special shows at his studio and does many private commissions. His watercolor paintings are in private and public collections, including the White House.

He and his wife, Nancy, conduct one personally-designed tour each year to Europe.

For current information on books, prints, shows and tours write to The Saturday Shop, P.O. Box 315, Clarkesville, Georgia 30523.

GOAT'S MILK ICE CREAM

½ cup honey
3 tablespoons unbleached white flour
3 eggs
5 cups goat's milk
1 cup heavy cream
1 teaspoon vanilla
2 cups of combined blueberries and sliced peaches

Place honey, flour, eggs, cream and 1 cup of milk in electric blender and blend until smooth. Pour into a saucepan. Heat, stirring until mixture thickens. Cool. Beat in remaining milk, vanilla and sliced fruit. Place in a hand-crank or electric ice cream freezer and proceed according to freezer instructions. Mix until firm. Scrape container and proceed to fill waiting bowls. Best when eaten right away but can be stored in the freezer. Yield: 6 servings.

Carey Kollock
The Saturday Shop

MEG'S MEAT LOAF

1 pound ground beef
1 egg
1½ cups bread crumbs
1cup milk
1¼ teaspoons salt
2 tablespoons soy sauce
One 10-ounce package frozen spinach, thawed, chopped and drained

Combine ground beef, egg, bread crumbs, milk, salt, soy sauce. Add spinach; mix well. Pat into a 9 x 5 x 3-inch loaf pan. Bake in 350-degree oven for 1½ hours.

Mushroom Sauce:
One 3-ounce can mushrooms, sliced, undrained
2 tablespoons all-purpose flour
1 cup sour cream
2 tablespoons snipped chives
¼ teaspoon dill weed

In saucepan combine mushrooms, flour, sour cream, chives and dill weed. Cook and stir just until mixture thickens. Do not boil. Yield: 5 servings.

Meg Kollock
The Saturday Shop

CAROB AND HONEY BROWNIES

½ cup butter or margarine
⅔ cup honey
2 eggs
1 teaspoon vanilla
½ teaspoon sea salt
½ cup carob powder
⅔ cup whole wheat flour
1 teaspoon baking powder
1 cup nuts or sunflower kernels, chopped
3 tablespoons milk

Preheat oven to 350 degrees. Cream butter with honey. Beat in the eggs, one at a time. Beat in the vanilla and salt. Sift together the carob powder, flour and baking powder and stir with the nuts or kernels and milk into batter. Turn into a well-oiled or buttered, 9-inch square baking pan and bake 30 minutes or until done. Cut into squares while still warm.

Kathleen Kollock
The Saturday Shop

SAUSAGE SQUASH CASSEROLE

1 pound sausage
1 clove garlic, crushed
4 cups squash, shredded
½ cup dry bread crumbs
½ cup Parmesan cheese, grated
½ cup milk
1 tablespoon parsley, chopped
½ teaspoon oregano
½ teaspoon salt
2 eggs, beaten

In a frying pan cook sausage and garlic. Drain. Cook squash in a little water. Drain. Combine sausage and squash. Add the remaining ingredients. Fold in the eggs last. Put in a greased 10 x 6 x 1½-inch dish and bake at 325 degrees for 25 to 30 minutes. You may substitute hamburger for sausage. Yield: 4 to 6 servings.

Meg and Nancy Kollock
The Saturday Shop

TANGY CLAM DIP

One 8-ounce package cream cheese
One 6-ounce can clams, minced and drained, reserving juice
1 to 2 tablespoons Worcestershire sauce
1/8 teaspoon cayenne pepper, or to taste
Lemon pepper, to taste

One day ahead: In a medium sized bowl, mash cream cheese with a fork, add drained, minced clams, Worcestershire sauce, lemon pepper and cayenne pepper. Cream all ingredients together. Adjust spices and slowly add clam juice to obtain desired consistency. Place in serving bowl, cover and refrigerate overnight. Garnish with paprika and serve with crackers.

Phoebe Martin
Cornelia Bank

RICE SALAD

3 cups hot white rice, cooked (do not use instant rice)
½ cup olive oil (can be a mixture of the oil in the artichoke jar and regular olive oil)
½ pound fresh mushrooms
3 tablespoons butter
1 cup marinated artichoke hearts, sliced
1 cup fresh tomatoes, chopped (peel and seed if you prefer)
½ cup black olives, sliced
1 teaspoon freshly cracked black pepper
Salt
½ purple onion, thinly sliced

Toss the hot rice with the oil in a large bowl, using 2 forks. Set aside to cool. Thinly slice the mushrooms; sauté briefly in the butter, add to the rice with the artichoke hearts, tomatoes, olives, pepper, salt to taste, and onion. Toss thoroughly. Serve at room temperature. Yield: 6 servings.

VARIATION: If fresh tomatoes are not available, slivers of sweet red peppers, either fresh or canned, make an acceptable substitute.

Excellent reheated as leftover and served as accompaniment.

Betty Gesbocker
Glenmeadow

COPE-CREST
A SQUARE DANCE RESORT

Nestled among the oldest mountains in the world, in a secluded and peaceful valley, lies Cope-Crest, a Square Dance Resort. Western square dancers from all over the world come to this retreat for a week of square dancing, fun, fellowship, and some of the best food the North Georgia hills can provide. Fresh vegetables, homemade cakes and pies, biscuits, yeast rolls, freshly-caught rainbow trout from Andy's Trout Farms next door—the food is truly part of the fun of spending a week at this resort!

Our Saturday Night Fish Buffet is a popular attraction for "one-day" visitors. We at Cope-Crest invite you to come share our mountains—our food—and enjoy, dancing or watching, our favorite activity—square dancing!

Cope-Crest, Betty's Creek Road, P.O. Box 129
Dillard, Georgia (404) 746-2134.

TERRY'S OATMEAL PANCAKES

2½ cups buttermilk
2 cups rolled oats, soaked overnight in buttermilk
1½ cups wholewheat pastry flour
1 teaspoon salt
1 teaspoon baking powder
3 eggs
1 tablespoon soda, dissolved in 2 tablespoons hot water
⅓ cup butter, melted
2 tablespoons brown sugar

Mix flour, salt, baking powder, eggs, soda, butter, and sugar and add to oatmeal mixture. Serve with maple syrup, molasses, or honey.

Becky Cope
The Square Dance Resort

CURRY DIP

1 cup mayonnaise
1 tablespoon curry
1 garlic clove, crushed
2 tablespoons catsup
1 teaspoon onion
Salt & pepper
1 teaspoon Worcestershire sauce

Mix all ingredients together. On a platter, arrange fresh vegetables suitable for dipping. Cauliflower, squash, carrot sticks, and cucumbers are great. Arrange them with the curry dip in the middle. This is excellent for the salad bar or for late night snacks after the dance.

Becky Cope
The Square Dance Resort

ANGEL BISCUITS

1 cup shortening
5 cups plain flour
¾ teaspoon baking powder
1 teaspoon salt
1 teaspoon soda
¼ cup sugar
1 package yeast, dissolved
2 cups buttermilk

Cut shortening into dry ingredients. Dissolve yeast in 2 tablespoons lukewarm water and add buttermilk. Mix all ingredients well. Roll to ½-inch thickness and use biscuit cutter. Refrigerate until needed. Bake at 400 degrees for 20 minutes.

Becky Cope
The Square Dance Resort

CRANBERRY SALAD

One 3-ounce package lemon flavored gelatin
1 cup boiling water
1 can cranberry sauce, frozen
One 8-ounce can pineapple, crushed
1 medium apple, chopped
½ cup celery, chopped

Dissolve gelatin in boiling water. Stir in sauce, fruit, and celery. Pour into quart pan. Chill until set.

Becky Cope
The Square Dance Resort

CHEESE BALL

One 8-ounce package cream cheese
1 cup Cheddar cheese, shredded
1 small onion, chopped
1 tablespoon Worcestershire sauce
½ cup pecans, chopped

Mix ingredients well and chill 3 to 4 hours. Serve with crackers. Decorate with parsley.

Becky Cope
The Square Dance Resort

CHOCOLATE PEANUT BUTTER PIE

2 pie shells, baked
½ cup peanut butter
1 cup powdered sugar
½ cup sugar
½ cup self-rising flour
2 tablespoons cocoa
2 egg yolks
4 cups milk

Mix peanut butter and powdered sugar together and smooth this mixture in bottom of shell. Make hot pudding by mixing remaining ingredients. Pour over filling.

Becky Cope
The Square Dance Resort

VEGETABLE STUFFED TROUT

½ can cream of mushroom soup
1 small carrot
1 medium stalk celery
¼ onion, golf ball size
1 teaspoon lemon juice
2 tablespoons butter
½ teaspoon salt
¼ teaspoon pepper
Dash of thyme
2 slices white bread, crumbled
Two 10-ounce rainbow trout
2 slices bacon

Mix first 9 ingredients and cook in pan with butter for 5 minutes. Mix with bread crumbs. Pack inside the fish. Grease pan. Place trout in pan, put 1 slice of bacon on top of each fish. Bake at 350 degrees for 25 to 28 minutes.

Mrs. Andy Cope
Andy's Trout Farms

BAKED RAINBOW TROUT WITH SEASONED SALT

4 rainbow trout
Seasoned salt, pepper
¼ cup margarine or butter
2 tablespoons onion, chopped
2 tablespoons celery, chopped
2 tablespoons lemon juice
¼ teaspoon Worcestershire sauce

Pat trout dry. Heat oven to 350 degrees. Sprinkle inside and out of trout with seasoned salt and pepper. Arrange fish in buttered baking dish. Cook onion and celery in margarine until lightly browned. Remove from heat. Add lemon juice and Worcestershire sauce. Spoon 1 tablespoon mixture in cavity of each fish. Bake 25 to 30 minutes. Yield: 4 servings.

Mrs. Andy Cope
Andy's Trout Farms

SYLVAN FALLS MILL

The Sylvan Falls Mill, Rabun Gap, Georgia, is located 4½ miles north of Clayton and 2 miles west of U.S. 441 on Wolf Fork Valley Rd. It is one of the beauty spots of North Georgia with the waterfalls cascading for over 100 feet. The 27 foot water wheel is used to grind corn meal and whole wheat flour which may be purchased at the mill. There has been a grist mill on this site since 1840 and the present mill was restored in 1978 by Maynard and Florence Murray.

The mill was purchased in 1983 by Dick and Isla June Davis and is now their permanent home. You are welcome to come and visit one of the most spectacular mills in Georgia, open from April through October.

Sylvan Falls Mill, Wolf Fork Valley Rd.,
Rt. 1, Box 548, Rabun Gap, GA 30568, (404) 746-2806

STONE GROUND WHOLE WHEAT BREAD

Dry Mix:
2½ pounds stone-ground flour
2½ pounds all-purpose flour
2 cups dry milk powder
2 teaspoons salt
5 packages yeast

Wet Mix: (should be very wet)
½ cup butter
½ cup honey
5 cups water, warm from tap
1 pound sunflower seeds (optional)

Combine dry and wet mix; knead 5 to 10 minutes. Let set in warm place until double in size. Knead 5 to 10 minutes. Cut into five parts for large bread tins. Let rise until double and then bake 45 minutes at 375 degrees or until brown to suit. Yield: 5 loaves.

Florence Murray
Sylvan Falls Mill

STONE GROUND WHEAT CRESCENT ROLLS

⅔ cup milk
½ cup butter
¼ cup sugar
1 teaspoon salt
1½ packages yeast
2 eggs, beaten
1½ cups stone-ground wheat
1½ cups all-purpose flour

Scald milk; add butter, sugar, and salt. Cool to lukewarm. Add yeast and let stand until dissolved. Add beaten eggs and stone-ground flour. Stir until thoroughly mixed. Gradually stir in enough all purpose flour to make soft dough. Place in greased bowl, cover and refrigerate overnight.

Remove from refrigerator and leave at room temperature for 2 hours. Roll into large circle, about ¼-inch thick, and spread lightly with melted butter. Cut into 16 pie-shaped wedges. Roll each wedge from outside towards point. Place on greased cookie sheet. Let rise until double, 1 to 6 hours. Bake 10 to 15 minutes at 400 degrees. Yield: 16 rolls.

Maynard Murray
Sylvan Falls Mill

CORN BREAD (CRISP STYLE)

½ teaspoon baking powder
1 teaspoon baking soda
½ teaspoon salt
½ cup all-purpose flour
1 cup corn meal
2 eggs
1⅓ cups buttermilk
2 tablespoons butter, melted
1 tablespoon honey

Sift together baking powder, soda, salt and flour. Mix in corn meal. Preheat oven to 425 degrees. In separate bowl beat eggs. Add buttermilk, melted butter and honey, beating to mix. Blend flour and egg mixture together. Batter will be thin. Grease large flat pan, 11 x 15, with lard. Put pan in oven until very hot. Pour batter into hot pan and bake until crisply done, about 20 minutes. Yield: 15 pieces.

Maynard Murray
Sylvan Falls Mill

STONE GROUND WHEAT PANCAKES

½ cup wheat germ
2 cups stone-ground wheat flour
2 teaspoons baking powder
1 teaspoon brown sugar
1 teaspoon salt
2 large eggs
2½ cups milk
2 tablespoons oil

Stir together all dry ingredients. Beat eggs lightly and combine with milk. Add to dry mix and stir lightly. Stir in oil. Heat griddle but do not grease. Pour onto griddle, turning once when bubbles come to surface and edges are slightly dry. Use syrup, yogurt, apple butter, or honey. Yield: 18 pancakes.

Maynard Murray
Sylvan Falls Mill

CORN MUFFINS

1 cup corn meal
1 cup all-purpose flour
¼ cup sugar
½ teaspoon salt
4 teaspoons baking powder
2 eggs
1 cup milk
¼ cup corn oil or melted butter

Sift dry ingredients into bowl; add eggs, milk, and shortening. Beat with fork until smooth. Do not over beat. Cook in greased muffin tins about 25 minutes at 400 degrees.

Maynard Murray
Sylvan Falls Mill

STONE GROUND WHEAT DINNER ROLLS

1½ cups milk
1 teaspoon salt
⅓ cup oil
⅓ cup honey
½ cup water
2 eggs, slightly beaten
2 packages dry yeast
3 cups stone ground wheat flour
3 cups all-purpose flour

Scald milk; add salt, oil, honey, water, eggs, and yeast in that order. (By the time yeast is added the milk should be cool.) Mix well. Beat in stone-ground wheat flour; let stand 15 minutes. Add enough flour for medium-stiff dough, knead 10 to 20 minutes until smooth and elastic. Place in lightly-greased bowl, turning once to grease top. Cover and let rise until double in size, about 45 minutes. Punch down and separate into 32 equal pieces. Shape into balls. Place in baking pans or on cookie sheets. Let rise until double in size, about 45 minutes. Bake 25 to 30 minutes in 375-degree oven.

Florence Murray
Sylvan Falls Mill

"OLDTIME SPOON ROLLS"

1 package dry yeast
2 cups warm water
¾ cup margarine, softened
1 egg
¼ cup sugar
2 cups stone-ground wheat
2 cups all-purpose flour

Dissolve yeast in warm water. Cream margarine with sugar and egg. Add yeast and water to mixture, then mix in flour, one cup at a time. Cook at 450 degrees for 5 to 10 minutes in greased muffin tins.

Florence Murray
Sylvan Falls Mill

SWEET POTATO SOUFFLÉ

3 medium sweet potatoes, boiled and mashed
5 eggs
2 cups sugar
3 teaspoons nutmeg
½ cup raisins
1 cup butter
Milk

Mix all of above and add enough milk to make mixture soft enough to pour into casserole which has been well buttered. Bake at 300 degrees until golden brown. Yield: 8 to 10 servings.

Minni Carver
The Hitching Post

TALLULAH GALLERY

Tallulah Gallery was established in 1973 as both a service and educational project of Tallulah Falls School. It continues today and is also rapidly becoming the hub of artistic activity in Northeast Georgia.

Tallulah Gallery represents an effort to collect and present the works of local artists and craftsmen as well as to present a wider selection to suit varied tastes.

The recent addition of the "gallery room" increases floor space and inventory and is a pleasant place to rock and enjoy the warmth from the wood heater. Free coffee and hot tea are available.

All proceeds and profits from gallery sales have helped provide a scholarship fund for deserving students at Tallulah Falls School. Art work represented in Tallulah Gallery includes batiks, watercolors, oil paintings, photographs and prints. Most are matted, framed and ready to hang. The staff is always available to help you with your selection or you may browse at your own pace.

Tallulah Gallery displays many styles of pottery including wind chimes, mugs, and pitchers. Since pottery is becoming more popularly used in home cooking, a selection of original casserole and quiche dishes is always on hand. Many visitors to Tallulah Gallery have found pottery to be a most appropriate gift for almost any occasion.

Weavings by local artists are carefully selected by Tallulah Gallery to blend with and highlight pottery displays. Many Gallery visitors have also used weavings as wall hangings and rugs.

Tallulah Gallery, US 441-23, Tallulah Falls, GA 30573 (404) 754-6020.

CARROT CAKE

1½ cups oil
2 cups sugar
4 eggs
2 cups plain flour
1 teaspoon soda
1 teaspoon salt
1 teaspoon baking powder
1 teaspoon cinnamon
½ teaspoon vanilla
1 cup nuts, chopped
2½ cups carrots, grated

Mix well oil, sugar, and eggs. Combine all dry ingredients and add to first mixture. Mix well. Add vanilla, nuts and carrots. Pour into pan and cook 30 minutes for layers and 50 minutes in a loaf pan at 350 degrees.

Tallulah Gallery

APPLE STRUDEL

½ cup butter
2 cups boiling water
1 cup sugar
1 teaspoon vanilla
3 tablespoons shortening
2 cups self-rising flour
Ice water
2 cups apples, chopped fine
¼ cup brown sugar
Cinnamon to taste

Mix butter, water, sugar and vanilla in baking pan and set aside. Cut shortening into flour and add enough ice water to form dough. Roll thin and spread evenly with mixture of apples, sugar, and cinnamon. Roll up as for jellyroll. Slice in ½-inch to ¾-inch pieces and place in pan of liquid mixture. Bake at 425 degrees until golden brown.

Tallulah Gallery

COUNTRY MEAT LOAF

1 pound ground beef
½ pound pork sausage
1 egg, beaten
1 cup cornbread crumbs
1 onion, finely chopped
1½ teaspoons salt
¼ teaspoon pepper
4 ounces tomato sauce

Mix all ingredients and shape into loaf. Put in shallow pan.

Sauce:
4 ounce can tomato sauce
2 tablespoons prepared mustard
¾ cup water
2 tablespoons brown sugar
2 tablespoons vinegar

Mix well and pour over meat loaf. Bake at 350 degrees for 1 hour. If a quantity of liquid is left when the loaf is done, thicken sauce and serve over loaf.

Tallulah Gallery

HOT CHICKEN SALAD

3 cups chicken, diced
2⅔ cups celery, diced
1 tablespoon onions, chopped
½ cup almonds, browned and chopped
1½ teaspoons lemon rind
2 tablespoons lemon juice
¼ teaspoon pepper
⅔ cup mayonnaise
2 cups cheese, shredded
2 ounces potato chips, crushed

Toss lightly all ingredients except cheese and potato chips. Place in casserole dish or pan. Sprinkle cheese, then potato chips over top of salad mixture. Bake at 350 degrees for 25 to 30 minutes. Serve hot!

Tallulah Gallery

TALLULAH SQUASH CASSEROLE

4 cups squash, cooked, drained, and mashed
1 medium onion, diced fine
½ green pepper, diced fine
¼ cup pimento, chopped
½ cup margarine, melted
1½ cups basic white sauce or 1 can celery soup
½ package herbed stuffing mix
Salt and pepper to taste

Mix all ingredients and place in 2-quart greased casserole. Heat thoroughly at 350 degrees until bubbly.

Tallulah Gallery

OATMEAL COOKIES

¾ cup shortening, softened
1 cup firmly-packed brown sugar
½ cup granulated sugar
1 egg
¼ cup water
1 teaspoon vanilla
1 cup flour, sifted
1 teaspoon salt
½ teaspoon soda
3 cups oats, uncooked

Beat shortening, sugars, egg, water, and vanilla together until creamy. Sift together flour, salt, and soda; add to creamed mixture. Blend well; stir in oats. Drop by teaspoonfuls onto greased cookie sheets. Bake in preheated oven, 350 degrees, for 12 to 15 minutes. (For variety, add chopped nutmeats, raisins, chocolate chips, or coconut.) Yield: 5 dozen.

Tallulah Gallery

CHUCK ROAST WITH CARROTS AND POTATOES

3 pounds chuck roast
1½ teaspoons salt
¼ teaspoon pepper
2 tablespoons oil
1 large onion, chopped
1 large clove garlic, crushed
One 16-ounce can tomatoes, cut up
One 10½-ounce can condensed beef broth, undiluted
½ cup dry red wine
1 bay leaf
½ teaspoon thyme
6 medium new potatoes, unpeeled
6 carrots, cut in 2-inch chunks

Sprinkle meat with salt and pepper. Brown on all sides in hot oil in Dutch oven. When meat is turned, add onion and garlic and sauté until onion is tender. Add tomatoes, broth, wine, bay leaf and thyme. Cover and simmer 2 hours. Add potatoes and carrots. Cover and simmer 45 minutes longer or until meat and vegetables are tender. (Or cook in slow cooker following manufacturer's directions.) Discard bay leaf. Slice meat and serve with vegetables and sauce. Yield: 6 to 8 servings.

Lucy Chance
Crafts by Chance

TALLULAH GORGE

The history and legends surrounding Tallulah Gorge reach back into the times of the Cherokee Indians. Before the construction of the system of dams on the Tallulah River, the thunder of the waterfalls 2,000 feet down in the gorge could be heard for miles away. A continuous veil of mist hung over the depths. From the 1880's until the passing of the resort hotels in the 1920's, visitors spent their days roaming the tiny paths that led to vistas of wildly romantic outcroppings or down into the depths of the precipice to stand in awe of one of the five major waterfalls that broke the flow of the river on its way through the one and one-half mile raceway. The Tallulah Falls Railroad connected the resort with the rest of the country and brought thousands of vacationers and honeymooners to the site. A hotel boom developed, beginning with the Shirley Hotel in 1870. Then came the Cliff House, the Grand View, Robinsons, the Glennbrook, Maplewood Inn, and many more. At the height of the resort development Professor Leon crossed the gorge one summer on a tight rope. This feat was accomplished a second time in recent years by Karl Wallenda on a cable stretching some 1,100 feet. Because the waters now create hydroelectric power the voice of Tallulah is silent, passing unnoticed by the visitor. Gone, too, are all the great hotels and even the railroad with its beautiful trestles.It is still possible to follow a dangerous trail to the bottom to get some idea of the spectacle that nature created, but it should be attempted with great care as there have been several fatal accidents.

FRESH APPLE CAKE

2 cups sugar
4 cups apples, chopped
2 cups plain flour
1½ teaspoons soda
1 teaspoon salt
1 teaspoon cinnamon
2 eggs
⅔ cup oil
2 teaspoons vanilla
1 cup nuts, chopped

Pour sugar over apples. Let stand for 30 minutes. Sift dry ingredients into apple mixture. Blend eggs and oil together. Combine with remaining ingredients. Bake in greased 9 x 13-inch or tube pan for 1 hour 15 minutes at 350 degrees.

Glaze:
1 cup powdered sugar
Juice of 1 lemon
1 teaspoon butter

Combine ingredients. Bring to a boil and pour over cake.

Linda Smart
Cornelia Bank

NOISETTES OF BEEF

Three 3-ounce prime filets of beef
Salt and pepper to taste
1 tablespoon butter
1 tablespoon oil
2 shallots, chopped fine
4 mushrooms, sliced
Parsley, garlic and leeks, chopped fine
½ cup Beaujolais wine
Rice or noodles

Season filets with salt and pepper. Place in preheated skillet with butter and oil. Brown on both sides. Remove filets from pan; using same skillet, add shallots, mushrooms, parsley, garlic and leeks. Sauté until vegetables are tender. Add wine. There will be a small flame in the pan. Place beef filets on plate. Pour sauce over filets and serve with rice or noodles. Yield: 1 to 2 servings.

Barbara Gray
Lake Rabun Hotel

TERRORA PARK AND VISITORS CENTER

Situated on US 441 and 23 in Tallulah Falls, Georgia Power's Terrora Park and Visitors Center provides recreation and discovery in the Northeast Georgia Mountains. Sitting on the northern rim of Tallulah Gorge and bordered by Tallulah Falls Lake, the Park offers free swimming, tennis, playground, picnicking, pavilion, nature trails, and a Tallulah Gorge overlook; 50 camp sites with electric and water hookups are available at a moderate charge. Animated exhibits in the Terrora Visitors Center explain the history of Tallulah Gorge. The highlights of hydroelectric development, how electricity is produced from all fuels, and Georgia Power's statewide recreation program. Travel information is also available at the Center, which is open year-round every day except Tuesday (open 7 days a week June 1st through September 1st).

Terrora Park & Visitors Center, US 441-23 at the Tallulah River, Tallulah Falls, GA 30573 (404) 754-3276

PEACH PIE

4 large peaches, peeled and sliced
One 9-inch pie shell, unbaked
1⅓ cups sugar
⅓ cup flour
2 eggs, beaten
¼ cup margarine, melted
¼ teaspoon almond flavoring

Put peaches in pie shell. Mix sugar and flour well. Add beaten eggs, margarine, and flavoring. Pour over peaches. Bake at 350 degrees until crust is brown.

Terrora Park and Visitors Center

SPICED APPLE MUFFINS

¼ cup margarine
½ cup sugar
1 egg
½ cup milk
1½ cups flour
1 tablespoon baking powder
½ teaspoon salt
1 cup apples, finely chopped
⅓ cup brown sugar
1 teaspoon cinnamon

Cream margarine and sugar. Beat in egg. Mix together dry ingredients and add alternately with milk. Fold in chopped apples. Fill muffin cups ½ full, mix brown sugar and cinnamon together, and sprinkle over batter in muffin cups. Bake in a 375-degree oven for 20 minutes.

Terrora Park and Visitor Center

APPLE CRISP

1 cup brown sugar
⅔ cup flour
½ teaspoon cinnamon
¼ teaspoon ginger
¼ teaspoon mace
½ cup margarine
6 apples
½ cup water or apple juice

Mix sugar, flour, and spices in large mixing bowl. Cut margarine into sugar mixture and blend until mixture is crumbly. Peel and slice apples into 1½-quart baking dish, which has been greased. Add water or juice. Sprinkle sugar mixture over top. Bake at 350 degrees for 1 hour.

Terrora Park and Visitors Center

SWEET POTATO AND APPLE CASSEROLE

4 large sweet potatoes or yams
4 large tart apples, peeled, cored, sliced thin
Brown sugar
Butter
Cloves, ground

Boil sweet potatoes in salted water until tender. Peel and cut in slices. In greased casserole, put a layer of apples; sprinkle well with brown sugar and butter and a pinch of ground cloves. Place a layer of sliced sweet potatoes and repeat the sugar, butter, and cloves until all apples and potatoes are used. Bake at 350 degrees for 30 to 40 minutes. Good with ham, pork, and duck. Yield: 8 servings.

Terrora Park and Visitors Center

DUTCH APPLE CAKE

1½ cups all-purpose flour, sifted before measuring
½ teaspoon salt
2 teaspoons baking powder
1 tablespoon sugar
4 tablespoons shortening
½ cup milk
1 egg, well beaten
4 large cooking apples, peeled and cut into eighths
2 tablespoons brown or granulated sugar
1 teaspoon cinnamon

Sift flour with salt, baking powder and sugar. Cut in the shortening. Add milk to beaten egg. Stir into flour mixture. This will make a soft dough. Spread dough in greased 7 x 11 x 1½-inch utility pan. Arrange apples, pointed sides down in parallel rows on dough. Mix sugar and cinnamon together and sprinkle on top. Bake uncovered at 400 degrees for 30 minutes. Serve hot with lemon sauce or cream.

Terrora Park and Visitors Center

GINGER PEACHY UPSIDE-DOWN CAKE

¼ cup margarine or butter
½ cup brown sugar, packed
1 package gingerbread mix
⅓ cup maraschino cherries
One 1-pound can sliced peaches, drained

Melt margarine in 9 x 9 x 1¾-inch pan. Blend in sugar with margarine and spread in pan. Sprinkle with cherries cut in half. Drain peaches well and arrange on top of sugar mixture. Prepare gingerbread mix as directed on package. Pour over peach slices and bake at 350 degrees for 40 minutes. Allow cake to stand in pan for five minutes before inverting.

Terrora Park and Visitors Center

GREEN BEAN CAESAR

2 cans cut green beans, cooked, drained
2 tablespoons salad oil or bacon fat
¼ cup vinegar
2 tablespoons onion, minced, or 1½ tablespoons instant onion
¼ teaspoon salt
2 to 3 cloves garlic, minced
⅛ teaspoon pepper
Parmesan cheese, grated
1 teaspoon sugar
Italian bread crumbs
Margarine

In ungreased casserole, toss beans with salad oil, vinegar, onion, salt, garlic, and pepper. Sprinkle top with cheese, sugar, and bread crumbs. Dot with margarine. Bake at 350 degrees for 20 to 25 minutes.

Barbara Gray
Lake Rabun Hotel

STAINED GLASS SALAD

1 can pineapple chunks, chilled
1 can mandarin oranges, chilled
2 or 3 bananas
1 package frozen strawberries, sliced
1 can peach pie filling

Chill canned fruit before mixing. Drain fruit, slice bananas, add strawberries and pie filling. Mix together and serve. Yield: 8 servings.

Joyce Adams
Cornelia Bank

FROZEN PUMPKIN SQUARES

One 1-pound can pumpkin (2 cups)
1 cup sugar
1 teaspoon salt
1 teaspoon ground ginger
1 teaspoon cinnamon
1 teaspoon nutmeg
1 cup pecans, toasted, chopped
½ gallon vanilla ice cream, softened
36 gingersnaps
Whipped cream
Pecan halves for garnish

Combine pumpkin, sugar, salt, ginger, cinnamon, and nutmeg; add chopped pecans. In a chilled bowl, fold pumpkin mixture into ice cream. Line bottom of 13 x 9 x 2-inch pan with half of the gingersnaps; top with half the ice cream mixture. Cover with another layer of gingersnaps; add remaining ice cream mixture. Freeze until firm, about 5 hours. Cut into squares; garnish with whipped cream and pecan halves. Yield: 18.

Barbara Gray
Lake Rabun Hotel

HAL WEST REAL ESTATE

A hometown business—owned and operated by Hal West and his wife Jackie, and ably assisted by their daughter, Sandi West Griffin—the office boasts a diversified and well-rounded staff whose dedication to serving their customers whenever and wherever needed is well known in Rabun County. Smack dab in the middle . . . of beautiful, bountiful Rabun County, this is the "bestest" busiest little real estate office you'll ever find. Like a memorable meal of unique dishes skillfully combined, each member of the staff offers something special, but knowledge of the area and of the properties that are for sale, skill and expertise in completing every step of a sale-purchase, and a willingness to serve the needs of everyone who comes in are ingredients common to all.

Come in and meet the talented folks who welcome you with a colorful map and tour guide of Rabun County at *Hal West Real Estate, Inc., US 441 South, P.O. Box 1234, Clayton, Georgia 30525, (404) 782-2222.*

HAL'S "DEER ME" HAMBURGERS

2 parts ground venison
1 part beef hamburger
1 egg
Hamburger seasoning or meat tenderizer with seasoning

Mix, make into patties and cook. Venison cooks quickly and loses its flavor. Do not overcook.

Hal West
Hal West Real Estate, Inc.

HAL'S SMOKED FISH (À LA GREAT)

1 pound uniodized, plain salt
1 cup honey
1 gallon water
Fish fillets
1 fresh coconut (or hickory chips)
Pepper
Italian salad dressing

For marinade, combine salt, honey and water. Soak fish fillets several hours, refrigerated. Place meat of fresh coconut or hickory chips on hot coals of barbecue grill or smoker on very low heat. Sprinkle with pepper and Italian salad dressing (or oil and vinegar). Cover with aluminum foil, tent-shaped cover, to allow air and smoke space over top of fillets. Smoke until done, usually 45 to 90 minutes when meat becomes flaky and non-translucent. It is almost impossible to undercook. Overcooking dries the meat but it still is excellent to snack on. Stores and freezes well.

Hal West
Hal West Real Estate, Inc.

HAL'S DEER MAN STEW

Venison stew meat, trimmed of fat and gristle
Peanut oil
Cans of bouillon
Water
Vegetables (your choice)
Rice, potatoes or pasta, cooked
Salt
Pepper
Italian seasoning
Bay leaves

Fry meat in oil until brown on outside and barely cooked. Put in large deep broiler. Add equal parts bouillon and water, enough to cover meat well. Simmer. Cook vegetables separately, then add to meat. Add rice, potatoes, or pasta. Season, to taste, with salt, pepper, and Italian seasoning. Simmer 30 minutes to all day.

Hal West
Hal West Real Estate, Inc.

HAL'S VENISON PARTY BALLS

1 pound venison
Beef fat
½ pound sharp Cheddar cheese
2 cups biscuit mix

Grind venison with beef fat. Hand mix cheese and venison together, then mix in biscuit mix. Hand roll in balls, size of cherry tomato. Bake on greased pan until light brown for about 35 minutes in 300-degree oven. Stores and freezes well!

Hal West
Hal West Real Estate, Inc.

HAL'S VENISON STEAK

Venison steaks
Salt
Pepper
Flour
Cooking oil
1 can beef bouillon soup
Onion, thinly sliced

Trim steaks of bones, fat and gristle; then salt, pepper and flour. Fry till lightly brown, not done, on medium heat. Pour off excess oil used in frying, and pour bouillon soup in pan. Lay thin slices of mild onion on top of steaks. Cover with lid or aluminum foil and reduce to low heat and simmer for 30 to 60 minutes. Serve plain, on rice, or toasted English Muffin. Stores well.

Hal West
Hal West Real Estate, Inc.

SALMON, SWORDFISH OR MARLIN
HAL'S "LIP PUCKER"

Fish steaks
Eggs
2 cups flour
1 tablespoon salt
1 teaspoon pepper
1 tablespoon Italian seasoning
Peanut oil

Pat dry ¾ to 1-inch steaks and dip in beaten raw egg. In a plastic bag place the flour, salt, pepper, and Italian seasoning. Shake to mix. Drop steaks in bag one at a time, shake, fry in peanut oil until coating is light brown. Use hot oil and fry only 1 at a time. Place on platter lined with paper towels in a preheated 350 degree oven until ready to eat.

Hal West
Hal West Real Estate, Inc.

BROWNIE PUDDING CAKE

1 cup enriched flour, sifted
2 teaspoons baking powder
¾ cup sugar
2 tablespoons cocoa
½ teaspoon salt
½ cup milk
1 teaspoon vanilla
2 tablespoons melted shortening
¾ to 1 cup walnuts, chopped
¾ cup brown sugar
¼ cup cocoa
1¾ cups hot water

Sift together flour, baking powder, sugar, cocoa, and salt. Add milk, vanilla and shortening; mix until smooth. Add nuts. Pour into greased 8 x 8 x 2-inch pan. Mix brown sugar and cocoa; sprinkle over batter. Pour hot water over entire batter. Bake at 350 degrees, 40 to 45 minutes. Yield: 6 to 8 servings.

Pat Marcellino
The Chik'n Coop, Inc.

TORTILLA CASSEROLE

2 cans cream of chicken soup
1 can evaporated milk
1 can green chilies, chopped
1 medium onion, finely chopped
16 to 18 tortillas
1 cup medium sharp cheese, shredded

Combine soup, milk, chilies and onions in large bowl. Dip half of the tortillas in soup mixture, then place in a 9-inch diameter x 3-inch casserole. Sprinkle with ¾ of the cheese. Dip remaining tortillas in soup mixture and place in casserole. Pour remainder of soup mixture over the casserole. Top with remaining cheese. Bake in 350 degree oven for 25 to 35 minutes or until bubbly. An inexpensive easy-to-fix casserole. Yield: 8 servings.

Pat White
Halls Boat House

WHITEWATER ON THE CHATTOOGA

In recent years Rabun County has come to be known for its whitewater activities. The wild and often dangerous Chattooga River became famous throughout the country after it was the main location for the film "Deliverance." The growing sport of whitewater rafting and canoeing has boomed the interest in this largely unspoiled section of rocks and rapids. From April through October, several professional operations are available to guide the visitors on a safe but thrilling adventure.

LAKE RABUN TOMATO PUDDING

1 cup brown sugar
¾ cup boiling water
½ teaspoon salt
One 10-ounce can of tomato purée
1 cup bread cubes
½ cup butter, melted

Add sugar, water and salt to tomato purée. Boil 5 minutes. In a casserole pour melted butter over bread cubes. Add hot tomato mixture and place cover on casserole. Bake at 350 degrees for 30 minutes. Serve with meats.

Barbara Gray
Lake Rabun Hotel

SPINACH BALLS (APPETIZER)

2 packages frozen spinach, chopped, cooked, drained
2 cups herb stuffing mix
2 medium onions, chopped fine
6 eggs, well beaten
¾ cup butter, melted
½ cup Parmesan cheese, grated
1 tablespoon garlic salt
½ teaspoon thyme
1½ teaspoons black pepper
1 tablespoon monosodium glutamate

Mix all ingredients together. Shape into small balls, ½ to ¾ inch, and place on cookie sheet. Bake at 350 degrees for 20 minutes. If spinach balls are to be frozen, bake only 10 minutes; cool and freeze. Bake, unthawed, at 350 degrees until hot and slightly brown, 10 to 15 minutes.

Betty Gesbocker
Glenmeadow

GLENDAL'S BEEF AND TOMATOES

1 to 2 tablespoons butter
1 medium onion, finely diced
2 tablespoons bell pepper, chopped
1 pound ground beef
3 to 4 medium-sized tomatoes, coarsely diced
1 small can mushrooms (or fresh)
½ cup sharp cheese, cubed
Salt and pepper
Rice, toast or noodles (optional)

In a skillet melt butter, add onions and bell pepper. Cook over moderate heat until tender. Add ground beef, cook until meat has lost red color, but is not yet brown; add tomatoes and mushrooms. Cover and simmer until tomatoes are tender. Stir in cheese cubes and salt and pepper to taste. Serve as soon as cheese is soft. May be served separately or over rice, toast or noodles.

Glen LaRowe

mark of the potter

THE YORK HOUSE

We invite you to relax on the wrap-around veranda of our 15 room historic country inn; rest in a comfortable rocker and allow the past to enhance the present. All rooms are furnished in antiques and each has its own private bath plumbed with natural spring water. Sit by the fireplace in our spacious formal lobby and living room while swapping stories about the day's adventures. A full continental breakfast is served to your room on a silver tray.

Rates are moderate. Open year-round. Located between Mountain City and Dillard, just off US 441/23 on York House Road. Jim and Phyllis Smith, owners.

York House, P.O. Box 126, Mountain City, Georgia 30562, (404) 746-2068.

JOHN'S CHICKEN PIE

2 to 3 cups chicken, cooked, cut into pieces
5 tablespoons butter or chicken fat
½ cup onion, sliced
4 tablespoons flour
2 cups chicken stock, more if needed
Salt and pepper
Celery salt
1 pastry shell, unbaked

Cook chicken; heat fat, add onion and cook over low heat about 10 minutes or until soft and lightly browned. Add flour; stir until blended. Slowly add stock; stir over low heat until thick and smooth; season to taste. Arrange chicken in casserole, cover with sauce and top with pastry. Bake in 425-degree oven until brown, about 30 minutes. Yield: 6 servings.

John Dillon
The York House

PIONEER BREAD PUDDING

2 cups bread cubes
2 cups milk
3 tablespoons butter
¼ cup sugar
2 eggs
1 teaspoon vanilla
½ to 1 cup raisins
Dash salt
½ teaspoon nutmeg (optional)

Use day-old bread, crusts and all, cutting into ¼ to ½-inch cubes. Put these in buttered one-quart baking dish. Scald milk with butter and sugar. Beat eggs slightly, add salt, and nutmeg, then stir in warm milk and vanilla; add raisins. Pour over bread cubes. Set baking dish in pan containing warm water to the level of the pudding and bake in 350-degree oven about 1 hour or until knife comes out clean when inserted in center. Serve hot or cold with plain cream or hard pudding sauce. Yield: 6 servings.

Hard Sauce:
4 tablespoons butter
1 cup powdered sugar
1 teaspoon boiling water
Few grains salt
1 teaspoon vanilla

Cream butter and sugar together thoroughly. Add boiling water, salt and vanilla. Beat until smooth and fluffy. Yield: 1 cup.

Mildred Dillon
The York House

OLD-FASHIONED BOILED CUSTARD

½ cup sugar
2 tablespoons cornstarch
3 eggs
4 cups milk, low-fat if desired
1 teaspoon vanilla
Dash salt

Mix sugar and cornstarch in top of double boiler. Beat eggs, add milk; add wet mixture to dry one, a little at a time. Cook over boiling water until custard coats wooden spoon. Remove from heat and strain into bowl to cool. Add vanilla.

Mildred Dillon
The York House

VEGETABLE SALAD

One package lemon gelatin
1 cup hot water
One 16-ounce can crushed pineapple
One 3-ounce package cream cheese, softened
⅓ cup mayonnaise
1 medium carrot, grated
1 cup celery, chopped
½ cup pecans

Combine gelatin with hot water. Drain pineapple and add cold water to juice to make 1 cup. Add to gelatin. Add cheese and mayonnaise to gelatin and stir well. Add carrot, celery and pecans. Chill.

John Dillon
The York House

PARTY ICED TEA

8 teaspoons tea
1½ cups sugar
One 6-ounce can frozen lemonade concentrate
1 large bottle ginger ale

Boil tea in water and let steep for 10 to 15 minutes. Strain into 1 gallon jug. Add sugar, lemonade and ginger ale. Fill jug with water.

Helen Whitney
Whitney Realty

CYNTHIA'S CHILI

3 pounds ground chuck, browned, drained
2 to 3 cloves garlic, minced
1 medium onion, chopped
1 tablespoon margarine
2 cans red beans
2 cans tomato sauce, or 2 cans tomato paste and 1 small can tomato juice
1 to 2 cans tomatoes
2 to 3 tablespoons cumin
¼ to ⅓ cup chili powder
1 to 2 tablespoons salt
1 to 2 tablespoons cracked pepper

Brown meat. Remove from pan. Add margarine to pan and sauté garlic and onion. Combine mixture with beans, tomato sauce, and tomatoes and place in crockpot or Dutch oven. Season with cumin, chili powder, salt, and pepper. Mix well with meat and simmer until flavors blend. Yield: 1 full large crockpot.

Cynthia Whitney
Cherokee Landing, Incorporated

SCALLOPED OYSTERS WITH CORN

⅓ cup butter, melted
1½ cup saltines, finely crushed
½ cup American cheese, grated
1 pint shucked 'standard' oysters
One 12-ounce can whole-kernel corn, drained
¼ cup half and half
¾ teaspoon salt
⅛ teaspoon pepper
½ teaspoon Worcestershire sauce
2 tablespoons parsley, chopped

Preheat oven to 400 degrees. In saucepan over low heat, stir saltines into hot butter until well mixed. In 10 x 6-inch baking dish arrange half of saltine mixture; top with ½ cup American cheese, then oysters, then corn. In small bowl, mix half and half, salt, pepper and Worcestershire sauce. Pour over oyster mixture. Sprinkle with parsley, then with remaining saltine mixture. Bake 20 to 25 minutes until lightly browned and bubbly.

Debbie Koenig
Chimney Mountain Fiberarts

Dahlonega through Cleveland to Helen

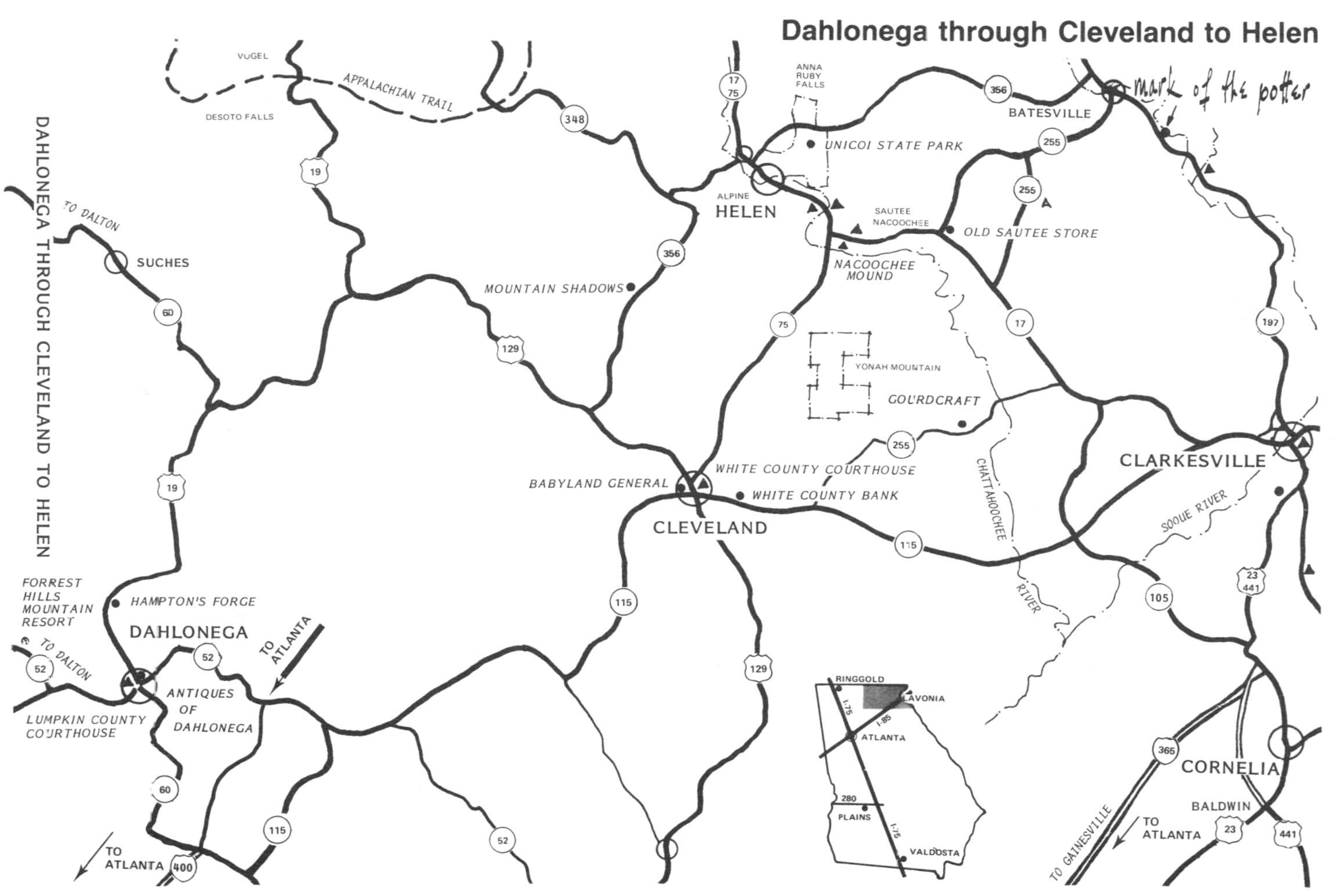

DAHLONEGA Through CLEVELAND To HELEN

WHERE TO SLEEP

Dahlonega Inn 864-4343
FORREST HILLS MOUNTAIN RESORT—
Page 154 GA 52
DAHLONEGA 864-6456
Gateway Inn 865-3121
Golden Inn Motel 864-6191
Mountain Creek Cottages 865-2515
Smith House Hotel 864-2348
Worley Homestead 864-7002

WHERE TO EAT

Beauregard Rippet's 864-7333
Cleve's Barbeque Kitchen 864-3730
Dagwood's Sandwich Shoppe . . . 865-4949
Dahlonega Gold Restaurant 864-2808
Dairy Queen & Brazier 865-2213
Dairy Queen of Dahlonega 864-3834
Daisy Burger 865-3843
Danny's Restaurant 864-6424
Eatery Restaurant, The 865-5505
Gateway Restaurant 865-2023
G & G Restaurant 865-3709
Gold City Cafe 864-4664
Golden Fried Chicken 864-6808
Haystack 864-4664
Huddle House 864-6512
Jake's Cafe 864-6433
KRAFT'S KOUNTRY KITCHEN (FORREST HILLS MOUNTAIN RESORT) GA 52, DAHLONEGA Page 154 864-6456
Lagniappe Restaurant 865-5504
Lodestone, The 864-2005
Louise's Food & Antiques 865-3709
Martha's Tea Room 864-2868
Mauney's House, The 865-4011
McDonald's 864-7600
Mint Sandwich Shoppe 864-4488
Mt. View Restaurant 865-3877
Mt. Yonah 865-2023
Sautee Barbecue 865-2987
Smith House 864-3566
Tastee-Freeze of Cleveland 865-4118
Tastee-Freeze of Dahlonega 864-2729
Trudy's Restaurant 865-4335
Wagon Wheel Restaurant 864-6677
Yonah Burger 865-4791

WHERE TO SHOP

Andy's Art Shop 864-6339
Antique House, The 864-6000
ANTIQUES OF DAHLONEGA—Page 168
NORTH PARK, DAHLONEGA . . 864-3637
Appalachian Adventures, Ltd. 864-3562
BABYLAND GENERAL™ HOSPITAL—Page 150, UNDERWOOD STREET
CLEVELAND 865-5164
Candles by Vera 864-4539
Capitol Antiques 864-6882
Cat's Meow 865-5218
Chattahoochee Country Store 865-5173
Cleveland Grocery 865-2155
Eddie's Kozy Home 864-6992
Fudge Factory 864-2256
G & G Restaurant & Bakery 865-3709
Gold City Mall 864-9915
Gold Shop, The 864-7227
Golden Memories 864-7222
GOURDCRAFT ORIGINALS—Page 158
BLUE CREEK, CLEVELAND . . . 865-4048
HAMPTON'S FORGE—Page 160
US 19 North DAHLONEGA 864-7393
Howard's Handcraft Shop 865-3844
Laurel Knob Jewelry 864-6799
Mountain Echoes Dulcimer Shop
Mrs. Plum's Country Things 864-2253
North Georgia Booksmith 864-6353
Original Appalachian Artworks . . . 865-5164
Rush's Miscellany 865-2155
Split Rail Antiques 864-6777
Timshel Traditions 864-4988
Towne Square Bakery 864-7681
Upstairs Antiques 864-4328
Wahoo Pottery
Yarn Station, The 865-6069

WHERE TO CAMP

Blackburn Park 864-4050
Camp Glisson 864-6181
Dahlonega Nuggett Campground . 864-4378
Mt. View Campground 865-3877

WHERE TO CAMP

MOUNTAIN SHADOWS JELLYSTONE PARK—Page 166 GA 356 CLEVELAND 865-4742
Yonah Mountain Campground . . . 865-6546

SERVICES

WHITE COUNTY BANK—Page 236 (See Helen North for the Branch at Helen, Georgia) 865-3151

WHAT TO SEE & DO

Crisson Mines—Gold Panning 2½ miles N. of Dahlonega off US 19
NACHOOCHEE MOUND—GA 17 at GA 75 Sautee—Page 246
LUMPKIN COUNTY COURTHOUSE—The square, Dahlonega—Page 164
Storyland 865-3613
WHITE COUNTY COUTRHOUSE—The square, Cleveland—Page 170

NOTICE: For your convenience we have listed all of the places to eat and all of the places to sleep in the area covered by this list. Quality is a personal concept and, although we have listed every place to eat or sleep known at the time of printing, some restaurants and some motels we recommend highly, while others do not quite meet our high standards of quality and we assume no responsibility for them. We would suggest that you inquire locally of any of the businesses in bold type listed above for their recommendations.

GEORGIA MOUNTAINS TRAVEL ASSOCIATION

With the growing travel industry in northeast Georgia it became evident that an organization was needed to promote the most beautiful region in the whole wide world as a place to visit or as a place to live.

In the winter of 1976 the merchants, the realtors, the bankers, the people of northeast Georgia formed the Georgia Mountains Travel Association. The organization acted quickly because there was a deadline to meet; the inauguration of their neighbor, Jimmy Carter in January 1977 in Washington, D.C. and the opening of the National Visitors Center there.

Following the October meeting the group signed up new members; designed and constructed an exhibition booth complete with photographs depicting our beautiful mountains; organized a narrated 10 minute slide presentation; designed and printed a brochure; drove to Washington, D.C.; set up the exhibit booth and manned it for the week of festivities during the inauguration.

Georgia Mountains Travel Association has grown through the years and serves the travel industry in 13 northeast Georgia counties. The exhibit is shown and brochures of member businesses are distributed at travel shows in Canada, Ohio, Pennsylvania, Florida, North Carolina, South Carolina, Alabama and Tennessee.

The Georgia Mountains Travel Association is a valuable source of information to the traveling public and its members are your hosts in these beautiful Northeast Georgia mountains.

Georgia Mountains Travel Association, P.O. Box 9, Tallulah Falls, Georgia 30573

WHY LEAVES CHANGE COLOR

Kay Blackwelder

Northeast Georgia is ablaze with color in the fall, and as the dazzling spectacle unfolds each year, two questions are most often asked by visitors: "When are the trees at their best?" and "What makes the leaves change color?" Or, to put it another way, "Is this going to be a good year for color?" and "When is the best time to come?"

People who live in the area have noticed that the middle two weeks of October in any year find the leaves at their peak of color. Whether to expect a super spectacular or an average display of leafy costume requires some understanding of leaf color processes.

Leaves appear green during spring and summer because their most abundant pigment is chlorophyll, the green food-making substance. However, other pigments are also present but masked by the doubly plentiful chlorophyll. In autumn, as food manufacture halts, the chlorophyll breaks down, revealing the hitherto unseen pigments carotene and xanthophyll, (pronounced "zan-tho-fill") which are bright yellow and orange. Thus appear the golden hues of hickories, tulip trees, elms, and some maples.

The autumn spectacular red color seen in maples, dogwoods, red oaks, sweet gums, and sourwoods is a different pigment, not present in summer but developing with the onset of fall. It is anthocyanin and is familiar to us as the red of summer flowers and certain vegetables, such as red cabbage.

What fall conditions cause chlorophyll to break down, revealing carotene and xanthophyll, and anthocyanin to form? Is it frost, or drought, or rain?

The bleaching of chlorophyll is part of the aging of the leaf and seems linked to the shortening of daylight hours. Some observers have noted that trees beside brightly lit streets stay green longer than their counterparts in the forest. Thus the yellowish pigments appear on schedule, more or less independently of weather conditions, barring some damage that would cause the leaves to die prematurely. Anthocyanin, however, requires light (the brighter the light, the more red pigment), and a cool temperature (but not cold enough to kill the leaf cells completely). Sugar is also needed to build the anthocyanin molecule (the more sugar the more red color). Cool temperatures seem to increase the sugar content of the leaf. With this knowledge it is clear that if autumn weather provides bright, sunny days and cool but not freezing nights, the red leaves should be especially brilliant. If autumn is warm and cloudy, however, little red will develop, limiting fall foliage to yellow and browns. Happily, the autumn weather in Northeast Georgia is usually just what is needed to generate a spectacular show.

BABYLAND GENERAL™ HOSPITAL

Since the fall of 1978, BabyLand General™ Hospital has been the birthplace for over 100,000 Little People™ soft sculpture babies.

Dr. Xavier Roberts, Chief of Staff at BabyLand, delivers his Little People™ creations in what once was a doctor's clinic built in 1919. Roberts transformed the aging clinic into the famous BabyLand General™ Hospital.

The Hospital's trained staff will guide you through the magic and fantasy of the Little People's world.

Visiting hours: Monday through Saturday, 9:00 to 6:00, Sunday, 1:00 to 6:00.

BabyLand General Hospital, 19 Underwood St., Cleveland, GA 30528 (404) 865-5164.

BABYLAND GENERAL'S™ RECIPE FOR FANTASY

Take one tour through BabyLand General™ Hospital, chock full of Little People™ soft-sculpture babies freshly delivered from the Cabbage Patch and dressed according to their dispositions.

Add a dash of gentle discipline and a generous sprinkling of Tender Loving Care from the specially trained Little People™ staff.

Whip in miniature nurses', doctors', and candy stripers' uniforms, mixed with a dollop of Xavier Roberts' designer genius.

Blend in slowly Otis Lee's Board Room, an authentic delivery room, stethoscopes, and a maternity ward with a smidgen of quintuplets in an isolette.

Fold in an over-running cup of Imagicillin.

Knead one or more loving persons and an Oath of Adoption into the dough. Then let the Fantasy rise.

Dr. Xavier Roberts
BabyLand General™ Hospital

BLACKBERRY CAKE

2 cups blackberries and juice
2 eggs
2 teaspoons ground cloves
2 teaspoons cinnamon
1 teaspoon baking soda
1 cup margarine
1½ cups sugar
Pinch of salt
1 cup buttermilk
3 cups self-rising flour

Mix all ingredients together and pour into 3 greased 9-inch round pans. Bake at 350 degrees for 35 minutes.

Frosting for Blackberry Cake:
1 large can evaporated milk
½ cup margarine
1 cup white sugar
2 cups brown sugar

Mix all ingredients together. Cook over low heat until soft ball stage. Spread on cake layers and sides.

BabyLand General™ Hospital

BLUEBERRY SALAD

2 packages black cherry gelatin
2 cups boiling water
1 can blueberry pie filling
1 No. 2 can crushed pineapple, undrained

Dissolve gelatin in water. Add the blueberry pie filling and crushed pineapple and mix well. Refrigerate until firm, overnight.

Topping:
One 8-ounce package cream cheese
1 cup sour cream
½ teaspoon vanilla
½ cup sugar
1 cup nuts

Blend together cream cheese, sour cream, vanilla, and sugar. Add nuts, then spread on top. Refrigerate.

BabyLand General™ Hospital

JAPANESE FRUIT CAKE PIE

4 eggs
1 cup coconut
1 cup pecans, chopped
1 cup raisins, yellow if possible
1 cup margarine
2 cups sugar
½ teaspoon vinegar
2 teaspoons vanilla
2 pie shells, unbaked

Beat eggs slightly; add other ingredients. Pour into 2 unbaked pie shells. Bake at 300 degrees for 50 to 55 minutes.

BabyLand General™ Hospital

CHOCOLATE OATMEAL CANDY

2 cups sugar
½ cup milk
½ pound butter
4 tablespoons cocoa
½ cup peanut butter
2 teaspoons vanilla
2½ cups quick oatmeal
2½ cups nuts (walnuts best)

Cook sugar, milk, butter and cocoa 1½ to 2 minutes. After mixture reaches a good rolling boil, remove from heat, add peanut butter and vanilla. Mix well. Add oatmeal and nuts. Drop heaping spoonfuls onto wax paper. Allow to cool.

BabyLand General™ Hospital

OKRA PICKLE

3¼ pounds small okra pods (3 to 4 inches)
5 cloves of garlic
5 small fresh red peppers
1 quart water
1 pint white vinegar (5% acidity)
⅓ cup pickling salt
2 teaspoons dill seed

Pack okra firmly in hot sterilized jars, leaving ¼ inch head space. Place a garlic clove and a hot pepper in each jar. Combine remaining ingredients in a saucepan and bring to boil. Pour over okra in jars and seal. Process in boiling water bath 10 minutes. Yield: 5 pints.

BabyLand General™ Hospital

SOUR CREAM BANANA PUDDING

1 large box instant vanilla pudding
2½ cups milk
One 8-ounce carton sour cream
1 large carton whipped topping
1 large box vanilla wafers
4 to 5 large bananas

Mix pudding with 2½ cups milk beating according to package directions. Add sour cream and ½ of the whipped topping. Mix well. Layer bananas and vanilla wafers in large bowl. Pour pudding over each layer. Put remaining whipped topping on top and sprinkle with crushed vanilla wafers. Chill thoroughly.

BabyLand General™ Hospital

FRESH STRAWBERRY PIE

1 quart fresh berries
2 tablespoons cornstarch
¼ teaspoon salt
1 cup sugar
½ cup boiling water
1 baked pie shell
Whipped cream

Wash, hull and sort strawberries. Save the big berries for placing in pie crust. Mash enough berries to make 1 cup. Mix sugar, salt, cornstarch; then add mashed berries and boiling water. Cook, stirring all the time, until thick. Cool. Just before serving, place reserved strawberries in pie crust. Pour cooled sauce over strawberries in pie crust. Add whipped cream.

BabyLand General™ Hospital

FORREST HILLS MOUNTAIN RESORT

Forrest Hills Mountain Resort is nestled in the forest on the southern slopes of the Blue Ridge Mountains. It is on GA 52 near Amicalola Falls State Park. The Kraft family hosts guests in two-, three-, and four-bedroom cottages which are beautifully appointed and completely supplied. For the romantic, a one-bedroom cottage with a large heated whirlpool spa and oversized canopy bed await you. On the weekends, our very own Kountry Kitchen is open, serving family-style meals with generous servings of garden-fresh vegetables and specially prepared meats.

For a truly relaxing and quiet vacation or honeymoon, write to Forrest Hills Mountain Resort, Route 3, P.O. Box 510, Dahlonega, Georgia 30533, or phone (404) 864-6456.

WHIPPED CREAM POUND CAKE

1 cup butter
3 cups sugar
6 large eggs
3 cups flour, sifted
½ pint whipping cream

Cream butter and sugar; add eggs one at a time, beating after each. Add flour and cream alternately, beginning with 1 cup of flour. Bake in preheated oven for 1 hour and 20 minutes at 325 degrees.

Katherine Partain
Forrest Hills Mountain Resort

HOT PECAN DIP

One 8-ounce package cream cheese, softened with 2 tablespoons milk
One 3-ounce package sliced dried beef, chopped fine
¼ cup green pepper, chopped
2 tablespoons dehydrated onion
½ teaspoon garlic salt
¼ teaspoon black pepper
½ cup sour cream
½ cup pecans, chopped
2 tablespoons butter

Mix all ingredients except pecans and butter. Before serving, lightly toast pecans in butter. Put mixture in baking-serving dish with pecans on top. Bake 20 minutes at 350 degrees. Serve in warmed dish. Will keep as long as one week in refrigerator.

The Kraft Family
Forrest Hills Mountain Resort

WILD RICE PILAF

1 cup wild rice
2¼ cups water
1 tablespoon instant chicken bouillon granules
½ pound fresh mushrooms
1½ cups celery, sliced
½ cup butter
One 10-ounce package frozen artichoke hearts
¼ cup green onions, sliced
1 tablespoon lemon peel, finely shredded
2 tablespoons pimento, chopped
1 tablespoon lemon juice
¾ teaspoon salt
½ teaspoon dried thyme, crushed
½ teaspoon pepper
Lemon slices and parsley for garnish

Run cold water over rice in strainer for 1 to 2 minutes, lifting rice with fingers to rinse thoroughly. In 3-quart saucepan combine rice, water and chicken granules. Bring to a boil; reduce heat and simmer for 30 minutes. (Rice should be undercooked.) Do not drain. Set aside. Cook mushrooms and celery in butter for 4 to 5 minutes until tender. In strainer rinse artichokes under hot water. Add artichokes, green onions, lemon peel, pimento, lemon juice, salt, thyme and pepper into mushroom mixture. Stir into rice. Turn into shallow 2-quart casserole or 12 x 7½ x 2-inch baking dish. Bake in 325 degree oven for 45 to 60 minutes. Garnish with lemon slices and parsley. Yield: 8 to 10 servings.

The Kraft Family
Forrest Hills Mountain Resort

TEXAS CHOCOLATE CAKE

2 cups plain flour
2 cups sugar
1 cup butter or margarine
1 cup water
4 tablespoons cocoa
2 eggs, well beaten
1 teaspoon soda
1 teaspoon vanilla
½ cup buttermilk
½ teaspoon cinnamon

Sift flour and sugar in large bowl. Bring to a boil butter, water and cocoa. Take from burner and pour over sugar and flour mixture, beating well. Add remaining ingredients; beat well again. Pour into greased and floured sheet pan. Bake at 350 degrees until done, approximately 15 to 20 minutes.

Icing for Texas Cake:
4 tablespoons cocoa
6 tablespoons milk
½ cup butter or margarine
1 pound powdered sugar
1 teaspoon vanilla
1 cup nuts

During last 5 minutes of cake baking, bring to a boil cocoa, milk and butter; remove from heat and add powdered sugar, vanilla and nuts. Beat well. Spread on hot cake.

Katherine Partain
Forrest Hills Mountain Resort

POTATO CASSEROLE

1 large sack of hash-brown potatoes (frozen)
1 teaspoon salt
¼ teaspoon pepper
½ cup onions, chopped
1 can cream of chicken soup
1 pint sour cream
2 cups Cheddar cheese, shredded
3 tablespoons butter
2 cups corn flakes, crushed

Mix all ingredients except butter and corn flakes. Melt butter, pour over potato mixture and sprinkle corn flakes on top. Cook 45 minutes at 350 degrees.

Katherine Partain
Forrest Hills Mountain Resort

CHICKEN KATHERINE

8 chicken breasts, skinned and boned
8 slices of bacon
One 4-ounce package dried beef
1 can cream of mushroom soup
½ pint sour cream

Wrap each chicken breast with slice of bacon. Cover bottom of greased 12 x 8 x 2-inch baking dish with chipped beef. Arrange chicken on top of beef. Mix soup and sour cream and pour over all. Bake, uncovered, 3 hours at 275 degrees.

Katherine Partain
Forrest Hills Mountain Resort

PEANUT BRITTLE

1½ cups sugar
½ cup white Karo syrup
¼ cup water
2 cups raw peanuts, shelled
1½ teaspoons soda
¼ teaspoon salt
Butter for greasing platter

Combine sugar, syrup and water. Bring to boil. Stir in peanuts gradually so as not to lose the boil of the liquid. Keep liquid at a rolling boil until peanuts pop open and turn brown. Remove from heat; add soda. Stirring well, add salt. Pour on a well-buttered platter. Allow room for candy to spread. When candy is cold, break into chunks.

Katherine Partain
Forrest Hills Mountain Resort

LAREDO SUPPER

1 pound ground beef
1 onion, chopped
1 bell pepper, chopped
1 can kidney beans
1 can tomatoes, cut up, drained
One 8-ounce jar processed cheese spread
1 tablespoon chili powder

Brown beef and drain. Add onion and bell pepper. Cook 10 minutes and add rest of ingredients; simmer 20 minutes. Serve with tortilla chips and green salad.

The Kraft Family
Forrest Hills Mountain Resort

GOURDCRAFT ORIGINALS

Gourdcraft Originals, owned and operated by Pricilla Wilson and Janice Lymburner, consists of the growing, crafting, and merchandising of one of the countryside's nearly-forgotten natural products. Our carved decorative gourds are unique as well as useful, and children of all ages enjoy their whimsical gourd toys. We also have gourd seeds and raw gourds available for "do-it-yourselfers" as well as a demonstration gourd patch and other interesting gourd exhibits.

Come and "have a gourd day," Saturday 10:00 to 6:00, Sunday 1:00 to 6:00, or call 865-4048 for weekday appointments.

Gourdcraft Originals, GA 225, at the foot of Yonah Mountain, 2 miles north of GA 115 or 5 miles south of GA 17, P.O. Box 412, Cleveland, Georgia 30528 (404) 865-4048.

GOURDCRAFT RICE CASSEROLE

1 cup uncooked rice
1 can onion soup
1 soup can of water in which 1 beef bouillon cube is dissolved
¼ cup of margarine, melted

Mix all ingredients in casserole dish. Bake at 350 degrees for 45 minutes.

Priscilla Wilson
Gourdcraft Originals

WALKING SALAD

Excellent for after-school snacks or hungry hikers.

Apples
Peanut butter
Raisins

Cut a small plug, 1 inch in diameter, from the stem end of each apple. Save to replace after stuffing. With paring knife or apple corer, remove core and as much of inside of apple as desired, leaving the bottom of the apple intact. Combine raisins and peanut butter. Stuff apple with the mixture and replace top.

Priscilla Wilson
Gourdcraft Originals

GREEN BEANS IN SOUR CREAM DRESSING

¼ cup onion, chopped
2 cups green beans, drained
½ cup water chestnuts, sliced, or less if desired
Salt and pepper to taste
⅓ cup sour cream
¼ cup mayonnaise
1 teaspoon lemon juice
¼ teaspoon dry mustard
½ teaspoon horseradish, if desired

Combine all ingredients and mix well. Refrigerate for at least 12 hours before serving.

Janice Lymburner
Gourdcraft Originals

HONEYED CHICKEN

2 frying chickens, 2½ to 3 pounds, cut into serving pieces
1 cup honey
1½ cups wheat germ
1 tablespoon parsley, chopped
½ teaspoon thyme
½ teaspoon basil
Sea salt and freshly ground black pepper to taste
Soy oil

Dip each piece of chicken in honey. Mix together all remaining ingredients except soy oil. Coat chicken with this mixture. Pour soy oil to depth of ½ to ¾-inch in a heavy skillet and heat. Add chicken pieces so that they make a single layer. Cook over medium to low heat until brown, turning several times. Cover skillet and cook until chicken is done, about 10 minutes. Yield: 6 servings.

HAMPTON'S FORGE

Located on US 19, 2 miles north of Dahlonega, this shop is owned and operated by Harold Hampton who specializes in custom-wrought iron work. He constructs items of varying sizes and designs, using the forge and anvil method of the early American smiths. Some of his creations are purely artistic while others are utilitarian. His designs are principally Early American although other styles are available.

As a rule, the shop is open from 10:00 a.m. until 4:00 p.m., Monday through Saturday. However, to be certain of finding someone there, it is advisable to call and make an appointment.

Hampton's Forge; Shop: US 19; Mailing Address: 105 Trahlyta Trail, Dahlonega, Georgia 30533, (404) 864-7393.

"POSSUM 'N' TATERS"

'possum
4 medium-sized sweet potatoes
Butter

Clean 'possum and cook in salted water until tender. Meanwhile, bake potatoes until soft. Peel and quarter them lengthwise. Place cooked 'possum and potatoes in baking dish. Dot with butter. Bake in 400-degree oven until brown.

Harold Hampton
Hampton's Forge

SCOTCH SQUARES

1 cup brown sugar
½ cup butter, melted
2 cups rolled oats, uncooked
1 teaspoon baking powder
½ teaspoon salt
1 cup nuts, chopped (optional)

Add brown sugar to melted butter and stir until sugar is dissolved. Add remaining ingredients and mix well. Pour into well-greased shallow pan and bake at 350 degrees for 30 minutes. When cool, cut into squares.

Harold Hampton
Hampton's Forge

STEWED FRUIT PIE

1½ cups dried fruit, stewed, sweetened
4 egg yolks
1 cup sugar
3 tablespoons cornstarch
3 tablespoons butter, melted
¾ cup canned milk
1 teaspoon vanilla
1 pie shell, unbaked

Line a 9-inch pie pan with pastry. Place a layer of fruit in bottom of pan. Beat egg yolks; add milk, sugar, cornstarch, vanilla, and butter. Pour this mixture on top of fruit. Bake in 350-degree oven for 45 minutes or until set. Top with meringue.

Meringue:
4 egg whites
8 tablespoons sugar
1 teaspoon vanilla

Beat egg whites until stiff, adding sugar and vanilla. Put on pie and bake at 300 degrees for 15 minutes.

Harold Hampton
Hampton's Forge

COCONUT PIE

3 egg yolks
2 tablespoons butter
1 cup sugar
3 tablespoons flour
2 cups milk
1 cup coconut, grated
1 teaspoon vanilla
1 pie shell, baked

Combine egg yolks, flour, sugar, butter and milk. Cook until thickened. Add coconut and flavoring. Pour into pie shell and top with meringue. (See meringue recipe for Stewed Fruit Pie).

Harold Hampton
Hampton's Forge

APPLE JACK SAUSAGE

1 to 2 pounds sausage
1 cup apple juice
1 to 2 ounces apple jack or apple brandy

Take a pound or two of good country bulk sausage and shape into patties about ½-inch thick and 2 inches in diameter. Place in large iron skillet and cover patties with apple juice. Cook until most of apple juice has cooked away. Remove from skillet and place on cookie sheet. Slide under broiler until sausage is browned. Place patties on large platter and saturate with the brandy. Ignite. When flame has burned out, sausage is ready to eat with hot homemade biscuits.

Harold Hampton
Hampton's Forge

HOT PEPPER JELLY

(Good with baked 'possum; also good with roast pork or lamb; and excellent with Ritz crackers and cream cheese.)

2 cups water
¼ cup hot pepper, chopped
¾ cup green bell pepper, chopped
1 cup white vinegar
6 to 8 drops green food color
6½ cups sugar
One 6-ounce bottle Certo

Boil chopped peppers and water for 5 minutes. Strain out peppers. If necessary, add enough water to the liquid to make 2 cups. Put this liquid, vinegar, green color, and sugar in large saucepan; bring to a boil. Add Certo. Bring to a full rolling boil and boil hard 1 minute. Pour into hot jars and seal. Yield: 9 half-pints.

Harold Hampton
Hampton's Forge

CANDY CHOCOLATE BALLS

1 cup butter, melted
1 teaspoon vanilla
½ cup peanut butter
1 can coconut
1 cup graham cracker crumbs
1 cup pecans, chopped
1 box powdered sugar
1 small package semi-sweet chocolate bits
½ stick paraffin

Mix first seven ingredients. In a double boiler, melt chocolate bits with paraffin. Roll first mixture into balls and dip in chocolate.

BabyLand General™ Hospital

BLACK WALNUT POUND CAKE

3 cups sugar
3 cups plain flour
⅔ cup self-rising flour
1 cup shortening
½ cup butter
1 cup milk
6 eggs
1 teaspoon vanilla
1 teaspoon black walnut flavoring
1 cup walnuts

Bake all ingredients at 300 degrees for 1½ hours.

Glaze:
1 cup sugar
½ cup buttermilk
¼ cup butter
½ teaspoon soda
2 teaspoons white corn syrup
1 cup black walnuts, chopped

Cook first five ingredients slowly for 5 minutes. Add walnuts. Glaze cooled cake.

Cream Cheese Icing:
One 8-ounce package cream cheese
½ cup butter
1 box powdered sugar
1 teaspoon vanilla
½ cup chopped walnuts

Mix cream cheese and butter. Add sugar, vanilla and nuts. Put on cooled cake.

BabyLand General™ Hospital

STRAWBERRY-NUT SALAD

2 packages strawberry gelatin
1 cup boiling water
Two 10-ounce packages frozen strawberries, sliced
One 1-pound can crushed pineapple, drained
3 medium bananas, sliced
1 cup nuts, chopped
1 pint sour cream

Dissolve gelatin in boiling water. Fold in strawberries. Mix pineapple, bananas, and nuts; add to gelatin. Pour half of mixture into a 9 x 13-inch pan; chill until firm. Spread with sour cream. Pour remaining mixture over sour cream. Refrigerate until congealed and ready to serve. Yield: 12 servings.

Barbara Dalton
Cornelia Bank

OLD LUMPKIN COUNTY COURTHOUSE

Dahlonega, Georgia, is on US 19 only a few miles from the northern terminus of Highway 400. Lying 70 miles northeast of Atlanta at GA 60 and GA 52, Dahlonega is 20 miles west of Cleveland and 29 miles from Helen, Georgia's Alpine Village.

In the late 1820's Dahlonega was the site of our young country's first gold rush. You can still find places where you, too, can pan for gold. A United States Government Branch Mint was located here in Dahlonega in 1835.

The Old Lumpkin County Courthouse was placed on the National Register of Historic Places in 1970, and The Georgia Department of Natural Resources currently administers it as an historic site and maintains the Gold Museum here.

Your trip to Dahlonega should include a walk around the restored village square surrounding the old court house, a visit to Price Memorial Hall, The Fields Place Vickery House, the campus of North Georgia College, Amicalola Falls State Park, the craft shops, the restaurants and the resorts.

YEAST ROLLS

- ¼ cup shortening
- ⅓ cup sugar
- ½ cup boiling water
- ½ cup warm water
- 1 package yeast
- 1 egg, beaten
- 3 cups plain flour
- ½ teaspoon salt

Mix shortening, sugar and boiling water. Allow to cool. Mix yeast, egg, and warm water. Add shortening mixture. Stir in flour, sifted with salt. Mix well. Put in refrigerator for at least 2 hours. Take out and knead and cut out. Allow to rise 2 hours. Bake at 400 degrees for 15 to 20 minutes.

BabyLand General™ Hospital

OYSTER PIE

- 1 quart oysters
- 1 teaspoon salt
- ¼ teaspoon pepper
- 3 tablespoons butter, or more
- 2 cups coarse soda cracker crumbs
- 1 egg
- ¾ to 1 cup milk or cream, or more
- ½ cup buttered bread crumbs

Preheat oven to 350 degrees. Remove any pieces of shell from oysters. Drain. Place layer of oysters in greased 2-quart casserole. Sprinkle with half the salt and pepper; dot with bits of butter; add layer of cracker crumbs. Add layer of oysters on top. Break egg in milk and mix well; pour over the oysters. Cover top with buttered crumbs and bake about 30 minutes. If the dish seems to dry out, add a bit more milk and butter. Serve at once. Yield: 6 servings.

Frances Mathis
Home Federal Savings & Loan Association

MOUNTAIN SHADOWS JELLYSTONE PARK CAMP-RESORT

Mountain Shadows Jellystone Park Camp-Resort is a stunning family recreation center surrounded by The Chattahoochee National Forest and The Blue Ridge Mountains. The resort, centered around the sparkling waters of Lake Qualatchee, features a beach, a heated swimming pool, hot tub, horseback riding, bass fishing, trout fishing, paddleboats, canoeing, teen center, adult lounge, motion picture theater, live bluegrass music (on some weekends), and daily activities including nature hikes and hayrides. A paradise for recreational vehicles. Six miles west of Alpine Helen, five miles north of Cleveland on GA 356.

For more information write Yogi Bear, P.O. Box 443, Cleveland, Georgia 30528. For reservations call (404) 865-4742.

FRENCH COCONUT PIE

¾ cup butter, melted
2½ cups sugar
5 eggs, beaten
One 7-ounce package flaked coconut
1½ tablespoons vinegar
2 pastry shells, unbaked

Combine first five ingredients and pour into pastry shells. Bake at 325 degrees for 1 hour. Yield: 2 pies.

COCONUT OATMEAL COOKIES

1 cup shortening
2 cups brown sugar
2 eggs, beaten
1 teaspoon soda
1 tablespoon hot water
1 cup flour
1 teaspoon baking powder
3½ cups oatmeal
1½ cups coconut
1 teaspoon vanilla
½ teaspoon salt

Mix all ingredients together and roll in small balls. Bake at 350 degrees for 12 to 15 minutes.

Shirley Lothridge
Mountain Shadows Jellystone Park

HOLIDAY FRUIT CAKE

½ pound butter
1 cup sugar
5 large eggs
1¾ cups flour
4 cups pecans, chopped
¾ pound candied cherries
1 pound candied pineapple
One 1-ounce bottle lemon flavoring
One 1-ounce bottle vanilla flavoring
1 teaspoon baking powder

Line tube pan with waxed paper.

Cream butter and sugar. Add eggs and ½ of the flour. Add chopped nuts and fruit and add remainder of ingredients. Start in cold oven at 300 degrees for 30 minutes. Reduce heat to 250 degrees for 3 hours.

Shirley Lothridge
Mountain Shadows Jellystone Park

GRANDMA'S POUND CAKE

A 100 year-old recipe.

10 eggs, separated
2 cups sugar
2 cups butter
4 cups plain flour

Beat eggs, yellows and whites separately. Cream butter and sugar, add egg yolks and mix well. Add stiffly-beaten egg whites alternately with flour. Bake from 1 to 2 hours at 325 degrees.

Shirley Lothridge
Mountain Shadows Jellystone Park

ANTIQUES OF DAHLONEGA

Antiques of Dahlonega was established in 1976 by Margaret Richards Owens. The shop, at 116 North Park, is housed on the ground floor of the two story brick Woodmen Of The World building one-half block north of the Public Square.

Antiques of Dahlonega features antiques, semi-antiques, collectibles, estate jewelry, exquisite replicas, memorabilia and reproductions. Here you can find everything a home needs or anything a person would want in town and country furniture and accessories from top to bottom (chandeliers to rugs, books, prints and linens to gold-miner's pans with everything in between).

Open every day, year round.

Antiques of Dahlonega, 116 North Park, Box 2046, Dahlonega, GA 30533 (404) 864-3356.

HOE CAKES

2 cups plain corn meal
½ teaspoon salt
1 cup hot water
1½ cups cold water
2 tablespoons bacon fat, or lard, melted

Mix salt in meal, then pour hot water on the mix; add enough cold water to thin the mush until it will pour slowly out of the bowl. Add melted fat. Drop batter by spoonfuls on a hot griddle or skillet, turn until both sides are brown.

CRACKLIN' CORN BREAD

1 cup cracklins, dry
½ cup warm water
4 handfuls water ground corn meal
1 teaspoon salt
Water to mix

Preheat oven to 450 degrees. Break cracklins into small pieces and pour over them ½ cup warm water and mix. Pour mix into meal and salt and add sufficient water to make dough. Let stand 5 minutes and if too stiff add a little water. Shape into small loaves and place on hot pan. Put into hot oven until brown on top. Reduce heat to 350 degrees and bake 30 to 45 minutes according to size of pone.

Margaret Owens
Antiques of Dahlonega

ICEBOX POTATO ROLLS

1 cup milk
2 cakes yeast
¼ cup warm water
1 cup potatoes, boiled & mashed
¾ cup shortening
½ cup sugar
1 tablespoon salt
2 eggs
4½ to 5 cups flour
1 teaspoon vegetable oil

Scald milk and cool to lukewarm. Dissolve yeast in warm water, add to milk. Add mashed potatoes, shortening, sugar, salt and eggs. Add flour and mix well. Dough will be stiff. Oil top of dough to keep from getting dry. Cover and place in icebox overnight and let rise. Dough may be kept in icebox 4 or 5 days and used as needed. Take out amount of dough desired and shape into rolls. Let rise for 2 hours. Bake in 400 degree oven about 15 to 20 minutes depending on size.

Margaret Owens
Antiques of Dahlonega

OLD WHITE COUNTY COURTHOUSE

The old White County Courthouse, located in the center of Cleveland on US 129 at GA 75 and GA 115, was built in 1859. It was contracted for U.S. dollars, but when completed it was paid for in Confederate money since the Civil War had begun in the meanwhile. White County was originally part of Habersham County, and the area around Cleveland was called Mt. Yonah. The courthouse was in use until 1965 and would have been lost to the area if it had not been for an energetic group of historians, who saved the building and established the White County Historical Society here. The site was placed on the National Register of Historic Places in 1970.

BUTTERMILK CUSTARD PIE

3 eggs
1¼ cups sugar
½ cup margarine, melted
1 tablespoon flour
1 cup buttermilk
1 lightly-baked pie shell

Beat eggs until light colored, add sugar and mix well. Stir in margarine, flour and milk. Pour into pie shell and bake in 350 degree oven for about 1 hour. Cool for 30 minutes before serving.

BabyLand General™ Hospital

CHICKEN BROCCOLI CASSEROLE

¼ cup margarine
1 cup stuffing mix
4 chicken breasts, cooked, salted, and diced
2 packages frozen broccoli, cooked, salted, and drained
1 cup sour cream
2 cans cream of chicken soup
1 cup onion, chopped
Cracker crumbs

Melt margarine in casserole and sprinkle with stuffing mix. Mix all other ingredients except crumbs and pour in casserole. Sprinkle with crumbs and cook 40 minutes at 350 degrees.

Shirley Lothridge
Mountain Shadows Jellystone Park

TWENTY-TWO-MINUTE CAKE

2 cups plain flour
1 teaspoon soda
2 cups sugar
½ cup butter
1 cup water
½ cup shortening
3 teaspoons cocoa
2 eggs
½ cup buttermilk
1 teaspoon vanilla

In a bowl, mix flour, soda and sugar. In a pan bring to a boil butter, water, shortening and cocoa. Pour into flour mixture. Mix well. Add eggs, vanilla and buttermilk. Mix well. Bake in greased and floured oblong pan at 400 degrees for 22 to 25 minutes. Ice while hot.

Icing:
½ cup butter
⅓ cup milk
3 teaspoons cocoa
1 teaspoon vanilla
1 box powdered sugar, sifted
1 cup walnuts

Bring to a boil butter, milk and cocoa. Only bring to a boil. Do not boil. Take off heat and add sugar, vanilla, nuts.

BabyLand General™ Hospital

Helen South

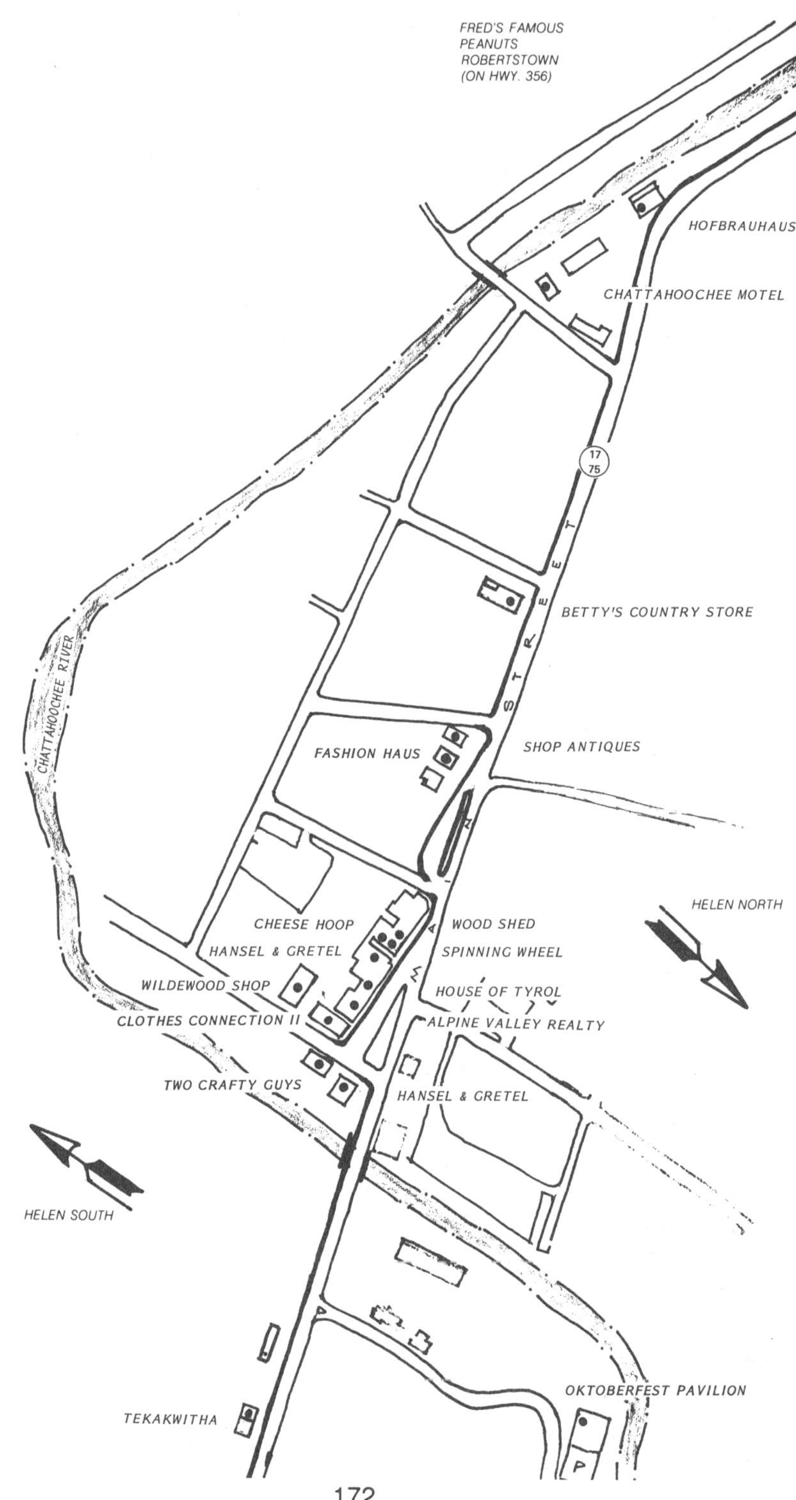
FRED'S FAMOUS PEANUTS ROBERTSTOWN (ON HWY. 356)
HOFBRAUHAUS
CHATTAHOOCHEE MOTEL
17
75
BETTY'S COUNTRY STORE
CHATTAHOOCHEE RIVER
FASHION HAUS
SHOP ANTIQUES
HELEN NORTH
CHEESE HOOP
WOOD SHED
HANSEL & GRETEL
SPINNING WHEEL
WILDEWOOD SHOP
HOUSE OF TYROL
CLOTHES CONNECTION II
ALPINE VALLEY REALTY
TWO CRAFTY GUYS
HANSEL & GRETEL
HELEN SOUTH
OKTOBERFEST PAVILION
TEKAKWITHA
P

HELEN SOUTH of Main Street

WHERE TO SLEEP

Alpenhof Motel 878-2268
Alpine River Lodge 878-2872
Chalet Khristy 878-2155
CHATTAHOOCHEE MOTEL—Page 178
MAIN STREET, HELEN 878-2184
HOFBRAUHAUS INN—Page 184
MAIN STREET, HELEN 878-2248

WHERE TO EAT

Alpine Valley Restaurant 878-2803
Christopher's 878-2453
HOFBRAUHAUS INN—Page 184—
MAIN STREET, HELEN 878-2248
KITCHEN, ETC (BETTY'S COUNTRY STORE)—Page 176 MAIN STREET, HELEN 878-2943
Mountain Valley Kitchen 878-3511
Paul's Restaurant 878-9922
Rathskellar 878-2967
Restaurant Edelweiss
River Haus Pizza 878-2382
Swiss Country Restaurant 878-3235

WHERE TO SHOP

Alpine Bake Shoppe 878-2987
Alpine Candle Cottage
Alpine Valley Complex 878-2803
Antiquity Realty 878-2252
Apple Tree, The 878-2552
Bears and Balloons
BETTY'S COUNTRY STORE—Page 176
MAIN STREET, HELEN 878-2943
Brookstown Fudge 878-2646
Candles by Anita 878-3214
CHEESE HOOP—Page 180
OLD STREET, HELEN 878-2924
Chief's Garage
China House 878-2999
CLOTHES CONNECTION II—Page 192—
HORSE & DUCK PLATZ,
HELEN 878-2857
Dulcimer Shop 878-3149
Fain's Antique Shop 878-2927
FASHION HAUS—Page 198 MAIN STREET,
HELEN 878-3321
FRED'S FAMOUS PEANUTS 878-3124
Gift World of Helen 878-2504
Gold & Silver Chalet 878-2352
HANSEL & GRETEL—Page 182
MAIN STREET, HELEN 878-2443
Helen Pharmacy 878-2889
Helen Travel & Convention
Service 878-2400
HOUSE OF TYROL—Page 188
MAIN STREET, HELEN 878-2264
Jolly's Toys 878-2262
Kennedy's Irish Cottage 878-2489
Lucky Duck, The 878-2838
Mathena's Handmade
Woodcrafts 878-3305
Music Box Plus 878-3428
Old Fashion Bakery 878-3455
Old Norway Imports 878-2475
Orbit Factory Outlet 878-2376
Perfect Cup, The 878-2259
Print Shop, The 878-2838
Roper's Taxidermy 878-2811
Shoe Corner 878-2616
SHOP ANTIQUES, THE—Page 194
MAIN STREET, HELEN 878-2359
South Main Street Arts Gallery
SPINNING WHEEL—Page 196
OLD STREET, HELEN 878-2764
TEKAKWITHA—Page 232 SOUTH MAIN
STREET, HELEN 878-2038
TWO CRAFTY GUYS—Page 204
RIVER ROAD, HELEN 878-3108
UPTOWN COUNTRY—Page 174—
MAIN STREET, HELEN 878-3215
WILDEWOOD SHOP—Page 202
RIVER STREET, HELEN 878-2541
WOOD SHED, THE—Page 206
MAIN STREET, HELEN 878-2586

WHAT TO DO & SEE

ALPINE HELEN—Page 212
Alpine Valley Trout Farm 878-2645
WILDEWOOD SHOP (CHATTAHOOCHEE OUTPOST)—Page 202, CANOE TRIPS, RIVER STREET, HELEN 878-2541

UPTOWN COUNTRY

Uptown Country strives to offer the finest quality country inspired giftware in the area.

Distinctive items are available for both men and women who appreciate accessories that add that certain "uptown" look to the home.

Linda and Tom Schoen and a friendly, knowledgeable staff are proud to represent fine craftsmen from the local area, across the country, and from around the world.

Be sure to visit both locations—the larger shop on Main Street and the Chattahoochee Street location for kitchen accessories and antiques.

Uptown Country, Main Street and Uptown Country Corner, Chattahoochee Street, P.O. Box 346, Helen, Georgia 30545, (404) 878-3215

ZABAGLIONE HORRWORTH

6 eggs (5 yolks plus 1 whole)
⅓ Cup sweet Marsala
2 tablespoons fresh orange juice
2 tablespoons sugar
1 tablespoon orange rind, grated

In a large enamel casserole combine 5 egg yolks, 1 whole egg, Marsala, orange juice, sugar to taste, and grated orange rind. With a wire whisk, combine the mixture thoroughly and beat over the lowest possible heat until thick and triple in bulk. Serve warm in parfait glasses.

Charles Horrworth
Alpine Valley Realty

CRAB MORNAY

¼ cup butter
⅓ cup flour
2 cups heavy cream
1 cup white veal or chicken stock or chicken broth
½ cup clam juice
¼ cup sweet sherry
3 tablespoons dry white wine
½ teaspoon lemon juice
Pinch nutmeg
1 cup Monterey Jack cheese, shredded
Salt and pepper to taste
3 pounds crab meat, cooked
Duchesse potatoes, cooked
¼ cup shallots, minced
1 tomato for garnish

In a saucepan melt butter and add flour. Cook the *roux,* stirring over moderate heat for 2 minutes. Remove the pan from the heat and stir in heavy cream and white veal or chicken stock or broth, both heated. Return the pan to the heat and cook the mixture, stirring, until it is thickened. Add clam juice, sherry, white wine, lemon juice, and nutmeg. Heat the sauce and add cheese and salt and pepper to taste, stirring until the cheese is melted and the sauce is smooth. Divide cooked crab meat among 6 lightly buttered individual au gratin dishes. With a pastry bag fitted with a decorative tube, pipe potatoes around the edges of the dishes. Sprinkle the crab meat with minced shallots. Spoon the sauce over the crab meat and top each dish with a thin slice of peeled tomato. Bake in a preheated oven at 400 degrees, for 20 minutes, or until it is bubbly.

Charles Horrworth
Alpine Valley Realty

"SCHNITZEL" BEANS

4 slices bacon, diced
3 medium onions, sliced
4 cups green beans, thinly sliced
2 cups tomatoes, peeled, seeded, diced
1 teaspoon salt
½ teaspoon pepper, freshly ground
⅓ cup boiling water

In a skillet sauté bacon until crisp; remove with a slotted spoon. Set aside. In the remaining bacon fat, sauté onions until tender and light brown. Add green beans and brown lightly. Add tomatoes, salt, pepper, and boiling water. Simmer the vegetables, covered, for 30 minutes, or until beans are tender. Stir in bacon bits.

Charles Horrworth
Alpine Valley Realty

BETTY'S COUNTRY STORE

For almost as long as there's been a Helen, there's been a country store at this site. Betty's, today, is a shoppers' paradise and you can find everything from hoop cheese to hard candy, picnic supplies to potatoes baked with dozens of different toppings, magazines to melons fresh from the farm, pots and pans to pumpkin heads made from clay, fresh coffee beans to freshly-baked carrot cake, hiking supplies to school supplies, fresh meats to fresh produce, and gasoline to gourds—all this and more under one low roof in one fun place to shop.

Betty's Country Store, Main Street,
Helen, Georgia, 30545 (404) 878-2943

BETTY'S BEEF STROGANOFF

1 tablespoon flour
½ teaspoon salt
1 pound beef sirloin, cut in cubes
2 tablespoons butter
1 cup mushrooms, thinly sliced
1 medium onion, chopped
½ clove garlic, chopped, minced
Rice or noodles

Combine flour and salt; dredge meat in mixture. Heat skillet; add butter. When melted, add the meat and brown quickly, browning all sides. Add mushrooms, onion, and garlic and cook 3 to 4 minutes or until onions are barely tender. Remove meat and mushrooms from skillet. Serve with sauce on rice or noodles.

Rich Sauce:
2 tablespoons butter
3 tablespoons flour
1 tablespoon tomato paste
1¼ cups beef stock or 1 can concentrated beef broth
1 cup sour cream
2 tablespoons cooking sherry

Add butter to pan drippings. When melted, blend in flour; add tomato paste. Now slowly pour in cold meat stock, stirring constantly, until mixture thickens with no lumps. Return browned meat and mushrooms to skillet. Stir in sour cream and sherry, heating briefly.

Betty Fain
Betty's Country Store

CHAMPAGNE PUNCH (For 10)

4 pineapples
1 pound sugar
1 pint light rum
1 pint brandy
4 jiggers Curaçao
Juice of 6 lemons
4 bottles champagne
Sliced fruits

Prepare pineapples, slice into a large bowl, toss with sugar, and leave until sugar has soaked thoroughly into the fruit. Pour in rum, brandy, Curaçao, and lemon juice. Place a block of ice in the bowl, and add champagne, pouring slowly along the side of the bowl in order to prevent too much effervescence. Decorate with sliced fruits and serve in champagne glasses.

Charles Horrworth
Alpine Valley Realty

CHATTAHOOCHEE MOTEL

The Chattahoochee Motel extends a warm invitation to visit picturesque Alpine Helen, Georgia. The lovely setting among the trees and the serenity of the Chattahoochee River, the swimming pool and tasteful rooms offer a vacation of pure relaxation.

There are a variety of rooms, most of which overlook the river. They feature balconies, heating and air conditioning, and color cable T.V. with 24 hour movie channel. The motel provides tubes for floating in the river.

Chattahoochee Motel, GA 17 and 75,
Helen, Georgia 30545. For reservations call (404) 878-2184.

FIG PRESERVES

3 cups figs
2 regular packages strawberry gelatin
1 cup sugar

Peel figs and mash fine with potato masher. Add sugar and gelatin. Boil hard for 5 minutes. Pour in sterilized jars and seal.

Ann Teems
Chattahoochee Motel

ANN'S FAVORITE COCONUT PIE

½ cup margarine or butter
2 cups sugar
4 eggs, beaten
2 cups heavy cream
⅓ cup milk
2 teaspoons vanilla
1 can coconut (or 1 package frozen)
2 pie crusts, unbaked

Cream margarine and sugar together; add beaten eggs, heavy cream, milk, coconut and vanilla. Pour into unbaked pie crusts. Bake at 375 degrees for 35 minutes. Yield: 2 pies.

Ann Teems
Chattahoochee Motel

SOUR CREAM CAKE

1¼ cups butter
3 cups sugar
6 eggs, separated
3 cups cake flour
¼ teaspoon baking soda
1 cup sour cream
3 teaspoons vanilla or 2 almond and 1 vanilla

Cream butter and sugar; add egg yolks, one at a time. Sift flour and soda; add alternately with sour cream to creamed mixture. Beat well. Fold in beaten egg whites and flavoring. Pour into 10-inch tube pan. Bake at 350 degrees for 1 hour and 15 minutes.

Ann Teems
Chattahoochee Motel

SOUTHERN CORNBREAD DRESSING

One 10-inch pone cornbread, crumbled fine
6 biscuits, crumbled fine
1 package cornbread stuffing
2 tablespoons poultry seasoning
2 large onions, chopped
4 eggs
½ pound melted margarine
8 cups chicken broth
1 stalk celery, chopped

Mix all ingredients together. Pour in large roasting pan. Bake at 400 degrees for 45 minutes. Great with baked hen or turkey. Enough to serve large family gathering at Thanksgiving or Christmas.

Ann Teems
Chattahoochee Motel

THE CHEESE HOOP

The Cheese Hoop is one of the original businesses of Helen. The shop is located on Old Street and is well stocked with unusual and hard-to-find products from around the world. The cheese is imported from thirteen countries and there are more than one hundred twenty varieties on display. A selection of imported wine is available to complement any palate. The Cheese Hoop packages and ships cheese. The atmosphere is warm and friendly and conducive to shopping.

The Cheese Hoop, Old Street, P.O. Box 123,
Helen, Georgia 30545 (404) 878-2924.

QUICK CHEESE DELIGHT

½ pound Dofino cheese
6 ounces of hot pepper jelly

Place the Dofino cheese on tray and place the pepper jelly on top of the cheese. Serve with a hard cracker.

June Parks
The Cheese Hoop

CHEESE FONDUE

1 clove garlic, cut in half
2 tablespoons cornstarch
3 tablespoons brandy, kirsch, or akvavit
1½ cups dry white wine
¾ pound Tybo, in small cubes
¾ pound Samsoe, in small cubes
Dash of white pepper, paprika, or nutmeg
French bread, in cubes

Rub inside of fondue pot well with garlic, then discard. Mix cornstarch and brandy; set aside. Pour the wine into fondue pot and heat at medium temperature until bubbles start to rise to the surface. Add the cheese by thirds, stirring constantly until all cheese is melted. When mixture starts to bubble, quickly add cornstarch mixture and spices, stirring until thickened. Serve fondue piping hot, with French bread cubes. Yield: 4 to 6 servings.

June Parks
The Cheese Hoop

THE CHEESE HOOP'S BLEU CHEESE DRESSING

½ pound Cove bleu cheese
1 pint mayonnaise
2 cups buttermilk

In a large jar or crock, mix together the mayonnaise and well crumbled bleu cheese. Add the buttermilk to desired consistency. Store in the refrigerator. Keeps well for several weeks.

June W. Parks
The Cheese Hoop

DEEP-FRIED DANISH CAMEMBERT CHEESE

Danish Camembert cheese, fresh or canned
Flour
Eggs
Bread crumbs
Oil

The cheese must be cold. Cut Camembert into small wedges. Lightly coat wedges in flour. Dip each wedge in slightly beaten eggs and coat in fine bread crumbs, then refrigerate. You can prepare the Camembert cheese several hours before frying. Fry cheese until golden in 1½ inches very hot salad oil about 1½ minutes. Drain briefly on paper towels. Serve hot as cocktail snacks or as a light dessert with toast and your favorite jam.

June Parks
The Cheese Hoop

HANSEL AND GRETEL CANDY KITCHEN

Hansel and Gretel Candy Kitchen is a family-owned candy business that started in Helen, Georgia in 1973. Created and still operated by Dave and Janet Jones, Hansel and Gretel produces candy that annually delights tens of thousands of tourists in the Alpine Village. Hansel and Gretel is noted for its imported candies, but it's the homemade candies that account for most of the business. The specialties are fudge, peanut brittle, divinity, and a variety of caramel delights. Hansel and Gretel is open 363 days a year, closing only on Thanksgiving and Christmas Days. The recipes that are prepared in their two locations in Helen are too large and cumbersome for production in a normal home. However, here are some recipes they think you might find easy to prepare at home.

Hansel and Gretel Candy Store, at the River and on Old Street, Helen, Georgia 30545, (404) 878-2443.

MARZIPAN

1 pound almond paste
⅓ cup light corn syrup
1 teaspoon vanilla
1¼ cups marshmallow creme
4 to 6 cups powdered sugar
Food coloring

Combine almond paste, corn syrup, vanilla, and marshmallow creme; mix well. Gradually add powdered sugar. Knead until uniform and smooth. Color as desired. Shape as vegetables, fruits, etc. Yield: 45 to 50 pieces.

Dave Jones
Hansel and Gretel Candy Kitchen

DATE NUT ROLL

2 cups sugar
1 cup heavy cream
1 cup milk
1 cup dates, chopped
1 cup nuts, chopped
1 teaspoon vanilla

Cook sugar, cream and milk to 230 degrees. Slowly add chopped dates so boiling does not stop. Occasionally stir mixture so the dates do not settle to the bottom of the pan and scorch. Cook to 238 degrees. Cool in the pan or pour out on a marble slab. When temperature is about 150 degrees, stir and work with your hands until it becomes creamy. Work nuts and vanilla into candy. Form into rolls, wrap tightly in waxed paper or plastic wrap until firm. Store in a tightly covered container. Yield: 30 pieces.

Dave Jones
Hansel and Gretel Candy Kitchen

COCONUT FUDGE

3 cups sugar
1 tablespoon light corn syrup
1 cup milk
One 8-ounce package shredded coconut

Place all ingredients in a 2-quart saucepan. Cook, stirring occasionally, until temperature is 237 degrees. Cool in the pan or pour out on a marble slab to cool. When warm, beat in pan or work with a spatula on a slab until candy turns dull and creamy. Spread in an 8-inch square pan. Cut into squares. Yield: 49 pieces.

Dave Jones
Hansel and Gretel Candy Kitchen

FIFTEEN-MINUTE PEANUT BUTTER FUDGE

1 cup sugar
1 cup light brown sugar
¼ teaspoon salt
½ cup milk
1 cup miniature marshmallows
½ cup peanut butter
1 teaspoon vanilla

In a saucepan, combine sugars, salt, and milk. Cook to 240 degrees. Remove from heat and add marshmallows, peanut butter, and vanilla. Beat with a wooden spoon several minutes until thick and creamy and gloss disappears. Spread in a buttered 8-inch square pan. Cut into squares. Yield: 48 pieces.

Dave Jones
Hansel and Gretel Candy Kitchen

HOFBRAUHAUS INN

The Hofbrauhaus Inn is the northernmost business in the Alpine Village of Helen, Georgia. This delightful "Old Country"-styled inn serves special German dishes as well as delicious American foods. Owned and operated by Chris & Mary Hammersen, both natives of the "Old Country," the inn offers an atmosphere of warmth and a friendly welcome. A German beer-garden is on the porch overlooking the Chattahoochee River. Upstairs, away from the hustle and bustle, are three beautiful guestrooms available by the day, weekend, week or longer.

Hofbrauhaus Inn, North Main Street, Helen, GA 30525 (404) 878-2248.

LOBSTER COCKTAIL

1 cup sour cream
2 teaspoons tomato catsup
Dash of Tabasco
Salt and pepper
1 jigger cognac
1 cup mushrooms
1 cup asparagus
1 can mandarin oranges
3 cups lobster, diced (preferably claws)

Mix sour cream and seasonings; add rest of ingredients and place in refrigerator to cool. Serve on lettuce cup with slice of lemon. For garnish, a small red meat claw on top.

Mary Hammersen
Hofbrauhaus Inn

GEFÜLLTE FISH ROULADER

2 pounds filet of sole or flounder
3 slices bacon, diced
1 small onion, minced
¼ pound mushrooms, chopped
¼ cup celery, chopped
2 tablespoons parsley, minced
Salt
Flour
3 to 5 tablespoons butter, melted
Cheese and paprika for garnish
½ cup white wine

Preheat oven to 350 degrees. Cut fish into six rectangular servings. Sprinkle filets with salt; let stand 15 to 30 minutes. Cook bacon, onion and mushrooms together, until bacon is crisp and onion soft; add celery and parsley; blend well. Sprinkle with salt. Spread the mixture over the filets; roll up each filet, fasten with toothpicks, dredge with flour. Brush half the melted butter over bottom of baking dish. Place stuffed fish in dish and dribble remaining butter over top. Sprinkle cheese and paprika over all. Pour wine in baking dish. Bake 20 to 30 minutes.

Mary Hammersen
Hofbrauhaus Inn

RHINELAND HERRING SALAD

1 jar pickled herring, drained
½ cup canned beets, diced
1 large apple, cored, diced
2 medium potatoes, cooked, diced
1 small onion, minced
Pickle, diced
½ cup sour cream
½ cup mayonnaise
1 teaspoon sugar
Vinegar
Salt and pepper to taste
Boiled eggs, sliced
Canned whole beets
1 tablespoon parsley, minced

Combine herring with beets, apples, potatoes, onion and pickle. Toss with sour cream, mayonnaise, sugar, vinegar, salt and pepper. Arrange in a salad bowl or platter. Place boiled egg slices over top and whole beets around the edges for garnish. Sprinkle with parsley before serving, if desired. Yield: 6 appetizer servings.

Mary Hammersen
Hofbrauhaus Inn

SCHASCHLIK SPRES
BEEF AND VEAL KEBABS

¾ pound tender beef
¾ pound lean veal
¾ pound lean pork or sausage, such as Mettwurst
½ pound calves' liver
8 strips bacon
2 large onions, thickly sliced
2 cups red or white wine, or vinegar marinade
3 or 4 tablespoons oil, or melted fat

The beef, veal and pork should all be cut into squares ½″ thick. The liver and bacon should be cut into squares of uniform size. Insert meat on 4 skewers, so that bacon and onion slices are added between cubes of meat with the pork on the end in each case. Marinate in wine or vinegar marinade for 24 hours in refrigerator. Remove from marinade. Grill over direct heat or under broiler until well browned on all sides, basting occasionally with oil or melted fat. Yield: 6 servings.

Mary Hammersen
Hofbrauhaus Inn

MEAT SALAD HORS D'OEUVRE BREMEN STYLE

¼ pound boiled ham, cut into thin strips
2 frankfurters, minced, or ½ cup bologna, minced
½ cup salami or other dry, firm sausage
3 sweet gherkins, diced
¼ cup mayonnaise
1 tablespoon vinegar
Salt to taste
Pepper, freshly ground

Combine all ingredients. Serve on bed of lettuce. Yield: 2 cups.

Mary Hammersen
Hofbrauhaus Inn

BASIC OMELET

2 eggs
2 tablespoons water
¼ teaspoon salt
1 tablespoon butter

Mix eggs, water and salt with fork. Heat butter in 8-inch omelet pan or fry pan over medium-high heat until just hot enough to sizzle a drop of water. Pour in egg mixture. Mixture should set at edges at once. With pancake turner turned over, carefully push cooked portions at edges toward center so uncooked portions flow to bottom. Tilt pan as necessary so uncooked eggs can flow. Slide pan rapidly back and forth over heat to keep mixture in motion and sliding freely. Cook until top is still moist and creamy-looking. With pancake turner, fold in half or roll, turning out onto plate with a quick flip of the wrist. Yield: 2 omelets.

Ann Teems
Chattahoochee Motel

STRAWBERRY OMELET

1 pint strawberries, washed and hulled
Sugar
⅔ cup sour cream
2 tablespoons powdered sugar
½ teaspoon orange peel, grated

Reserve 4 strawberries for garnish. Slice the remaining berries, sprinkle with sugar to taste and set aside. Combine sour cream, powdered sugar and orange peel; set aside. Make omelets, using Basic Omelet recipe, for each serving. To serve, spoon about ½ cup sliced berries on each folded omelet. Spoon sauce over the tops and garnish with the reserved berries. Yield: 4 omelets.

Ann Teems
Chattahoochee Motel

HOUSE OF TYROL

The House of Tyrol, established in 1970, is Alpine Helen's specialty German gift shop. The owners, Bernd Nagy, from Tyrol, Austria, and his wife, Linda, travel extensively to find unusual imports for the shop.

Browse through the House of Tyrol while German folk music creates a holiday mood. The shop includes a wide variety of household items, crystal, beer steins, cuckoo clocks, Hummel figurines and alpine fashions.

House of Tyrol also has a full color mail order catalog available upon request.

House of Tyrol, Main Street, P. O. Box 180,
Helen, GA 30545 (404) 878-2264.

PARISER SCHNITZEL

5 to 8 pieces (1½ pounds) veal cutlet or pork tenderloin
2 large eggs
Seasoned salt
Parmesan cheese, grated
Flour
Oil
Lemon slices, for garnish

Pound meat slightly and knick edges. Beat eggs well and add seasoned salt and 1 teaspoon or more Parmesan cheese to taste. Dip meat into flour and then into the egg mixture. Deep fry in hot oil for 2 to 3 minutes on each side or until golden brown. Drain and serve. Garnish with lemon slices. This schnitzel is much lighter than the traditional Viennese Schnitzel, but has plenty of flavor and aroma.

Linda Nagy
House of Tyrol

EINGERBRANNTE ERDAPFEL
(POTATO SALAD)

5 potatoes
1 small onion
1 teaspoon parsley, chopped
½ teaspoon salt
½ teaspoon caraway
¼ teaspoon marjoram
1 bay leaf
2 tablespoons butter
2 tablespoons flour
1 tablespoon vinegar

Peel and cut raw potatoes into quarters and then into ½″ slices. Put in pot and barely cover with water. Add onion, parsley, salt, caraway, marjoram, and bay leaf. Cook until potatoes are soft. Make a roux from the butter and flour and add a little water from the cooked potatoes to thin. Add this back to the potato mixture to thicken. Stir in vinegar as desired for taste. By serving with two or three sliced smoked sausages, this recipe can be turned into a hearty meal. Yield: 4 servings.

Linda Nagy
House of Tyrol

VANILLEKIPFEL
(VANILLA CRESCENT COOKIES)

½ pound unsalted butter, softened
½ cup sugar
2 cups all-purpose flour, sifted
1 cup ground hazelnuts or pecans
1 teaspoon vanilla
½ teaspoon salt
Powdered sugar or vanilla sugar

Cream butter and sugar until light and fluffy. Beat in flour ½ cup at a time; then add nuts, vanilla and salt and continue beating until mixture becomes a slightly stiff dough. Shape dough into a ball, wrap in plastic and refrigerate for about an hour. Preheat oven to 350 degrees. Lightly butter two 12 x 15″ baking sheets. Pinch off walnut-sized pieces of dough and roll them on floured board to form small crescents about 1½ inch long. Arrange crescents ½ inch apart on baking sheets. Bake for 15 to 20 minutes until lightly colored. While still warm, roll cookies in sugar. Cool completely and roll again in sugar. Yield: 36 crescents.

Linda Nagy
House of Tyrol

MARILLENKNODEL
(POTATO DUMPLINGS WITH APRICOTS)

1 package potato dumpling mix
8 fresh apricots
8 sugar cubes
4 tablespoons butter
¾ cup fine bread crumbs
2 tablespoons powdered sugar

Prepare potato dumpling mix according to directions on package. (Add 1 egg for lighter dumplings.) Remove pits from apricots and replace the pit with a sugar cube. If apricots are large, use half only. Divide mix into 8 dumplings, place apricot in center of dough and roll in hands to form two 3-inch balls. Drop prepared dumplings in boiling salted water and continue cooking for 15 minutes. While dumplings are cooking, heat butter in a large skillet, add bread crumbs and mix until golden brown. Remove cooked dumplings with a slotted spoon and roll in bread crumbs. Top dumplings with powdered sugar and serve. Yield: 4 servings.

Linda Nagy
House of Tyrol

SCHINKENFLEKERLN
(HAM AND NOODLE CASSEROLE)

8 ounces broad egg noodles
3 tablespoons butter
1 cup sour cream
3 eggs
1 cup ham, diced
3 tablespoons bread crumbs
Freshly ground pepper
Salt

Preheat oven to 350 degrees. Break the noodles into square pieces and cook in boiling salted water for approximately 10 minutes; don't overcook. Drain noodles. Melt butter in pot where noodles cooked. Add noodles and toss until well coated. With a wire whisk or fork, beat the sour cream and eggs in a mixing bowl. Stir in ham, pepper, salt and noodles. Generously butter a 2-quart casserole, sprinkle with bread crumbs, tip from side to side to coat with crumbs. Fill with noodle and ham mixture. Bake uncovered for 35 to 45 minutes. To unmold, run a sharp knife around the casserole and invert on a warm plate. Serve with bottom side up. Schinkenflekerln is great for a light lunch or supper accompanied with a green salad.

Linda Nagy
House of Tyrol

GURKEN SALAT
(CUCUMBER SALAD)

3 medium cucumbers, peeled, scored, and sliced
1 clove garlic, pressed or finely chopped
Salt
2 tablespoons oil
2 tablespoons vinegar
Fresh parsley, chopped (optional)
Freshly ground pepper
Paprika

Peel cucumbers, score with a fork and cut paper thin. (Use a food processor, if you have one.) Sprinkle with salt, add pressed or finely chopped garlic; allow to stand in refrigerator approximately one hour. Pour off some of the accumulated juice. Mix oil and vinegar together and toss with cucumbers. Divide into four small servings and garnish with parsley, paprika and pepper. Yield: 4 servings.

Linda Nagy
House of Tyrol

EASY CHEESE STRAWS

Equal quantities of shredded cheese, margarine and flour
Red pepper
Salt

Mix margarine and flour together in a bowl with seasonings. Add the cheese. When well mixed, roll it out thin and cut into strips, then place on a tin and bake in a moderate oven until pale brown.

June Parks
The Cheese Hoop

DAVE'S PEANUT BRITTLE

3 cups sugar
1¾ cups light corn syrup
1 cup water
5 cups (1½ pounds) raw peanuts
2 tablespoons butter
¾ tablespoon soda
1 teaspoon salt

Cook sugar, syrup, and water to 240 degrees and add peanuts. Cook to 295 degrees, stirring constantly. Remove from heat; add butter, soda, and salt. Stir, mixing in well, until butter melts. Stir very hard. Pour on a buttered slab and spread as thinly as possible. Break into pieces when cool. Store in airtight container or wrap.

Dave Jones
Hansel and Gretel Candy Kitchen

CLOTHES CONNECTIONS I & II

These two shops, owned and operated by Susan Horrworth, offer name brand clothing for men and women at discount prices. Brands include Levi's, Lee, Lady Arrow, Gunne Sax and Dee-Cee.

Clothes Connection I for men, White Horse Square, Helen, Georgia 30545 (404) 878-2734
Clothes Connection II for women, Horse & Duck Platz, Helen, Georgia 30545 (404) 878-2857.

GAZPACHO

4 cups tomatoes, diced
1½ cups green pepper, chopped
¾ cup onion, chopped
2 cups beef bouillon
½ cup lemon juice
½ cup olive oil
1 tablespoon paprika
1 tablespoon salt
Freshly ground pepper
18 blanched almonds, chopped
1 tablespoon parsley
½ cup cucumber, thinly sliced

Combine all ingredients except cucumber. Let stand at room temperature 1 hour, stirring frequently. Chill for at least 2 hours. Garnish with cucumbers. Yield: 6 to 8 servings.

Sue Horrworth
Clothes Connection I

BEER CHEESE

1 pound sharp Cheddar cheese
1 pound mild American cheese
2 to 3 garlic cloves, to taste
3 tablespoons Worcestershire sauce
1 tablespoon salt
1 teaspoon dry mustard
Dash of Tabasco sauce
¾ of a 12-ounce bottle of beer, about 1 cup

Grind the cheeses with garlic. Mix Worcestershire sauce, salt, mustard and Tabasco with ground cheese. Put into mixing bowl and mix on slow speed. Gradually add beer to make a paste smooth enough to spread. Store in covered jars. Refrigerate until needed.

Sue Horrworth
Clothes Connection

MARINATED ARTICHOKE CHICKEN

6 chicken breasts
Garlic salt
1 package onion soup mix, mixed with small amount of water
Soy sauce
2 jars marinated artichokes, reserving oil
One 8-ounce can mushrooms, chopped
Small amount of water

Preheat oven to 325 degrees. Put chicken breasts in long baking casserole, skin side up. Sprinkle garlic salt and soup mix on top of chicken. Sprinkle soy sauce over all of the chicken mixture. Evenly distribute the artichokes with some of the oil. Place mushrooms on the top. Bake uncovered for 1¾ hours.

Sue Horrworth
Clothes Connection

RIVER ROAD RICE

1 cup rice, raw
1 can onion soup
1 cup chicken gumbo soup
1 small can mushrooms chopped
¼ pound butter

Preheat oven to 325 degrees. Put all ingredients into casserole and cover. Bake 1 hour. Mix before serving. Yield: 6 servings.

Sue Horrworth
Clothes Connection

THE SHOP ANTIQUES

The Shop Antiques specializes in 19th century American furniture and accessories. Established in 1980 in Helen, Georgia, in one of the 1912 Morse Brothers Lumber Company houses, the shop is the home of Loris and Tom Mann. Their interest in antiques and their wish for a shop dates back to their days of personal collecting of pieces throughout the midwest.

In their shop you will find walnut, cherry, maple, chestnut and birch tables, washstands, night stands, and chairs. All of the pieces are ready to use, having been refinished and restored under Tom's careful work or supervision. The shop also has a selection of old linens, handkerchiefs and coverlets. There is an attractive selection of antique Japanese Imari as well as other china and glass for your delight and purchase. Paintings, etchings, prints by area artists and a unique selection of gift items, miniature lamps, baskets, porcelain, note paper, napkins, gift wrap and cards are also available.

The Shop Antiques is open every day, except Monday, from 10:00 a.m. to 5:00 p.m. and is located one block north of the center of town on Main Street.

The Manns will be pleased to assist you in obtaining items suited to your specific needs and you are always WELCOME to browse and enjoy treasures of the past!

The Shop Antiques, North Main Street, Helen, GA 30545 (404) 878-2359.

COMPANY BREAKFAST EGGS

Wonderful on a cool mountain morning.

8 slices of white bread, crust trimmed
4 slices ham
1 cup Cheddar cheese, or 4 slices, shredded
4 eggs, beaten
2 cups milk
Dash of pepper
½ teaspoon salt
¼ teaspoon dry mustard

Arrange bread slices in bottom of 8-inch pan, cover with cheese, ham and again bread. Combine eggs, milk and seasoning. Pour over bread and let stand in refrigerator overnight. Bake in 325-degree oven about 1 hour or until lightly browned and puffy. Remove from oven and let stand a few minutes, then cut into squares and serve.

Loris Mann
The Shop Antiques

BEETS AND BING CHERRIES

¼ cup vinegar
⅔ cup sugar
3 tablespoons cornstarch
½ cup beet juice
½ cup bing cherry juice
Juice of 1 orange or ½ tablespoon frozen orange juice
2 cans small whole beets, if large cut in half
1 can bing cherries

Combine everything *except* beets and cherries. Cook until thickened, add beets and cherries and heat until beets and cherries are hot. Marvelous hot or cold.

Loris Mann
The Shop Antiques

GRANNY'S APPLE CAKE

¾ cup margarine
1½ cups sugar
2 eggs
2½ cups flour
1½ teaspoons soda
¾ cup strong coffee
3 cups apples, chopped
1 teaspoon vanilla
½ cup brown sugar
½ cup pecans

Mix together thoroughly all except last 2 ingredients. Pour into greased 9 x 13-inch pan. Combine brown sugar and pecans. Sprinkle on top of cake. Bake in 350-degree oven for 30 to 45 minutes.

Loris Mann
The Shop Antiques

THE SPINNING WHEEL

At the corner of Main Street and Old Street in the center of Helen, Georgia, lies the pretty little shop of Tony and Nancy Roberts. Yarns for knitting and needles to boot, latchhook kits and Helen T-shirts, ski sweaters and stationery and notepapers to write home—they're here at the Spinning Wheel.

The Spinning Wheel, Main Street at Old Street,
Helen, Georgia, 30545 (404) 878-2762.

SPAGHETTI WITH WHITE CLAM SAUCE

3 cloves garlic, peeled
½ cup butter or margarine
Two 6½-ounce cans minced clams, undrained
¼ cup parsley, chopped
¼ teaspoon basil or thyme leaves
1 pound spaghetti, cooked

Sauté garlic in the butter in saucepan until lightly browned; discard garlic. Add clams and heat, then add parsley and seasonings and serve on hot cooked spaghetti. Yield: 4 servings.

Nancy Roberts
The Spinning Wheel

PORK CHOPS SORRENTO

6 pork blade, rib, loin or sirloin chops (each cut about ¾-inch thick)
One 8-ounce can tomato sauce with mushrooms
1 small green pepper, cut into ¼-inch strips
½ teaspoon oregano leaves
One 8-ounce package mozzarella cheese, cut into 6 slices

About 55 minutes before serving:

Trim several pieces of fat from edges of pork chops. In 12-inch skillet over medium high heat, heat fat until lightly browned; using spoon, press and run fat over bottom of skillet to grease it well; discard fat. Add chops to skillet and cook until browned on both sides. Add tomato sauce, green pepper and oregano. Reduce heat to low; cover and simmer 30 minutes or until meat is fork tender. Top each chop with cheese slices; allow to cook 5 more minutes. Yield: 6 servings.

Nancy Roberts
The Spinning Wheel

RITZ CRACKER PIE

20 Ritz crackers, crushed
1 cup sugar
3 egg whites, beaten
1 teaspoon vanilla
1 cup pecans, chopped
Whipped topping

Beat together first five ingredients. Bake at 300 degrees for 45 minutes. This pie makes its own crust. Can be made a day ahead. Serve with whipped topping.

Nancy Roberts
The Spinning Wheel

FASHION HAUS

The Week Ender's Fashion Haus is located in one of the 1912 Morse Brother's Lumber Company houses. In this unique shop you will find name brand ladies clothing at 10% to 75% below retail prices. Such names as Evan Picone, Nancy Greer, Peter Popovitch, Act I, Kayser, Howard Wolf and many more are found here—at last count—39 name brands.

The Fashion Haus in Helen is open each year from mid April through November. The Week Ender, located at 12 Executive Park Drive Northeast, Atlanta is open all year.

The Fashion Haus in Helen is open Friday, Saturday and Sunday 10:00 to 6:00. The Week Ender in Atlanta is open Monday through Saturday 10:00 to 6:00.

Fashion Haus, Main Street, Helen, Georgia 30545, (404) 878-3321.

STRUDEL HAUS "HOUSE DRESSING"

6 tablespoons dry mustard
6 tablespoons celery seed
5 tablespoons salt
8 cups sugar
1 quart cider vinegar
1 gallon vegetable oil

Mix all ingredients except oil. Slowly add the oil and mix continuously for 10 minutes.

For your convenience, the following recipe will yield about 1¾ cups.

½ cup sugar
1 teaspoon dry mustard
1 teaspoon salt
1 to 2 teaspoons celery seed
⅓ cup cider vinegar
1 cup vegetable oil

Follow directions for above recipe.
Variation: add 1 teaspoon onion, grated.
Garnish with lemon thyme sprigs finely chopped.

STRUDEL HAUS BISCUITS

20 cups flour (self-rising)
7 tablespoons dry chives
3 tablespoons ground oregano
1½ pounds butter, softened
5¼ cups milk

Glaze:
2 eggs
2 tablespoons water

Mix dry ingredients together. Mix in butter, using low speed of mixer. Add milk, mixing thoroughly. Roll out on floured board to ½-inch thickness. Cut with 2-inch biscuit cutter. Beat eggs and water thoroughly. Brush tops of biscuits with egg mixture. Bake at 425 degrees until done. Yield: 200 biscuits.

We have reduced the following to yield approximately 20 biscuits.

1¾ cups flour (self-rising)
2 teaspoons dry chives
1 teaspoon ground oregano
¼ cup butter softened
¾ cup milk

Glaze:
1 egg
1 tablespoon water

Follow directions for above recipe.

PARMESAN CHICKEN

One 2½ to 3 pound chicken, cut up
⅓ cup water
½ teaspoon seasoned salt
½ cup Parmesan cheese, grated

Place chicken in a 13x9x2 inch baking dish, adding water. Sprinkle seasoned salt and Parmesan cheese over chicken, making sure that you have a good coating of cheese on chicken. Bake in 475 degree oven for 20 minutes, reducing heat to 375 degrees, cooking for an additional 10 minutes. Yield: 4 to 6 servings.

Ann Head
Mark of the Potter

JOHN'S CROCKPOT LAMB OREGANO

2 lamb shanks
2 tablespoons olive oil
1 small clove garlic, minced
1 to 1½ teaspoons oregano
2 medium tomatoes, diced
1 cup beef broth
3 tablespoons lemon juice
salt and pepper

Brown shanks in oil with garlic and oregano. Remove shanks to crockpot. Add tomatoes, beef broth and lemon juice to pan drippings. Simmer until tender. Strain tomato pulp into crockpot. Add beef broth to cover shanks. Salt and pepper to taste. Cook on high for 1 hour and on low 7 to 8 hours. Cool; refrigerate 4 hours or more to solidify fat. Remove solid fat, reheat and serve with oven roasted new potatoes, hot buttered beets, green salad and hot home baked bread.

John E. LaRowe

SPINACH SALAD DRESSING

1 cup granulated sugar
1 tablespoon dry mustard
1 tablespoon sweet basil
1 tablespoon salt
1 tablespoon marjoram
4 garlic cloves, minced
1½ cups salad oil
1½ cups red wine vinegar

Combine all ingredients well and serve over spinach salad.

Liz McFerrin
The Potter's Place

FRUIT BARS

Bars keep, pack and ship well.

½ cup margarine, softened
1⅓ cups brown sugar (½ box)
2 eggs
1 cup flour
1 tablespoon vanilla
2 cups nuts, chopped
6 slices canned pineapple, diced
½ pound citron
½ pound cherries

Cream brown sugar with margarine. Add eggs. Add remaining ingredients. Grease and flour 12 x 14 x 1-inch pan. Cook at 350 degrees about 1 hour. Cool; cut into 1- to 2-inch squares. Store in container with tight lid, adding sliced apples placed on waxed paper before closing. After two weeks discard apples, roll bars in powdered sugar.

Anne Askew
Village Realty

ORANGE MERINGUE PIE

3 egg yolks
½ cup sugar
3 tablespoons flour
1 cup orange juice
Juice of 1 lemon
1 pie shell, baked

Preheat oven to 325 degrees. Beat yolks; add sugar and flour. Add juices, stir and cook over hot water until thick. Fill pie shell.

Meringue:
3 egg whites
¼ teaspoon cream of tartar
4 tablespoons sugar
½ teaspoon vanilla

Whip egg whites until frothy, add cream of tartar and whip until soft peaks form. Beat in sugar, one tablespoon at a time, until blended; then add vanilla. Do not over beat.

Cover pie filling with meringue. Bake 10 to 15 minutes.

Elva Davidson
Village Realty

THE WILDEWOOD SHOP

Just down River Street a few feet, you'll find Helen's unique shop for outfitting the entire family for outdoor fun. Hiking shoes and shorts and shirts and socks; new canoes and canoes to rent; back packs and everything to fill them from dried soup to nuts and fruits to eat along the trail are only a part of the Wildewood's stock. Find the trails yourself or let Dave Gale lead you and your party on a hike or a canoe trip for a never-to-be-forgotten adventure in the beautiful Northeast Georgia mountains. The *Kite Site* is now a part of this wonderful shop.

Visit Ann and Dave Gale's new outpost "Chattahoochee Outfitters" on GA 115 at the Chattahoochee River, formerly Mrs. Fred Wikes' Store.

The Wildewood Shop, River Street, P.O. Box 119,
Helen, Georgia, 30545 (404) 878-2541.

PECAN PIE

½ cup sugar
1 cup light corn syrup
1 cup nuts
1 tablespoon margarine
1 teaspoon vanilla
1 teaspoon flour
1 pie shell, uncooked
3 eggs

Mix all ingredients. Bake in 400-degree oven in uncooked pie shell for 10 minutes. Then cook at 325 degrees until firm.

OYSTERS "ROCKYFELLOW"

1 bunch green onions
1 stalk celery
1 bunch parsley
½ teaspoon anise
1 tablespoon anchovy paste
Dash of Tabasco
2 packages frozen spinach, cooked
¾ cup butter
2 ounces Worcestershire sauce
Salt and pepper to taste
4 dozen oysters, in shells

Grind all ingredients except oysters. Place oysters in shells in oven at 350 degrees until edges crinkle and get watery. Pour water off. Put the ground mixture on top of oysters. Put into oven until slightly brown.

Anne Gale
The Wildewood Shop

ANNE'S LEMON CAKE ICING

½ cup flour
1 cup sugar
3 eggs, beaten
¼ cup lemon juice
Rind of one lemon, grated
¼ cup butter

Mix flour and sugar and beaten eggs, then add other ingredients. Cook in double boiler until thick. Yield: enough icing for top and sides of 8-inch cake.

Anne Gale
The Wildewood Shop

SHRIMP MARINADE

2½ pounds shrimp
4 medium onions, thinly sliced
1 box bay leaves
1¼ cups salad oil
¾ cup vinegar
1½ teaspoons salt
2½ teaspoons celery seed
2½ tablespoons capers and juice
Dash of hot sauce
¼ cup Worcestershire sauce

Put shrimp in cold water. Bring to a boil and set aside to steep for 6 minutes. Peel shrimp and remove veins under running water. Arrange shrimp and onions in layers with bay leaves. Mix remaining ingredients; pour over shrimp and let stand overnight or longer. Stir several times.

Anne Gale
The Wildewood Shop

TWO CRAFTY GUYS

Located in one of Helen's few remaining landmark buildings, Two Crafty Guys offers a wide selection of distinctive gifts for the entire family.

Unique creations by area craftsmen and Northeast Georgia's largest collection of wooden decoy ducks highlight this relaxed and rustic shop owned by Peter and Becky Fiero.

Two Crafty Guys features a select line of favorite collectibles: Wildlife sculptures in bronze, pecan and ceramic; calico cats, dogs, and ducks; dolls in porcelain and patchwork. We also carry Helen's largest selection of stained glass.

Two Crafty Guys, 1 River Road, P.O. Box 575,
Helen, GA 30545, (404) 878-3108.

VICHYSSOISE

4 leeks, white parts only, sliced
1 medium onion, sliced
¼ cup sweet butter
4 medium potatoes, thinly sliced
1 quart chicken broth
1 tablespoon salt, to taste
3 cups milk
2 cups heavy cream
Chopped chives

Brown the leeks and onions very lightly in butter. Add the potatoes, broth and salt. Boil for 35 minutes or until tender. Purée in blender. Return mixture to the soup kettle, add milk and 1 cup of the cream. Bring to a boil. Cook and purée in blender again. Chill. Add the remaining 1 cup cream. Chill thoroughly and serve, using chives as garnish. Yield: 8 servings.

Becky Fiero
Two Crafty Guys

THEM HAM BALLS

1 pound ground ham
1 pound ground lean pork, beef, or veal
2 eggs
1 cup canned milk
1 cup bread crumbs

Mix together and shape into small meat balls. (Make very tiny balls if using for appetizer). Arrange in a large baking pan. Now mix together in bowl:

1½ cups brown sugar
1½ cups vinegar
½ cup water
1 tablespoon dry mustard
1 small can crushed pineapple

Pour over meat balls. Bake in 275-degree oven in uncovered pan for 3 hours. Tiny size; a scrumptious appetizer, hot or cold; regular size, a dinner delight.

Loris Mann
The Shop Antiques

THE WOOD SHED

The Wood Shed offers its visitors a wide assortment of accessories at discount prices. Located in the heart of Helen on GA 75 and GA 17, the main showroom contains wooden items for use in the vacation cabin as well as back home. In the back gallery the theme turns to brass. You can find many more beautiful items for yourself and the gift items you need for a special occasion. Drop in on your next visit and plan to spend some time absorbing the variety of things that can be made in these materials.

The Wood Shed, Main St., P.O. Box 42, Helen, GA 30545 (404) 878-2586.

SHRIMP & SQUASH CASSEROLE

1 package stuffing mix
2 pounds cooked squash, drained
2 carrots, grated
1 onion, grated
1 can cream of chicken soup
One 8-ounce carton sour cream
1 can pimento, chopped
16 ounces chopped shrimp

Grease baking dish. Cover bottom with ½ package of stuffing mix. Mix all other ingredients and pour over stuffing in dish. Top with remaining stuffing and bake at 350 degrees for 30 minutes.

The Wood Shed

BROCCOLI AND SPINACH MOLD

2 cans beef consommé
3 boxes frozen broccoli, chopped
2 boxes frozen spinach, chopped
2½ cups mayonnaise
7 tablespoons Worcestershire sauce
1 teaspoon Tabasco
Juice of 4 lemons
1½ teaspoons salt
4 envelopes gelatin, plain
1 cup water
8 eggs, hard boiled, chopped

Heat consommé with broccoli and spinach until vegetables are completely thawed. Add mayonnaise, Worcestershire sauce, Tabasco, lemon juice and salt. Mix well. Soften gelatin in water, add gelatin and eggs to vegetable mixture. Pour into large ring mold. Chill. Remove from mold. Serve with Seasoned Cottage Cheese. Yield: 12 servings.

Seasoned Cottage Cheese:
One 24-ounce carton cottage cheese, cream style
4 tablespoons canned pimento, chopped
4 tablespoons green onion or chives, chopped
4 tablespoons green pepper, chopped
2 teaspoons prepared horseradish
½ teaspoon salt

Combine ingredients. Chill. Place in center of mold. Yield: 5 cups.

The Wood Shed

WILD RICE AND SEAFOOD CASSEROLE

1½ pounds fresh mushrooms, sliced
1 cup celery, sliced
1 green pepper, chopped
1 onion, chopped
Butter
3 packages wild & white rice, mixed, cooked
4 pounds shrimp and crab, mixed, cleaned
1 jar pimento, chopped
2 cans mushroom soup
1 cup milk
½ cup sherry
1 cup slivered almonds

Sauté mushrooms, celery, pepper and onions in butter. Stir into cooked rice with seafood and pimento. Dilute soup with milk and sherry. Stir into rice mixture with almonds. Pour into oiled casserole and bake at 350 degrees for 45 minutes. Yield: 12 servings.

The Wood Shed

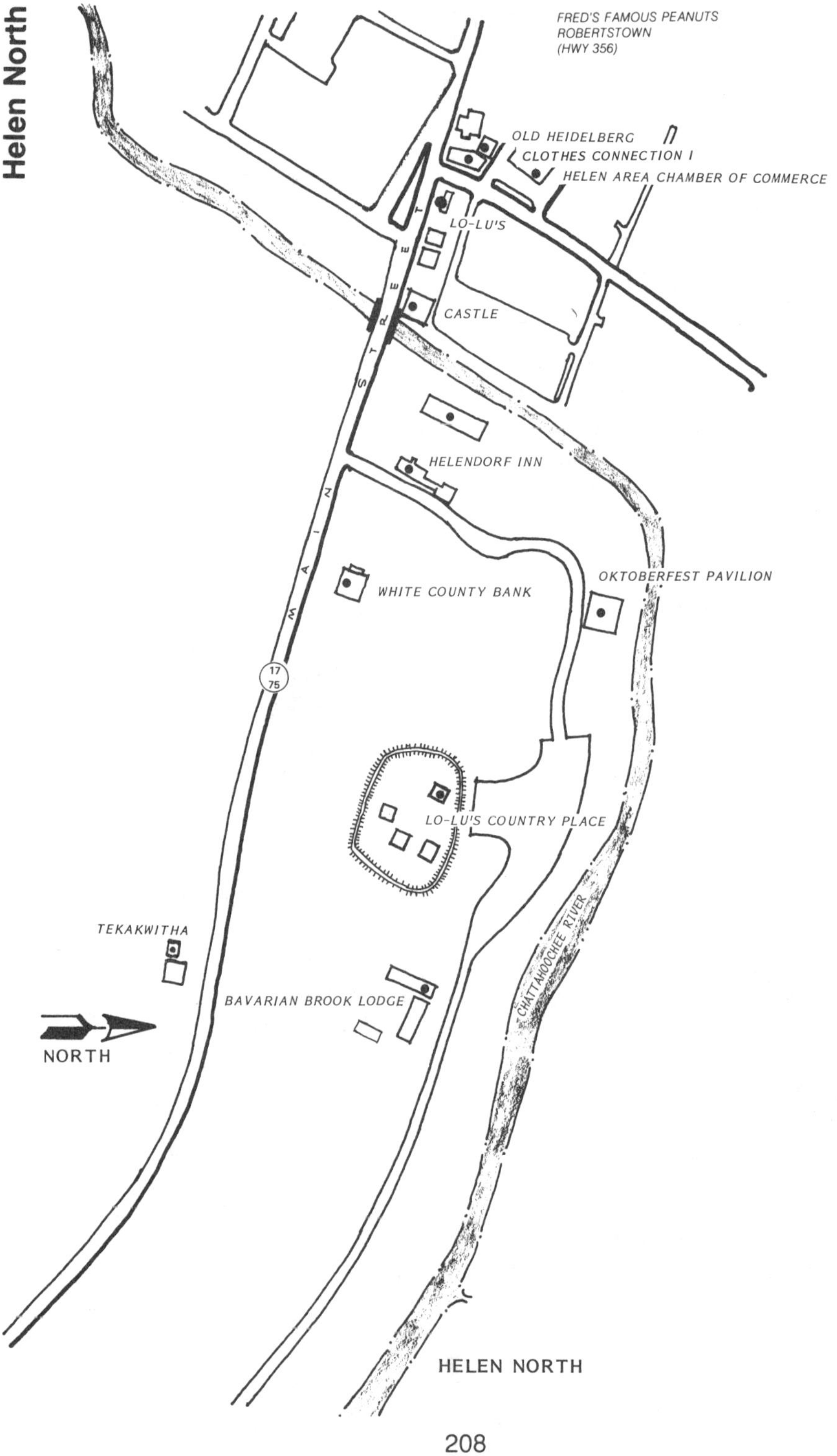

Helen North

FRED'S FAMOUS PEANUTS
ROBERTSTOWN
(HWY 356)

OLD HEIDELBERG
CLOTHES CONNECTION I
HELEN AREA CHAMBER OF COMMERCE
LO-LU'S
MAIN STREET
CASTLE
HELENDORF INN
OKTOBERFEST PAVILION
WHITE COUNTY BANK
17
75
LO-LU'S COUNTRY PLACE
CHATTAHOOCHEE RIVER
TEKAKWITHA
BAVARIAN BROOK LODGE
NORTH

HELEN NORTH

HELEN NORTH of Main Street

WHERE TO SLEEP

Alpenhof South 878-2191
BAVARIAN BROOK LODGE—Page 214
BROOK LANE, HELEN 878-2840
CASTLE INN—Page 216
MAIN STREET, HELEN 878-3140
Derdenhof Inn 878-2141
HELENDORF INN—Page 220—
MAIN STREET, HELEN 878-2271
Hilltop Haus 878-2388
Motel Heidi 878-2689
Village Inn, The 878-2296

WHERE TO EAT

Cafe International 878-3102
Colonel's Carriage Haus 878-3399
DELI, THE (OLD HEIDLEBERG)—
Page 228—MAIN STREET,
HELEN 878-2986
Flossie's Funnel Cakes 878-3181
Gesellschaft Haus 878-2136
Grannie's Cupboard 878-2656
Hickory Mountain BBQ 878-3543
Kuntry Ham Kitchen 878-3552
Mountain Valley Kitchen 878-2508
OLD HEIDELBERG RESTAURANT—
Page 228—MAIN STREET,
HELEN 878-2986
Rosel's Deli and Restaurant 878-3483
Sullivan's Pub 878-2895
Wurst Haus Restaurant 878-2647

WHERE TO SHOP

Ace Hardware 878-3230
Alpine Putt Putt
Balloons by Bernandette
Bavarian Bottle 878-2690
Bavarian Stein 878-2410
Bavarian Castle 878-2314
Bavarian Village
—Cafe International 878-3102
—Ice Cream Store 878-2092
—Sigmaringen Sports &
Rentals 878-2673
Burlwood Gallery
Christmas Factory, The 878-2540
CLOTHES CONNECTION I—Page 192—
WHITE HORSE SQUARE,
HELEN 878-2734
Corner Market
Das 1st Leather 878-3534
Der Bootsee
Earth Treasures 878-3192
FRED'S FAMOUS PEANUTS 878-3124
For Heaven's Sake
French Quarter, The 878-3302
Gesellschaft Haus 878-2136
—Alpine Glass Engraving
by Damron 878-2087
—Alpine Sportsman 878-3544
—Art & Decorating Accessories
—Bavarian Glass Blower 878-3156
—Country Touch, The 878-3583
—Doll & Toy Museum 878-3192
—Magic Touch, The 878-3155
—Mouse Trap, The 878-3288
—Small Treasures 878-2421
—True Vine, The 878-3488
—1890 Photo Shop 878-3297
Gift World 878-2504
Glass Spectrum, Inc. 878-3287
Gold Reflections 878-3200
Harris, Ltd. 878-2599
Helen Celler 878-2651
Hunt's Old Tyme Store 878-2447
Ice Cream, Inc.
Mount'neer Plants & Crafts 878-2736
Mr. B's
MUSEUM OF THE HILLS, THE CASTLE—
Page 216—MAIN STREET,
HELEN 878-3140
Nature's Store House 878-2990
RIVER PALACE, THE CASTLE—Page 216—
MAIN STREET, HELEN 878-3140
Rocks to Riches 878-3415
Scottish Store, The 878-3103

WHERE TO SHOP

Sign Shop .878-3153
Strawberry Junction 878-3151
Sullivan's Game Room
Swiss Alps Kandle Shop
Tobak Haus 878-2956
Underground Gallery 878-2627
UPTOWN COUNTRY CORNER—
Page 174—CHATTAHOOCHEE STREET, HELEN 878-3215
Windmill Shop, The 878-3444
Ye Olde English Shoppe 878-3394

SERVICES

All-Region Realty 878-2102
Balok Printing 878-3500
City Hall 878-2733
Dee's Hair Designs 878-2060
Guy's & Gal's Hairstyles 878-2512
HELEN AREA CHAMBER OF COMMERCE—Page 218 MAIN STREET, HELEN 878-2521
Helen Pavilion
Helen Small Engine Service
Helen Wash & Dry 878-2934
Loreley Center 878-2238
Only Kids Allowed
People's Bank, The 878-2294
Vagen Vaschen
Village Health Clinic 878-2207
WHITE COUNTY BANK—Page 236 MAIN STREET, HELEN (CLEVELAND) 865-3151

WHAT TO DO & SEE

ALPINE HELEN—Page 212
CASTLE, THE—Page 216—MUSEUM OF THE HILLS & RIVER PALACE, MAIN STREET, HELEN 878-3140
OKTOBERFEST PAVILION—Page 208— MAIN STREET, THE ISLAND, HELEN

WHERE TO CAMP

HELENDORF INN—Page 220— MAIN STREET, HELEN 878-2271

discover
the northeast
GEORGIA
MOUNTAINS

NOTICE: For your convenience we have listed all of the places to eat and all of the places to sleep in the area covered by this list. Quality is a personal concept and, although we have listed every place to eat or sleep known at the time of printing, some restaurants and some motels we recommend highly, while others do not quite meet our high standards of quality and we assume no responsibility for them. We would suggest that you inquire locally of any of the businesses in bold type listed above for their recommendations.

CONTENTED CONTEMPLATION

I remember from childhood visits the excitement of catching the first glimpse of distant peaks. Traveling up from the sandy, pine-covered coastal plains through the undulating Piedmont, we would search to the north for the ancient sentinels of a strange and beautiful land.

Its isolation guarded this old Cherokee homeland from the abuses of civilization. Its mysteries were held secure by the Blue Ridge pickets.

Now there is convenient access to accommodate the tempo of the age. The frustrating, impatient anticipation is modified somewhat. Nevertheless, there is still a sense of homecoming when I sight Wauka and Black Mountain from 365 south of Gainesville.

To some, intimacy engenders indifference and they become inured, or at least oblivious to the symmetry of the ridges and valleys. But, like a faithful though unappreciated companion, absence rejuvenates adolation. The veiled mountains, cloaked in forest green, offer, perchance subliminally, security and tranquility. Possibly this is all an illusion, but many share the experience.

Living in the mountains perpetuates this euphoria. Here, where seasons are definite but not severe, time is sipped and savored.

Spring slips out of its cocoon as quietly as the moth. Red buds whisper in the cool, clear mornings of fields to be turned and cobwebs to be cleared. The "new green," accompanied by the crow's anticipatory caws, heralds planting time.

Summer's appearance is announced by the joy of freed school children splashing carefree in the sparkling brook, or on some distant rise plucking berries for an evening cobbler.

CARROLL PROCTOR "SCOOP" SCRUGGS

ALPINE HELEN

No visitor to the mountains should fail to see Helen, located on GA 75 and GA 17 north of Cleveland. Here on the remains of a defunct lumber mill village, the community has created a theme town in the style of a Bavarian resort. The shops are alive with colorful gingerbread and murals; the air is filled with music; and some shopkeepers dress in authentic costumes. Throughout the year there are festivals and sporting events. From Winter Carnival to Oktoberfest, there is always something doing in Helen—and everyone is welcome to join in the fun and goodwill.

VENISON CHILI

2 pounds ground venison
1 pound ground beef
Three 16 ounce cans tomato sauce
Three 16-ounce cans kidney beans
Three packages chili seasoning mix

Brown venison and beef in Dutch oven. Add tomato sauce, beans, chili seasoning and mix. Cover and simmer 15 minutes.
The Wood Shed

ARROZ CON POLLO

Chicken with Rice, but a lot fancier!

1 large onion, chopped
1 large green pepper, chopped
2 stalks celery, chopped
1 clove garlic, minced
Spanish olive oil
1 frying chicken, cut up
2 cups tomatoes
Pinch of oregano
Pinch of thyme
Salt and pepper to taste
1 bay leaf
Small box long grain wild rice
2 cups peas, cooked, reserve juice
One 16-ounce can white asparagus, drained, reserve juice
1 can of beer
½ cup water
1 package of saffron mixed with 1 drop of boiling water to make a paste
1 small can pimentos
1 jar mushroom caps

Sauté onions, pepper, celery and garlic in oil for 5 minutes. Add chicken. Sauté 10 minutes longer. Transfer to a large casserole. Spread tomatoes over chicken, and sprinkle with seasonings. Add bay leaf. Pour rice over tomatoes. Mix liquid from the peas and asparagus with the beer and pour over rice. Add ½ cup water to saffron paste and spread over rice. Cover and bake at 350 degrees for 45 minutes. Remove from oven and spread drained peas over top. Add drained asparagus spears "spoke fashion." Cut poinsettias from pimentos and arrange on top using mushroom caps as center of flowers. Cover and return to oven for 15 minutes. Yield: 4 to 6 servings.

Sue Horrworth
River Road Shoppe

SOUR CREAM DRESSING FOR FRUIT SALAD

¾ cup sour cream
1 tablespoon mayonnaise
1 tablespoon lime or lemon juice
Grated rind of lime or lemon
1 teaspoon sugar, or to taste

For fresh fruit salad, cut up fruit in advance. Sprinkle lime or lemon juice over fruit so it will not turn brown. Combine ingredients; fold dressing into fruit very gently until fruit is well coated. Cover container and chill until ready to serve.

Betty Boysen
Village Realty

BAVARIAN BROOK LODGE

Located on the Chattahoochee River as you come into Helen is Bavarian Brook Lodge, an authentic copy of a Bavarian Country Mountain complex. The setting in these Blue Ridge foothills with the cool river and lush green surroundings, as well as the neighboring home copied from its twin in Berchtesgaden, Germany, insure that your stay here seems like a trip abroad to the old country.

The Lodge offers a variety of rooms: rustic Bavarian motel rooms, rooms with wood burning fireplaces, studio rooms and full apartments, along with extras such as private pool, tennis court, riverbank and cable T.V.

The convenience of a pleasant stroll into the village and, most important, reasonable rates and seasonal specials make for a special vacation here.

Bavarian Brook Lodge, P.O. Box 333,
Helen, Georgia 30545; reservations (404) 878-2840.

CROCKPOT BARBECUE CHICKEN

One 2- to 3-pound chicken

One 18-ounce bottle barbecue sauce

Cut up chicken. Place layer of chicken in crockpot; cover with barbecue sauce; then add another layer of chicken and barbecue sauce. Place cover on top. Turn on high for 15 minutes, then cook on low heat overnight.

Janie Woodcock
Bavarian Brook Lodge

JANIE'S SQUASH CASSEROLE

2 cups yellow squash, cooked
1 cup cheese, shredded
1 tablespoon onion, minced
1 can mushroom soup
3 eggs, slightly beaten
Salt and pepper to taste

Mix together and bake in a 1-quart casserole at 350 degrees for 45 minutes or until firm.

Janie Woodcock
Bavarian Brook Lodge

CHEESE BISCUITS

½ cup butter
2 cups sharp cheese, shredded
2 cups cake flour
Salt
Red pepper

Have all ingredients at room temperature. Use *no* liquid. Cream butter and cheese; add flour and seasonings. Shape into 2 rolls. Chill and cut. Bake at 450 degrees for 5 to 10 minutes.

Janie Woodcock
Bavarian Brook Lodge

"GREEN BEAN" CAKE

1 box yellow cake mix
4 eggs
¾ cup plus 1 tablespoon water
¾ cup oil
1 box instant pistachio pudding mix
¼ teaspoon green food color
1 cup nuts

Mix all ingredients; put in well greased 13 x 9 x 2-inch pan. Sprinkle chopped nuts on top of batter. Bake at 350 degrees for 30 to 45 minutes.

Topping for Cake:
3 tablespoons butter
1⅓ ounces unsweetened chocolate
⅓ cup water
2 cups powdered sugar
1 teaspoon vanilla

Melt butter, chocolate and water in saucepan on very low heat. Add sugar and vanilla, beating until creamy. Place on cooled cake.

Miriam Lovell
Bavarian Brook Lodge

THE CASTLE

Right at the Helen Square and on the edge of the beautiful Chattahoochee River, the Castle Inn has 11 deluxe guest rooms with private balconies overlooking the many activities of the City or the beauty and serenity of the river. Old Fashioned ceiling fans, Cable T.V. and complimentary morning coffee are all part of the plan to make your stay as comfortable, unique and enjoyable as possible. Shops, Restaurants, and entertainment are only a few steps away.

Also located in the 'Castle' on the Main Street level is the "Museum of the Hills", a one of a kind presentation depicting life in North Georgia at the turn of the Century. You will walk through a typical farm of the times and a complete old town with its various shops, a grist mill, whiskey still, sawmill and much more to reflect the early life in the hills. A 'World of Fantasy' area is a delight for children of all ages and adds to the overall theme of "Family Entertainment".

On the lower floor, the River Palace Music Hall offers the visitor a program of light musical entertainment set in a jewel box theatre that captures the "Good Old Days" of song and dance when everyone was young and happy. Shows are performed on a regular afternoon and evening schedule—available on request.

The Castle, North Main Street at the river, Helen, GA, 30545, (404) 878-3140

ZUCCHINI CASSEROLE

4 medium zucchini, sliced
3/4 cup carrots, shredded
1/2 cup onion, chopped
6 tablespoons butter
2 1/4 cups herb stuffing cubes
1 can cream of chicken soup
1/2 cup sour cream

Boil zucchini until tender. In saucepan, sauté carrots and onions in 4 tablespoons of the butter until tender. Add 1 1/2 cups of the bread crumbs and soup and sour cream. Stir in zucchini. Place in casserole. Melt remaining butter and add rest of bread cubes. Sprinkle on top of casserole. Bake at 350 degrees for 30 to 40 minutes. Yield: 8 servings.

Kathy Hawthorne
The Castle

CEYLON CHICKEN

1 chicken fryer, cut up
1/8 teaspoon pepper
1 teaspoon salt
4 tablespoons salad oil
2 small onions, diced
2 medium apples, chopped
2 tablespoons curry powder
1 tablespoon cornstarch
1 1/2 cups water
2 chicken bouillon cubes
Cooked rice

Sprinkle chicken with salt and pepper; brown in salad oil and drain well. Sauté onions and apples in oil until tender. Add curry powder, cornstarch, water and bouillon cubes. Stir until cubes are dissolved. Add chicken. Cover and cook over low heat for 35 minutes or until chicken is tender. Serve over rice.

Kathy Hawthorne
The Castle

HELEN AREA CHAMBER OF COMMERCE

The Greater Helen Area Chamber serves the needs of the busy and beautiful Alpine Village of Helen and the surrounding Sautee and Nacoochee Valleys. The once thriving lumbering business of the early 1900's petered out, "gold fever" came and went but Helen lives on as the most charming and most often visited theme town in the southeast. Beginning in January with the *Fasching Karnival,* the *Kite Festival* in March, the *Canoe Races* in April and May, the *Trout Festival* in May, the *Helen Balloon Festival* in June, *Oktoberfest* in September and the *Fall Leaf Spectacular* in October, there is always *"Somethin' Cookin'"* in the greater Helen area. Visit the Chamber office or write or telephone for *current information.*

Greater Helen Area Chamber of Commerce,
Helen, Georgia 30545 (404) 878-2521.

SWISS CHARD PIE

12 ounces (12 cups) Swiss chard, torn
4 eggs
3 ounces feta cheese, crumbled
½ cup milk
½ cup Swiss cheese, shredded
½ teaspoon salt
⅛ teaspoon pepper
3 tablespoons grated onion
One 9-inch unbaked pastry shell
Cherry tomatoes and parsley, for garnish

Wash and cook chard in the water that clings to leaves, about 10 minutes or until tender; drain well, pressing out excess water. In small mixer bowl beat eggs. Stir in milk, feta cheese, Swiss cheese, salt, pepper, and onion. Stir in chard. Turn into pastry shell.

Bake at 375 degrees for 25 minutes. Let stand 10 minutes before serving. Top with halved cherry tomatoes and parsley, if desired.

Fay Parks
Helen Area Chamber of Commerce

SESAME SEED COOKIES

1 cup sesame seeds
½ cup coconut
½ cup butter
1 cup brown sugar
1 egg
2 teaspoons vanilla
2 cups flour
½ teaspoon baking soda
1 teaspoon baking powder
⅛ teaspoon salt

Preheat oven to 350 degrees. Grease 2 cookie sheets. Spread seeds and coconut on sheets and toast 8 minutes. Stir with fork and cool. Beat butter and sugar until light and creamy. Fold in egg and vanilla. Sift together flour, soda, baking powder, salt. Fold into butter mixture. Fold in sesame seeds and coconut. Form into small balls, about ½-inch around. Chill 1 hour, then bake 10 minutes. Cool. Yield: 3 dozen.

PANOCHA SQUARES

¼ cup butter, melted
1 cup brown sugar
1 egg
½ teaspoon vanilla
1 cup plain flour
1 teaspoon baking powder
¼ teaspoon salt
1 cup semi-sweet chocolate bits
¾ cup chopped nuts

Blend all ingredients. Pour into greased 8-inch square pan. Bake for 30 minutes at 350 degrees. Cut into squares.

Vivian Adams
Helen Area Chamber of Commerce

HELENDORF INN

The Helendorf Inn both outside and inside reflects the Alpine image of Helen. The lobby sitting room is a warm and friendly place for meeting folks, with a big fireplace, comfortable furniture and the coffee is always on. Books and table games are available to be enjoyed with new friends or checked out for use in your own room.

Set aside for private functions is a lovely room which can accommodate up to 100 people for meetings or parties. This room has fireplace, exposed beam ceiling, many windows and a kitchen for catered or do-it-yourself food.

Thirty three of the rooms have private sitting areas a few feet from the crystal clear Chattahoochee River providing entertainment for the observer or participant in swimming, tubing, fishing or canoeing. These rooms are decorated with John Kollock watercolors and floral painted furniture. Kitchenette, private bath, phone, cable T.V., and individual temperature control units add to your comfort.

The Helendorf Inn is within easy walking distance of all shops and restaurants and activities.

Helendorf Inn, Main Street at the river, P.O. Box 305,
Helen, Georgia 30545 (404) 878-2271.

BLEU CHEESE SAUCE FOR MEATS AND VEGETABLES

¼ cup butter or margarine
4 tablespoons flour
1 clove garlic, minced and washed
1 cup half and half
1½ cups chicken broth
4 ounces bleu cheese, crumbled
Salt

Heat butter in pan. Stir in flour and garlic and cook until blended and bubbly. Gradually stir in half and half and chicken broth, stirring until thickened. Add bleu cheese and stir until blended. Add salt if needed.

Dick Gay
Helendorf

FRUIT CAKE

¾ cup flour
¾ cup sugar
½ teaspoon baking powder
½ teaspoon salt
2 cups brazil nuts, whole
1 cup maraschino cherries, whole
Two 7-ounce packages or 1 pound pitted dates, whole
3 eggs, beaten
1 teaspoon vanilla

Sift together flour, sugar, baking powder, and salt. Add nuts, cherries and dates and stir well until coated. Add eggs and vanilla and mix well. Pour into 4 x 8½ x 2½-inch pan lined with brown paper and oiled. Bake at 300 degrees for 1½ hours.

Genie McCoy
Helendorf

SOUTHERN PECAN PIE

⅓ cup butter
½ cup brown sugar, firmly packed
1 cup light brown corn syrup
1 teaspoon vanilla
3 eggs, slightly beaten
1 cup pecans, chopped
1 unbaked 9″ pie crust

Cream butter and brown sugar well. Blend in and mix thoroughly corn syrup and vanilla. Add eggs and pecans. Pour into pie crust. Bake at 450 degrees for 10 minutes, then at 350 degrees for 25 minutes more.

Barbara Gay
Helendorf

PIQUANT SAUCE

3 tablespoons brown sugar
½ cup catsup
¼ teaspoon nutmeg
1 teaspoon dry mustard

Combine all above and pour over meat loaf before or after baking.

Barbara Gay
Helendorf

MEAT BALL HORS D'OEUVRES

2 pounds ground beef
½ cup bread crumbs
½ cup milk
2 eggs
1½ teaspoons salt, or part garlic salt

Mix all ingredients well; form into small balls and cook at 500 degrees for 5 to 6 minutes in baking dish.

Sweet and Sour Sauce:
One 14-ounce can pineapple chunks, drained (save juice)
¼ cup chicken broth
¼ cup brown sugar
½ cup vinegar
1 tablespoon soy sauce
1 tablespoon catsup
1 tablespoon cornstarch
1 cup onion, thinly sliced
1 green pepper, seeded, cut in 1″ squares

Combine pineapple juice, broth, sugar, vinegar, soy sauce, catsup and cornstarch. Cook, stirring until thickened. Add onion and green pepper and cook 1 minute longer. Remove from heat and add pineapple chunks and meat balls.

Genie McCoy
Helendorf

MEXICAN CORN BREAD

1 cup self-rising corn meal
½ cup self-rising flour
1 cup sweet milk
1 cup onion, chopped
½ cup sharp cheese, grated
½ cup cooking oil
2 eggs
1 teaspoon cayenne pepper
Dash of salt
1 cup canned cream style corn

Mix all ingredients and bake at 350 degrees until golden brown.

Janie Woodcock
Bavarian Brook Lodge

SOUTHERN CHEESE LOG

1 cup pecans
2 cloves garlic
8 ounces cream cheese
⅛ teaspoon Worcestershire sauce
⅛ teaspoon soy sauce
⅛ teaspoon salt
4 drops Tabasco
3 teaspoons chili powder

Chop pecans and garlic. In medium bowl mix cream cheese, Worcestershire sauce, soy sauce, salt and Tabasco; add pecans and garlic. Mix very well. Shape into 2 rolls, 4″ x 1½″. Sprinkle 1½ teaspoons chili powder on waxed paper for each roll; roll logs coating evenly and wrap, twisting ends. Chill 4 hours or more. Best made in advance. Keeps 2 weeks or more in the refrigerator. May freeze.

Betty Higgins
Helendorf

COUNTRY CAPTAIN

3 pounds chicken pieces
¼ cup butter
1 onion
1 green pepper
1 garlic clove
1 cup chicken broth
1 teaspoon salt
½ cup almonds
3 tablespoons currants
6 strips bacon, fried crisp
Rice, cooked

Brown chicken in butter. Remove to a baking dish. In same pan, cook onion, pepper and garlic until limp. Stir in chicken broth and salt. Pour over chicken in baking dish and bake 45 minutes at 350 degrees. Stir in almonds and currants. Sprinkle crumbled bacon on top. Serve with rice. Yield: 4 servings.

The Wood Shed

CHOCOLATE POUND CAKE

1 cup shortening
3 cups sugar
6 eggs
3 cups cake flour
½ cup cocoa
½ teaspoon baking powder
1¼ cups milk
2 teaspoons vanilla
¼ teaspoon salt

Cream shortening and sugar; add eggs one at a time. Add other ingredients. Preheat oven to 325 degrees. Cook 1 hour and 25 minutes or until done.

Daisy Dorsey
Bavarian Brook Lodge

BROWN SUGAR PIE

2 tablespoons flour
¾ cup brown sugar
1 cup milk
2 eggs, separated
1 tablespoon margarine
1 cup nuts
1 teaspoon vanilla
1 pie shell, baked
4 teaspoons sugar

Mix flour and brown sugar; add half of milk, beaten egg yolks and remainder of milk. Add margarine, nuts and vanilla. Cook over low heat until thick. Pour in baked pie shell. Beat egg whites; add sugar to make meringue. Spoon on top. Bake at 400 degrees until brown.

Anne Gale
The Wildewood Shop

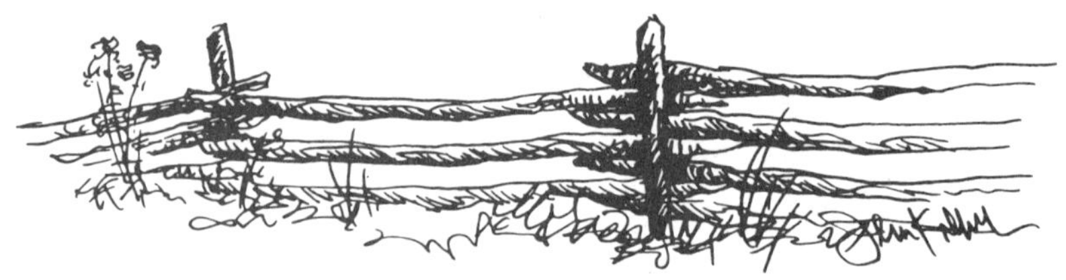

CARROTS SUPREME

5 large carrots, scraped, coarsely grated
2 eggs
2 tablespoons flour
Salt and pepper to taste
¼ cup nuts, chopped (optional)
2 tablespoons cooking oil
2 onions, sliced
2 celery stalks, finely sliced
1 green pepper, seeded, sliced
1½ cups tomatoes, peeled, seeded, chopped
¼ cup tomato paste
¼ cup brown sugar

In a bowl, combine carrots with eggs, flour, salt and pepper to taste. If desired, stir in chopped nuts. Drop the mixture by teaspoons into oil in a skillet and fry the patties until they are brown on both sides. Drain on paper towels and reserve. In another skillet sauté onions, sliced celery, and green pepper until the vegetables are soft. Add tomatoes, tomato paste and brown sugar. Salt and pepper to taste. Simmer the mixture, stirring occasionally, for 10 minutes. Carefully add the carrot patties, and simmer the mixture, covered, for 10 minutes more.

Charles Horrworth
Alpine Valley Realty

MRS. ALDRIDGE'S CRISP COOKIES

2 eggs
2½ cups dark brown sugar, packed
1 cup butter, melted
3½ cups flour, unsifted
1 teaspoon soda
½ teaspoon salt
1 teaspoon vanilla
¼ to ½ cup pecans, chopped

Beat eggs well; add sugar and butter; mix again. Add remaining ingredients and mix thoroughly. Divide into 4 parts. With hands, shape each part into a roll, 2 inches in diameter. Wrap each roll in waxed paper; chill 3 hours or overnight. Slice as needed; bake on greased tin at 325 degrees for 15 to 20 minutes. Keeps indefinitely. Yield: 36 cookies per roll.

Marion Tidmore

MARION'S CHEESE CAKE

1 cup graham cracker crumbs
¼ cup butter
4 eggs, separated
1½ cups sugar
¼ teaspoon salt
Three 8-ounce packages cream cheese at room temperature
1 tablespoon lemon juice

Mix graham cracker crumbs and butter for crust. Press into springform pan. Beat egg yolks with ½ cup of the sugar and salt. Add cream cheese, ½ cup sugar and lemon juice. Beat egg whites until soft peaks form; gradually add ½ cup sugar and fold into the egg yolk mixture. Pour over crust in pan. Bake at 400 degrees for 30 to 35 minutes. Remove from oven and turn oven up to 550 degrees.

Topping:
½ pint sour cream
½ cup sugar

Stir and pour over top of cake. Bake 5 minutes at 550 degrees. Cool thoroughly. Refrigerate any remaining cheese cake.

Marion Tidmore

OKTOBERFEST PAVILION

OKTOBERFEST: This early September to mid October event is not only the biggest and best happening of the year in Helen...but, it's bigger and better than any OKTOBERFEST anywhere outside of Bavaria itself.

Not only does Helen go "all out" for OKTOBERFEST but look at what else there is to do and to see—so many ways to become involved and so many ways for you to take a part—come enjoy all of these annual activities.

Each Saturday during the summer at high noon watch or join our Sidewalk Parade.

JANUARY
Fasching "Mardi-Gras" Karnival
Hogpen Hill Climb

FEBRUARY
Fasching "Mardi-Gras" Karnival
Fireside Arts & Craft Show

APRIL
Canoe & Kayak Classics
Passion Play
Trout Festival & Fish Fry

MAY
Mayfest in the Mountains
Clogging Convention
Hot Air Balloon Festival

JUNE
Summer Theater
Indian Day
Helen Arts Council Craft Show
Helen Antique Show

JULY
Summer Theatre
July 4th Activities

AUGUST
Summer Theatre

SEPTEMBER
OKTOBERFEST & Parade

OCTOBER
OKTOBERFEST
Antique Show

NOVEMBER
Christmas Lighting of Helen

DECEMBER
Christmas in Helen

For further information contact:
The Helen Area Chamber of Commerce, P.O. Box 192, Helen, Georgia 30545, (404) 878-2521

SPAGHETTI AND MEAT SAUCE

2 pounds ground beef
1 large onion
1 green pepper
1 cup mushrooms
One 16-ounce can tomatoes
Two 6-ounce cans tomato paste
2 tablespoons sugar
2 bay leaves
2 teaspoons sage
Dash red pepper
2 teaspoons salt
Dash black pepper
1 cup water
1 pound spaghetti, cooked

Brown ground beef, onion and pepper. Add mushrooms. Add remaining ingredients, except spaghetti. Simmer for two hours. Pour over cooked spaghetti.

CHEESE CAKE MARTHA

1 pound ricotta cheese, shredded
Two 8-ounce packages cream cheese
1½ cups sugar
4 eggs
1 teaspoon vanilla
2 tablespoons lemon juice
⅓ cup cornstarch
½ cup margarine, melted and cooled
1 pint sour cream
½ cup graham cracker crumbs

Mix in mixer one at a time, in the order listed, all ingredients except graham cracker crumbs. Grease spring-form pan lightly with margarine. Dust with graham cracker crumbs. Carefully spoon cheese mixture onto crumbs. Bake at 325 degrees for 1 hour and 10 minutes. Turn off oven and leave in oven for 2 hours more. Cool and refrigerate.

Martha Drzyzga
Lo-Lu's Country Place

BANANA SPLIT CAKE

3 cups graham cracker crumbs
1 cup margarine, melted

Combine crumbs and melted margarine. Make graham cracker crust by pressing crumb mixture into pie plate. Bake 10 minutes at 350 degrees. Cool crust before adding filling.

Filling:
3 or 4 bananas
3 or 4 tablespoons lemon juice
1 cup margarine
2 cups powdered sugar
2 eggs
1 teaspoon vanilla
One 16-ounce can unsweetened crushed pineapple, drained
One 13½-ounce container of whipped topping
Walnuts
Cherries, halved for garnish

Slice bananas and soak in lemon juice to keep them from turning dark. Mix margarine, sugar, eggs and vanilla and beat at high speed about 20 minutes until thick and creamy. Spread filling in crust, drain bananas and spread on top of filling. Spread pineapple on top of bananas. Spread whipped topping on bananas. Sprinkle chopped walnuts on top. Garnish with cherries cut in half.

Martha Drzyzga
Lo-Lu's Country Place

OLD HEIDELBERG

Old Heidelberg Restaurant and Lounge with its castle-like interior serves fine German cuisine. There, German born owners Harold and Theresia Link, take great pride in serving Germany's best known meals. Old Heidelberg specializes in Wiener Schnitzel, Sauerbraten and Rouladen. Our courteous staff is ready to serve you whether it be in our newly opened Deli located on the first floor, in our dining room, or in our lounge where one can hear Harold's Oomp-Pa band entertain for listening or dancing pleasure.

Old Heidelberg is located in White Horse Square, Helen, Georgia. Open for lunch and dinner with entertainment on the weekends.

Old Heidelberg, White Horse Square, Main Street,
Helen, Georgia 30545 (404) 878-2986.

HIMMEL UND ERDE EINTOPF
(Potatoes and Apples in one pot)

3¼ pounds potatoes
⅔ pint water
Salt
1⅛ pounds apples, peeled and quartered
Sugar
Vinegar
4 ounces fat bacon, cut into cubes
2 onions, sliced

Put potatoes in boiling salt water and cook gently for 15 minutes. Add apples, bring back to boil and cook gently until done. Season with salt, sugar and vinegar. Fry bacon. Add the onions and brown them; pour over the dish and serve. Total cooking time, approximately 45 minutes. Yield: 4 servings.

Theresia Link
Old Heidelberg Restaurant and Lounge

BUTTERCREMETORTE

3 eggs, separated
1 cup sugar
3 to 4 tablespoons water
1 lemon rind, grated
1 cup plain flour
1 cup cornstarch
3 teaspoons baking powder

Beat together egg yolks, sugar and water until foamy; add lemon rind. Mix flour, cornstarch, and baking powder added by spoonfuls. Beat egg whites until stiff and fold into mixture. Put dough in a wax paper-lined springform pan and bake 40 minutes at 350 degrees. When cooled, cut cake into 3 layers and fill with buttercreme.

Buttercreme Filling:
1 cup butter
2 cups powdered sugar
1 egg yolk
2 tablespoons lemon juice
3 tablespoons strong coffee
2 tablespoons liquor of your choice

Beat butter until foamy and add 1 cup powdered sugar. Mix egg yolk, remaining cup of powdered sugar, lemon juice, coffee and liquor. If necessary, add 1 to 2 tablespoons hot water and mix.

Theresia Link
Old Heidelberg Restaurant and Lounge

FRED'S FAMOUS PEANUTS

Fred and Dianne Jenkins have tried their hands successfully at many crafts and projects including stained glass, basket weaving and soft sculpture. Their forte, however, is definitely peanuts—ALL FORMS OF PEANUTS: boiled peanuts, roasted peanuts, peanut brittle, and best of all, Fred's Famous Fried Peanuts.

Naturally, there is more to do at Fred's Famous Peanuts than just enjoy the free samples Fred and Dianne offer. Take your picture with the old folks (life size soft sculptures) that are always sittin' around the peanut shack or by the old wagon full of flowers. You may even catch a quick game of Racquetball on famous Fred's court.

In season you can find apples and cider, pumpkins, and all sorts of mountain products. There are always new peanut products and crafts so you really never know just what to expect.

Fred's Famous Peanuts opens with the Spring blossoms and closes with the last falling leaf of Autumn.

PEANUT BUTTER PIE

4 ounces cream cheese
1 cup 10x sugar
1/2 cup peanut butter
1/2 cup milk
1 (8-ounce) container cool whip
1 graham cracker pie crust

Cream cheese and sugar and peanut butter. Add milk then cool whip. Pour into pie crust and refrigerate for three hours before serving.

Fred's Famous Peanuts, Hwy 356,
Robertstown, Georgia 30545 (One mile north of Helen)

SPINACH-CHEESE CASSEROLE

1 cup biscuit mix
¼ cup milk
2 eggs
¼ cup onion, chopped
2 packages spinach, thawed, drained and chopped
½ cup Parmesan cheese, grated
6 ounces Monterey Jack cheese, cut into ½-inch cubes
One 12-ounce container cottage cheese
½ teaspoon salt
2 cloves garlic, minced
2 eggs

Grease a 9 x 12-inch baking dish. Mix biscuit mix, milk, 2 eggs and onion. Spread batter into baking dish. Mix remaining ingredients and spoon over batter. Bake for 30 minutes at 375 degrees. Yield: 6 servings.

Liz McFerrin
The Potter's Place

BLACKBERRY-SOUR CREAM PIE

¾ cup sugar
1 cup sour cream
3 tablespoons flour
¼ teaspoon salt
4 cups fresh blackberries
¼ cup bread crumbs, finely chopped
2 tablespoons sugar
1 tablespoon butter, melted
One 9-inch pie shell, unbaked

Combine sugar, sour cream, flour and salt. Place berries in pastry shell. Spread sour cream mixture over berries. Combine bread crumbs, 2 tablespoons sugar and butter. Sprinkle atop pie. Bake at 375 degrees for 40 to 45 minutes.

Liz McFerrin
The Potter's Place

McFERRIN'S SCOTCH SHORTBREAD COOKIES

½ cup finely granulated sugar
½ cup butter, softened
2 cups all-purpose flour, sifted

Mix all ingredients together and knead on lightly floured surface. Knead until texture becomes smooth—the longer, the better. Roll in ½-inch balls and flatten with fork onto ungreased cookie sheet. Bake at 275 degrees for 20 to 25 minutes.

Liz McFerrin
The Potter's Place

TEKAKWITHA

For over 10 years Tekakwitha has been a vital force in the marketplace of the Greater Helen area and of the Northeast Georgia trading area. Tekakwitha has introduced thousands of people to the beautiful handmade arts and crafts of the American Indian. Represented are over 50 American Indian tribes whose craftsmen produce functional and decorative jewelry, pottery, beadwork, sand paintings, moccasins, prints, paintings, carvings, pipes, baskets, kachinas, molas, books, wall hangings, carved gourds, cards, dolls and much, much more.

Tekakwitha is located on the south side of Main Street next to Fain's Antiques, and is a Member of the Indian Arts and Crafts Association.

Tekakwitha, South Main Street, P.O. Box 338,
Helen, GA 30545, (404) 878-2038.

POSOLE OR HOMINY

2 pounds frozen posole or two 16-ounce cans hominy
2 pounds pork roast
Dash of oregano
3 to 4 dry red chili pods, broken up

Rinse posole well. Put all ingredients except the meat into a large pot. Fill the pot with water about 2 inches above the corn. Heat to boil and cook for 20 minutes. Add meat, reduce heat and simmer for about 3 hours until meat is cooked and kernels are soft, but not mushy. Stir frequently and add water as needed. Salt to taste at the end. Posole is uncooked hominy.

INDIAN BREAD PUDDING

1 large loaf white bread, sliced
1 cup raisins
1½ pounds Longhorn cheese, thinly sliced
2 cups brown sugar, packed
1 tablespoon cinnamon
2½ quarts water
1 tablespoon butter

Lightly toast the bread slices. Soak the raisins in a little warm water until they are puffy. In a large ovenproof baking dish layer the slices of bread, cheese and raisins, starting with the bread and repeating the layers until the ingredients are used up. In a large saucepan dissolve the brown sugar and cinnamon in water. Add butter and bring to a boil. Simmer for about 15 minutes. Pour the hot syrup slowly over the layers in the baking dish until all ingredients are completely soaked and covered. Cover with lid or foil. Bake in a 350-degree oven for 1 hour. Serve hot or cold, plain or with cream. Yield: 8 servings.

Ruth Lammers
Tekakwitha Indian Crafts

CORN-ZUCCHINI DISH

1 pound small zucchini, thinly sliced
4 to 5 medium-sized ears corn (2½ to 3 cups kernels)
¾ cup onion, finely chopped
⅓ cup green pepper, chopped
3 medium-sized tomatoes, peeled and coarsely chopped
2 tablespoons vegetable oil
¼ teaspoon sugar
1 teaspoon salt
¼ teaspoon black pepper, freshly ground
1½ cups stale bread, diced
⅓ cup sharp cheese, diced

Preheat oven to 350 degrees. In flameproof casserole, combine zucchini, corn, onion, green pepper, tomatoes, oil, sugar, salt and pepper. Cook, stirring gently over medium heat for about 10 to 12 minutes or until zucchini and corn are just cooked. Sprinkle vegetables with bread and cheese cubes and bake until cheese melts and bread is crisp. Serve hot. Yield: 6 servings.

Ruth Lammers
Tekakwitha Indian Crafts

APPLESAUCE NUT BREAD

2 cups all-purpose flour
¾ cup sugar
3 teaspoons baking powder
½ teaspoon baking soda
½ teaspoon salt
½ teaspoon cinnamon
1 egg, beaten
1 cup applesauce
2 tablespoons shortening, melted
1 cup walnuts, chopped

Preheat oven to 350 degrees. In a large bowl, sift together flour, sugar, baking powder, baking soda, salt and cinnamon. Set aside. In a small bowl combine egg, applesauce, shortening and walnuts. Add to flour mixture, stirring just enough to moisten. Spoon batter into a greased 9 x 5 x 3-inch loaf pan. Bake 1 hour or until done. Yield: one 9-inch loaf.

Ruth Lammers
Tekakwitha Indian Crafts

FAT CAKE

1 cup flour
½ cup margarine
1 cup nuts, chopped
One 8-ounce package cream cheese
1 cup powdered sugar
One 9-ounce carton whipped topping, thawed
One 3-ounce package instant vanilla pudding
One 3-ounce package instant chocolate pudding
3 cups milk
Additional chopped nuts for garnish

Mix together flour, margarine and nuts. Spread in 9 x 13 x 2-inch pan. Bake at 350 degrees for 15 minutes. Cool.

Blend together the cream cheese, powdered sugar and 1 cup of the whipped topping. Spread on crust. Mix together the vanilla pudding, chocolate pudding and milk and spread over the cream cheese layer. Cover pudding layer with remainder of whipped topping. Sprinkle more chopped nuts on top and refrigerate.

Martha Drzyzga
Lo-Lu's Country Place

SPANISH CHICKEN

Two 2½- to 3-pound fryers, cut up
½ cup flour
⅓ cup salad oil
¾ cup onion, chopped
1 garlic clove, minced
½ pound fresh mushrooms, sliced
One 12-ounce can tomatoes, cut up
1 cup dry white wine
½ teaspoon pepper
2 crumbled bay leaves
½ teaspoon of basil and thyme

Coat chicken with flour and brown in oil. Remove and set aside. Brown onions, garlic and mushrooms in drippings. Replace chicken; add tomatoes, wine, salt, pepper and herbs. Cover and simmer for approximately 1 hour, until tender. Sauce is excellent over brown or yellow rice. Yield: 6 servings.

Liz McFerrin
The Potter's Place

SCHWEINGULASCH MIT PAPRIKA
(Pork Goulash with Paprika)

2 ounces lard
1½ pounds sauerkraut
1 apple, cut up
1½ pounds pork, cut in cubes
1 onion, chopped
2 tablespoons flour
Salt, paprika
1 tablespoon sour cream
1½ pounds Irish potatoes, peeled and sliced

Melt fat; add sauerkraut and apple. Cook a few minutes, add enough water to cover kraut, and cook covered for 45 minutes. Brown the meat and onion in small amount of fat. Dust meat with flour and add paprika, salt and enough water to half cover meat. This will give you a nice red gravy. Cook on low, covered, and let simmer for 30 minutes, adding water as needed. Add kraut and sour cream and stir; top with peeled potatoes; cover and simmer 30 minutes more or until potatoes are done. Yield: 4 servings.

Theresia Link
Old Heidelberg Restaurant and Lounge

WHITE COUNTY BANK

The White County Bank was formed in 1975 and opened for business on October 19, 1976, at its main office in Cleveland, Georgia. It has approximately 400 stockholders and started with an initial investment of $600,000.00 in capital. Today the bank has assets of over $19,000,000.00 and has opened a branch office in Helen. The Helen office opened for business on November 19, 1980. This office has helped the White County Bank better serve its customers.

WHITE COUNTY BANK, South Main Street, Helen, Georgia 30545; P.O. Box 709, Cleveland, Georgia 30528, (404) 865-3151.

CRUNCHY POUND CAKE

1 cup shortening
2 cups sugar
2 cups flour, plain
6 eggs
1 teaspoon vanilla flavoring
1 teaspoon lemon flavoring

Mix shortening and sugar thoroughly; add eggs alternately with flour. Add flavorings. Bake in a tube pan 1 hour at 350 degrees. Remove from oven and let cool not more than 10 minutes. Remove from pan.

Eddy Jackson
White County Bank

BLITZ TORTE

½ cup butter or margarine
½ cup sugar
4 egg yolks, beaten lightly
1 teaspoon vanilla
3 tablespoons milk
1 cup flour
1 teaspoon baking powder

Cream the butter; gradually beat in the sugar, egg yolks, vanilla, milk and flour, sifted with the baking powder. Spread the mixture in two greased round shallow baking pans.

5 egg whites
¾ cup sugar

Beat the egg whites until soft peaks form. Add the sugar gradually, continue to beat until egg whites are stiff but not dry. Spread on the unbaked mixture in the pans.

½ cup blanched almonds, chopped
1 tablespoon sugar
½ teaspoon cinnamon
1 box instant vanilla custard

Sprinkle with almonds, sugar and cinnamon mixed. Bake at 350 degrees approximately 15 to 20 minutes or until meringue is brown. When cool put 1 top down and spread with custard, prepared according to package directions.

Ann Stamey
White County Bank

APPLE RAISIN BREAD

⅓ cup butter or margarine, softened
⅔ cup sugar
2 teaspoons lemon peel, grated
¼ teaspoon cinnamon
2 eggs
3 tablespoons milk
1 teaspoon lemon juice
2 cups flour
1 teaspoon baking powder
1 teaspoon salt
½ teaspoon baking soda
1½ cups apple, peeled and shredded
1 cup raisins or currants, chopped
½ cup nuts, chopped

Cream together butter, sugar, lemon peel and cinnamon. Beat in eggs until light and fluffy. Beat in milk and lemon juice. Stir together dry ingredients; add to creamed mixture, stirring until moistened. Fold in apple, raisins and nuts. Spoon batter into greased 5 x 9-inch loaf pan. Bake at 350 degrees 1 hour 40 minutes, or until toothpick inserted in center comes out clean.

Pat Welborn
White County Bank

BROCCOLI PUFFS

½ cup butter
1 cup water
1 teaspoon salt
Pinch garlic powder
1 cup all-purpose flour, sifted
4 eggs
1 package (10 ounce) frozen chopped broccoli, cooked & well drained
½ cup Parmesan cheese, grated

Combine butter, water, salt and garlic powder in saucepan. Heat until water is boiling and butter is melted. Add flour all at once. Remove from heat. Stir mixture quickly until dough comes away from sides of pan. Add eggs one at a time, beating well after each addition. Stir broccoli into dough. Chill 2 hours or overnight.

Pour oil into deep skillet and heat to 375 degrees. Drop heaping teaspoonfuls into oil, brown on one side about 2 minutes, then turn and brown on the other side. Drain. Sprinkle with Parmesan cheese and serve hot.

Puffs may be fried day before. Heat on cookie sheet in 350 degree oven for 10 minutes.

Ann Stamey
White County Bank

CHINESE PEPPER STEAK

2 pounds boneless round steak
¼ cup soy sauce
1 beef bouillon cube
½ teaspoon ginger
½ teaspoon garlic powder
2 tablespoons shortening
3 large green peppers, seeded, cut into large pieces
3 tablespoons cornstarch
4 cups cooked rice
2 cups boiling water

Cut meat into long thin strips. For marinade, combine soy sauce, bouillon cube, ginger, garlic and 1 cup boiling water. Add beef; cover and refrigerate for several hours. Drain meat, reserving ½ cup marinade. Cook meat in hot shortening until it loses its red color. Add marinade and 1 cup boiling water. Reduce heat and simmer, covered, 1 hour. Add green peppers and cook 15 minutes. Thicken with cornstarch and serve over cooked hot rice. Yield: 4 servings.

The Wood Shed

VENISON SHISH KABOBS TERIYAKI

Teriyaki Sauce:
1 cup soy sauce
½ cup vegetable oil
4 tablespoons molasses
4 teaspoons dry mustard
4 teaspoons ginger
8 garlic cloves, minced

Combine all sauce ingredients and set aside.

Kabob Ingredients:
Two 2½-pound round or flank venison steaks, cut in ½-inch cubes
1 fresh pineapple
1 pound whole fresh mushrooms
12 small whole onions

Marinate venison cubes in teriyaki sauce for six hours. Cut pineapple into 1½-inch cubes. Alternate venison, pineapple, mushrooms and onions on skewers. Grill over medium heat for 10 to 20 minutes or until meat is done. Yield: 4 to 6 servings.

Liz McFerrin
The Potter's Place

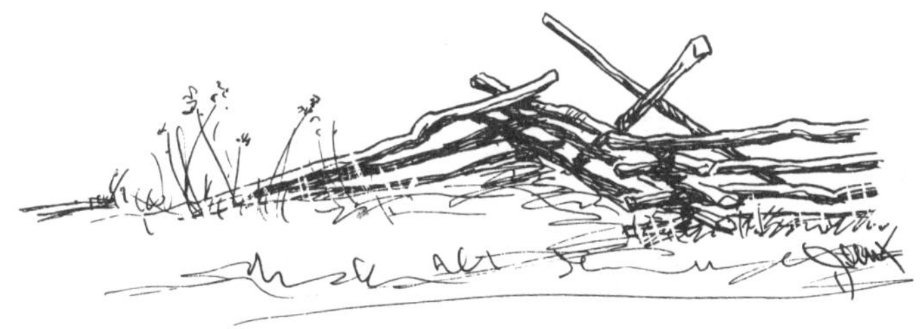

BLACK RUSSIAN PIE

1 4½-ounce package instant chocolate pudding
1 cup milk
1½ cups whipped topping, thawed
¼ cup nuts, chopped
2 tablespoons Kahlúa
2 tablespoons Creme de Cacao
Pie shell, baked

Prepare instant pudding with milk. Blend in whipped topping and nuts. Fold in Kahlúa and Creme de Cacao. Spoon into cooled pie shell. Chill. Yield: 8 servings.

The Wood Shed

Sautee-Nacoochee Valley

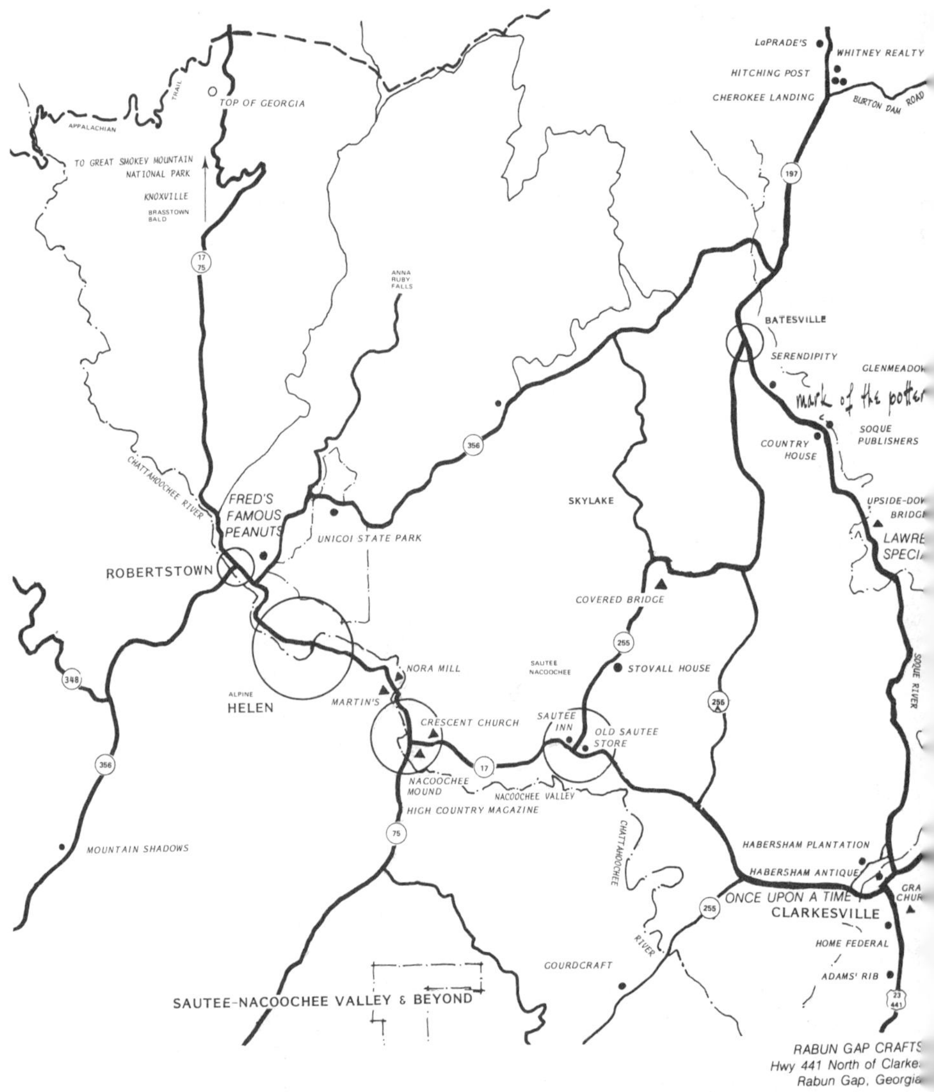

SAUTEE-NACOOCHEE VALLEY AND BEYOND

WHERE TO SLEEP

Cherokee Ridge Cabins 878-2380
Hickory Nut Mountain Camp & Cabins 878-2772
Koenig's Mountain Madness 878-2851
STOVALL HOUSE—Page 264 GA 255 SAUTEE 878-3355
Skyridge Cabins 878-3244
Tanglewood Cabins 878-3286
UNICOI STATE PARK—Page 266 GA 356 878-2201

WHERE TO EAT

SAUTEE INN—Page 258 GA 17 at GA 255, SAUTEE 878-2940
STOVALL HOUSE—Page 264 GA 255 SAUTEE 878-3355
UNICOI STATE PARK—Page 266 GA 356 878-2201

WHERE TO SHOP

Carriage Trade 878-2603
Chattahoochee Pottery 878-2807
Critters & Crafts 878-2802
FRED'S FAMOUS PEANUTS. 878-3124
GOURDCRAFT ORIGINALS—Page 158 BLUE CREEK 865-4048
Homestead House Antiques 878-3252
Old & Gold 878-2603
OLD SAUTEE STORE—Page 254 GA 17 at GA 255, SAUTEE 878-2281
RABUN GAP CRAFTS 746-5343
Sautee Valley Pottery 754-6356
Skylake Country Store 878-2934
Tribble Tree House 878-2890
UNICOI STATE PARK CRAFT SHOP—Page 266 GA 356 878-2201
Wind Vane, The—GA 255A 754-9225

WHERE TO CAMP

Hickory Nut Mountain Camp & Cabins 878-2772
MOUNTAIN SHADOWS JELLYSTONE PARK—Page 166 GA 356 865-4742
UNICOI STATE PARK—Page 266 GA 356 878-2201

WHAT TO DO & SEE

ALPINE HELEN—Page 212 GA 17 & GA 75
Chattahoochee Stables 878-2742
COVERED BRIDGE—Page 262 GA 255
CRESCENT CHURCH—Page 242 GA 17 just off of GA 75
Sunburst Stables 878-2095
NACOOCHEE MOUND—Page 246 GA 17 at GA 75
NORA MILL—Page 252 GA 75 on the Chattahoochee River
MARTIN'S HOTEL—Page 250 GA 75 just across from Nora Mill

NOTICE: For your convenience we have listed all of the places to eat and all of the places to sleep in the area covered by this list. Quality is a personal concept and, although we have listed every place to eat or sleep known at the time of printing, some restaurants and some motels we recommend highly, while others do not quite meet our high standards of quality and we assume no responsibility for them. We would suggest that you inquire locally of any of the businesses in bold type listed above for their recommendations.

CRESCENT HILL CHURCH

Crescent Hill Church, nestled in the fold of a hill just off GA 75 on GA 17, is perhaps the most photographed and best-loved church in our mountains. Built in the early 1870's at the same time as the Hardman house around the bend, it employed the best craftsmen available to create this "carpenter gothic" gem. The church was originally on the land owned by Captain Nichols, a planter and mining speculator from Milledgeville. Nichols is responsible for most of the appearance of this end of Nachoochee Valley. His home, "West End," and the summer house atop the Indian mound in the center of the valley, were part of a grand setting which satisfied the romantic nature of this gentleman. He also had fountains and deer parks surrounding his home, and it is to him that we are indebted for naming the beautiful twin falls in Unicoi Park. His daughter's name, you see, was Anna Ruby. Dr. L. G. Hardman later bought the property and gave the church to the Baptist congregation, and they still maintain it.

CORN CASSEROLE

1 can cream-style corn
1 can whole corn
2 eggs
1 cup sour cream
1 package corn muffin mix
½ cup butter, melted
1 cup Cheddar cheese, shredded

Mix together all ingredients except cheese and bake 30 minutes at 350 degrees. Take out of oven and sprinkle cheese over top. Return to oven and bake another 15 minutes, or until center is firm. Delicious served hot or cold.

Loris Mann
The Shop Antiques

PEACH COBBLER

¾ cup sugar
2 cups sliced peaches or cherries
½ cup butter or margarine
¾ cup sugar
¾ cup flour
2 teaspoons baking powder
¾ cup milk
Pinch salt

Pour ¾ cup sugar over peaches and let stand. Melt butter or margarine in a casserole. Make a batter of sugar, flour, baking powder, milk, and salt. Pour batter into casserole. Then pour peaches over batter. Bake one hour at 350 degrees.

Frances Mathis
Home Federal Savings & Loan Association

COLE SLAW

1 large head white cabbage
1 large onion
1 large green pepper
1 cup sugar
¾ cup salad oil
1 cup vinegar
1 teaspoon dry mustard
1 teaspoon celery seed
1 tablespoon salt

Shred cabbage and chop onion and green pepper in large container. Bring remaining ingredients to a boil and pour over cabbage mixture while hot. Do not stir. Refrigerate at least 4 hours in airtight container. Keeps for at least 2 weeks. Yield: 8 servings.

Frances Mathis
Home Federal Savings & Loan Association

RABUN GAP CRAFTS

Rabun Gap Crafts is owned by Rabun Gap-Nacoochee School, a coeducational college preparatory boarding school serving grades 8 through 12.

Located on US 441, 7 miles north of Clayton, Georgia, Rabun Gap Crafts specializes in authenic Appalachian crafts and handwoven items from their own looms.

For many years one of the favorite foods in the Rabun Gap-Nacoochee School dining hall has been the delicious yeast rolls made by the former head dietician, Mrs. Mary Brown. "Aunt Mary" has kindly reduced her recipe to family size for you to enjoy.

AUNT MARY BROWN'S YEAST ROLLS

1 package dry yeast
1 cup warm milk
1/3 cup melted butter or shortening
4 tablespoons sugar
1 teaspoon salt
3 1/2 to 4 cups plain flour

Dissolve yeast in 1/3 cup warm water. Mix together milk, butter, sugar, and salt. Add dissolved yeast and flour. Cover and let rise until double in bulk. Roll out into rolls and let rise again for 1-1/2 hours. Dough should be kept warm from mixing until baking. Bake 25 minutes in 350 degree oven.

DANDELION SALAD

4 to 6 strips bacon, cut up
1 egg
1 cup water
1 tablespoon flour
Vinegar to taste
2 tablespoons sugar
Pinch of salt
Milk
2 quarts young tender dandelion greens (picked before blossom appears)

Brown bacon. Mix egg with bacon in drippings. Pour in water. Mix flour and water to thicken; add to above mixture. Add vinegar, sugar and salt. Put in milk for desired thickness. Cut up dandelion greens and add just before eating.

Debbie Koenig
Chimney Mountain Fiberarts

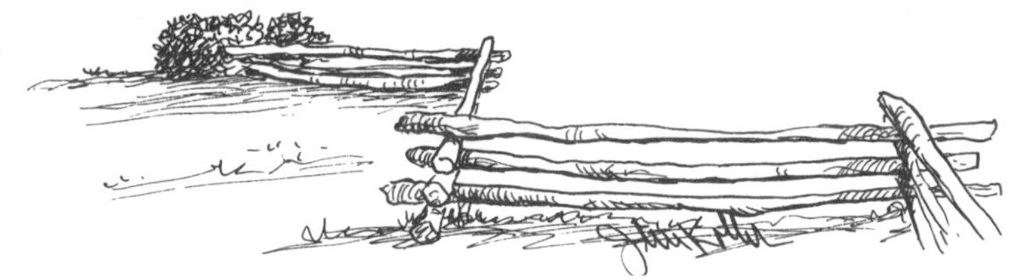

CREAM CHEESE RHUBARB PIE

⅔ cup sugar
2 tablespoons cornstarch
3 cups rhubarb, finely diced
9-inch unbaked pie crust
8-ounce package plain or orange cream cheese, softened
1 egg
½ cup sugar
⅛ teaspoon nutmeg
1 cup sour cream
1 teaspoon orange peel, grated
2 tablespoons brown sugar
¼ cup slivered toasted almonds

Preheat oven to 425 degrees. Mix sugar and cornstarch; add to rhubarb, blend well. Turn into pie crust; bake 15 minutes. Meanwhile, whip cream cheese with fork until fluffy. Add egg, sugar and nutmeg. Blend well. Remove pie from oven. Reduce oven heat to 350 degrees. Spread cream cheese layer on baked rhubarb filling. Bake pie 20 minutes longer; cool. Chill several hours. Top with sour cream mixed with orange peel and sugar; sprinkle on almonds. Keep refrigerated until served.

Debbie Koenig
Chimney Mountain Fiberarts

NACOOCHEE MOUND

One of the best landmarks in White County is the Indian Mound rising from the valley floor of Nacoochee. Here the Chattahoochee River makes a wide sweeping curve around the pasture land before making its way to join Sautee Creek and the other tributaries that make up Lake Lanier a few miles to the south. Atop the mound, which predates the Cherokee Indians, sits a white gingerbread summer house built in the 1870's. The creator of this touch of Victorian elegance was Captain Nichols who built the mansion West End which can just be glimpsed in its setting of dense magnolias across the highway. It was Captain Nichols' daughter Anna Ruby for whom the twin waterfalls in Unicoi Park were named.

Although the valley at this point is surrounded by mountains, one alone stands out in dramatic solitude. This is Yonah, which in Cherokee means the "Bear." Looking south from Highway 17 the mountain does indeed look like a great crouching bear watching over the valley.

SORGHUM OATMEAL COOKIES

1/3 cup butter, softened
1/2 cup sorghum
2 eggs, lightly beaten
1 cup all-purpose flour
1 teaspoon baking powder
1/2 teaspoon cloves
1/2 teaspoon cinnamon
1/2 teaspoon allspice
2 1/2 cups oats, rolled
1/4 teaspoon salt
1/4 cup raisins or dates
1/4 cup nuts, chopped

Preheat oven to 375 degrees. Cream the butter and sorghum. Beat in the eggs one at a time. Stir in the flour, baking powder and spices. Combine with the rolled oats, salt, raisins and nuts. Drop by teaspoons onto a greased cookie sheet and bake 8 or 9 minutes. Cool on a rack. Yield: 36 to 48 cookies.

Bruce Mitchell
Nacoochee Mound

HIGHLANDS STACK CAKE

4 cups flour
1/4 teaspoon salt
3 teaspoons baking powder
1/2 cup butter
4 eggs
2 cups sugar
1 cup milk
1 teaspoon vanilla

Combine flour, salt and baking powder, mix in butter. Beat eggs, add sugar and beat thoroughly, then add to mixture enough milk and vanilla combined to make a stiff dough that can be rolled out. Pinch off small fist-size pieces of dough, roll out and cut about 6 inches in diameter by 1/4-inch thick (use 6-inch saucer for pattern). Bake on top of stove in heavy iron skillet until brown. Turn once.

Filling:
3 pounds dried apples
1/2 to 1 cup sugar (to taste)

Cook apples together with sugar until soft and spread between layers of cake, except the top. These are best when stored for two or three days before eating.

Bruce Mitchell
Nacoochee Mound

CORN FRITTERS

1 cup corn, fresh, cut from the ear
2 eggs, slightly beaten
½ cup all-purpose flour
½ teaspoon baking powder
¼ teaspoon salt

Combine the corn with the eggs. Stir in the flour, baking powder and salt. If the batter is too thin, add a bit more flour. Mix the batter until smooth. Drop by heaping tablespoons onto a greased griddle and fry like pancakes. Serve with meat or alone with syrup or sorghum.

Bruce Mitchell
Nacoochee Mound

MOUNTAIN CAVIAR
(PICKLED BLACKEYED PEAS)

2 cups blackeyed peas, cooked
½ cup bell pepper, thinly sliced
3 medium onions, thinly sliced
½ cup oil
¼ cup vinegar
⅛ teaspoon dried red pepper, crushed
¼ teaspoon salt
1 clove garlic, smashed

Drain the peas. Combine all the ingredients and refrigerate overnight. Keep covered. Remove the garlic if desired. Serve from a relish dish with a slotted spoon. Yield: 10 to 12 servings.

Bruce Mitchell
Nacoochee Mound

APPLE POUND CAKE

2 cups sugar
1½ cups cooking oil
3 eggs
3 cups all-purpose flour
1 teaspoon baking soda
1 teaspoon salt
1½ teaspoons vanilla
¾ cup coconut
3 cups tart apples, peeled, cored and diced
1 cup pecans, chopped

Preheat oven to 350 degrees. Combine the sugar and oil. Beat with an electric mixer until well blended. Add the eggs one at a time and beat until fluffy. Combine the flour, baking soda and salt. Add to the sugar mixture and blend well. Beat in the vanilla and coconut. Fold in the apples and nuts. Pour into a greased 9-inch tube pan. Bake for 80 minutes, or until the cake tests done. Turn onto a wire rack to cool.

Bruce Mitchell
Nacoochee Mound

ASPARAGUS PARMESAN

16 asparagus spears, cooked
3 tablespoons butter
½ cup Parmesan cheese, freshly grated
Black pepper

Arrange the asparagus in a baking dish. Sprinkle with the butter and cheese. (Try grating your own Parmesan cheese. You won't believe the difference in taste between the cans of already grated cheese and the wedges you grate yourself.) Sprinkle with black pepper to taste and run under the broiler until the cheese melts. You won't need salt because the cheese has plenty.

Bruce Mitchell
Nacoochee Mound

HONEY WHOLE WHEAT BREAD

2 cups milk, scalded
1 tablespoon sea salt
½ cup honey
3 tablespoons oil
2 tablespoons active dry yeast
⅓ cup lukewarm water
4½ cups whole wheat flour, unsifted
½ cup wheat germ (optional)
½ cup soy flour (optional)
2 tablespoons brewer's yeast (optional)
Heavy cream, oil or fat

Place milk in a large bowl. Add salt, honey and oil. Mix well and set aside to cool to lukewarm. Dissolve the dry yeast in the warm water. Set in a warm place for 10 minutes. Add yeast to cooled milk mixture. Beat in three cups of the flour and continue beating until smooth. Work in wheat germ, soy flour, brewer's yeast and enough of the remaining flour to make a dough that can be kneaded. Knead the dough on a lightly floured board until smooth and elastic. This will take at least 10 minutes. Place the dough in a clean oiled bowl; oil the top. Cover and set in a warm place to rise until doubled in bulk, about 1 hour. Punch down, knead until smooth, pat back in bowl. Cover and let rise again, about 45 minutes. Punch down and divide into two. Shape dough into two loaves and place in oiled 8 x 4½ x 2½-inch bread tins or five-cup capacity deep round cake tins or charlotte molds. Cover and let rise in a warm place until loaves reach top of pans. Do not let over-rise. Preheat oven to 375 degrees. Bake loaves 45 minutes or until loaves sound hollow when tapped on the bottom. Cool on rack. Brush with heavy cream, oil or fat for a soft crust. Yield: 2 loaves.

Berry Wright

MARTIN'S

Across the road from Nora Mill on GA 75 and 17 stands a large frame house with two levels of porches running around the front and south elevations. The building was constructed by John Martin about 1876. Mr. Martin also built Nora Mill. Since Mr. Martin was involved in the gold mining operations, many of which took place in the immediate area, the house was used as both a headquarters and rooming house for miners. There is still much evidence to be found in Nacoochee Valley, Bean Creek and along the Chattahoochee River of the extent of the hydraulic mining that took place following the discovery of gold in the area of Dukes Creek in 1828. Less than a mile up the river a man-made valley runs back into the mountain following a vein of gold until it "pinched off." Within the forest one can still follow the depressions of ditches that were once lined with timber to carry the water down to power the giant hoses that ate away the mountainside. "Martin's" as the house came to be known, is remembered by some for its festive evenings of square dancing when the owners ran it as an early tourist hotel, following the turn of the century.

CHEESE ROUNDS

1 cup sharp Cheddar cheese, shredded
6 tablespoons butter
⅓ teaspoon Tabasco
Dash salt
1 cup flour
1 cup rice crispies

Allow cheese and butter to soften to room temperature and combine them. Stir in remaining ingredients. Make balls, place on a greased cookie sheet, then flatten them. Bake at 350 degrees for 10 to 15 minutes. Stored in a tightly covered container they will keep several months.

Sally Hart
Helendorf

MARZIPAN "POTATOES"

1¾ cups almonds or hazelnuts, ground, grated
1 cup powdered sugar
1 egg yolk
1 tablespoon butter, melted
1 tablespoon rum or cognac
Cocoa

In a bowl, combine almonds, powdered sugar, egg yolk, butter and rum. Mix the ingredients with the hands until they form a ball. Pinch off small pieces about the size of walnuts and shape them into slightly elongated balls to simulate small potatoes. With a toothpick, poke eyes in the marzipan "potatoes." Dust them generously with cocoa and chill.

Mary Hammersen
Hofbrauhaus Inn

VENISON CHOPS IN CLARET

Venison chops, 1-inch thick
Butter
Salt and pepper to taste
¼ teaspoon basil
⅓ cup currant jelly
½ cup claret or Madeira
Juice of 1 lemon
Wild rice
Mushrooms

Sauté chops in butter until nicely browned. Add salt, pepper, and basil. Stir in currant jelly, wine and lemon juice. Simmer for 3 minutes, turn and simmer 3 minutes more. Serve with wild rice and mushrooms. Venison steaks should always be broiled and served medium to very rare.

Charles Horrworth
Alpine Valley Realty

NORA MILL

Nora Mill is one of those rare historic locations that is still functioning with its original purpose. Since 1876 there has been a mill at this location on the Chattahoochee River on GA 75, just north of the intersection of GA 17.

John Martin, an Englishman who had come to North Georgia as a miner, had the mill built using the best heart pine and blue poplar. Over the years the overshot wheel ground not only corn and wheat, but rice grown on the Hardman farm. Small amounts of beautiful white rice flour were available during the First World War. The mill was purchased by Dr. Lamartine G. Hardman in 1905. Some years later he named the mill "Nora" in memory of one of his sisters. The mill has been converted into a turbine operation, and the dam has been replaced a number of times.

Nora Mill had its most dramatic moment in the summer of 1950 when it was used as the site of the "drowning scene" in the movie "I'd Climb The Highest Mountain." The passing tourist today can still walk across the porch and into yesterday to purchase a few sacks of fresh waterground meal from the miller, Grandpa Fain.

Grandpa Fain, born in Robertstown only a few miles from Nora Mill, also sells cider, mountain honey, sorghum syrup, jams and jellies, country cured hams and bacon, hard candy, cheese and crackers and other country fare.

Grandma Fain's freshly baked carrot cake is, by far, the best in these hills. Every nook and cranny of the old mill and store is filled with home baked pies and cookies and lots of old-timey goodies.

Nora Mill, GA 17
Sautee Nacoochee, Georgia 30571

FRUIT CAKE PUDDING

1 can cherry pie filling
1 can crushed pineapple
½ box yellow cake mix
1 cup pecans, chopped
½ cup margarine
1 can coconut

Pour cherry pie filling in 12-inch cake pan, spread pineapple and juice over pie filling. Sift ½ box yellow cake flour over this, then spread pecans and cover with margarine. Bake at 350 degrees for approximately 30 to 35 minutes. Remove from oven and sprinkle coconut over top; return to oven for approximately 10 minutes.

BabyLand General™ Hospital

HUSHPUPPIES

½ cup self-rising flour
1½ cups self-rising corn meal
1 egg
1 onion, chopped
¾ cup buttermilk

Mix and drop by the teaspoonfuls into deep hot fat until done.

BabyLand General™ Hospital

MEXICAN CORNBREAD LOTHRIDGE

1½ cups self-rising corn meal
3 eggs, beaten
1 cup cream style corn
⅔ cup cooking oil
1 cup buttermilk
1 large hot pepper, chopped fine
½ large sweet pepper, chopped fine
1 teaspoon salt
1 cup sharp cheese, grated

Mix all ingredients, except cheese. Pour ½ batter on greased and floured pan. Sprinkle cheese on top and then add remaining batter. Use a 9 x 14 x 1½-inch pan. Cook at 375 degrees until golden brown.

Shirley Lothridge
Mountain Shadows

OLD SAUTEE STORE

The Old Sautee Store is a country store museum, built over a century ago, located in the mountains of Northeast Georgia, at the intersection of Georgia Highways 17 and 255, four miles southeast of Helen. Admission free.

Where the old Post Office used to be, there is a Scandinavian Gift Shop. There you will find high-quality, beautifully finished arts and crafts of Norway, Denmark, Sweden, Finland and Iceland. We have a great selection of Norwegian and Icelandic sweaters, jackets and coats, crystal, dinnerware, sterling, gold and enameled jewelry, needlework, gourmet foods and books.

Visit our Christmas Shop—Yule Log, next door.

Old Sautee Store, GA 17 at GA 255, Sautee-Nacoochee, Georgia 30571. Open all year. Monday through Saturday 9:30 a.m. until 5:30 p.m.; Sundays 1:00 p.m. until 6:00 p.m. Phone: (404) 878-2281.

ABLESKIVER
(PANCAKE BALLS)

Set an ableskiver pan* over low heat.

2 cups flour, sifted
2 tablespoons sugar
1 teaspoon baking soda
1 teaspoon cardamom
¾ teaspoon salt
1 pint thick sour cream
4 egg yolks
2 tablespoons butter, melted
4 egg whites
Powdered sugar

Sift together first 5 ingredients and set aside. Combine sour cream, 4 beaten egg yolks and melted butter. Make a well in center of dry ingredients. Add liquid mixture all at once, stirring until well blended. Beat 4 egg whites until rounded peaks are formed. Gently spread batter over egg whites and fold together. Heat the ableskiver pan and test by dropping on it a few drops of cold water. (If drops dance around in small beads, temperature is right). Grease the wells with shortening. Pour batter into wells, filling about one half full. With a fork, turn ableskivers frequently to allow even browning. Do not pierce. Ableskivers are done when a wooden pick inserted in center comes out clean.

Serve immediately, sprinkled with powdered sugar. If desired, accompany with lingonberries, jam or syrup. Yield: 4 dozen balls.

*Available at the Old Sautee Store.

Marie Resager
Old Sautee Store

FISH BALLS IN WHITE SAUCE
(FISKEBOLLER I HVIT SAUS)

2 tablespoons butter
4 tablespoons flour
2 cups milk
***20 fish balls**
1 cup fish broth
½ teaspoon salt
2 tablespoons sherry (optional)

Melt butter and add flour, stirring well. Add milk gradually and stir until thickened. Heat fish balls in fish broth; add salt and add to white sauce. Just before serving, add sherry. Yield: 4 to 5 servings.

*Available at Old Sautee Store.

Astrid Fried
Old Sautee Store

CUCUMBER SALAD
(AGURKSALAT)

1 large cucumber
⅓ cup cider vinegar
5 tablespoons water
5 tablespoons sugar
½ teaspoon salt
Few grains white pepper
1 tablespoon parsley, chopped

Rinse, pare, and score cucumber by pulling the tines of a fork the length of the cucumber. Cut into very thin slices. Put into a shallow bowl. Thoroughly mix vinegar, water, sugar, salt, and white pepper. Pour over the cucumber slices and toss lightly to coat evenly. Cover and put in refrigerator for several hours to chill and allow sweet-sour flavors to blend. Garnish cucumbers with 1 tablespoon finely chopped parsley. Yield: 8 to 10 servings.

Astrid Fried
Old Sautee Store

KRUM KAKE

3 eggs, well beaten
1 cup sugar
½ cup heavy cream, whipped
½ cup butter, melted
½ teaspoon vanilla
1¾ cups flour
¼ teaspoon salt

Beat the eggs with the sugar until very light and fluffy. Fold in the cream, butter and vanilla. Mix well. Fold in the flour mixed with the salt. Heat a *Krum Kake Iron over the burner slowly. Brush lightly with shortening. Place a rounded teaspoonful of the batter in the center of the iron. Close the iron and cook about 45 seconds or until cookie is lightly colored. Turn the iron and cook about one-half minute longer or until golden. It requires two to three "cookings" to season the iron and adjust heat, especially with a new iron, so don't expect a perfect cookie on the first try. Form cake on wooden cone, immediately on removing from iron. Yield: 3 dozen.

*Available at Old Sautee Store.

Astrid Fried
Old Sautee Store

NORWEGIAN RICE CREAM

6 cups milk
1 cup regular long-grain rice
½ teaspoon salt
2 teaspoons vanilla, or
1 teaspoon almond extract
or 2 tablespoons sherry
1 cup cream, whipped
raspberry syrup

In large heavy sauce pan over medium heat, heat milk, rice, sugar and salt until simmering and bubbles form. Reduce heat to low, cover and cook 45 to 50 minutes until rice is tender; stirring occasionally. Chill. Whip the cream, add the flavoring and gently fold into rice. Serve topped with raspberry syrup if desired. Yield: 10 to 12 servings.

Astrid Fried
Old Sautee Store

ICE BOX FRUIT CAKE

1 pound pecans
1 pound English walnuts
1 pound cherries, candied
1 can flaked coconut
1 pound pineapple, candied
1 box white raisins
Two 12-ounce boxes vanilla wafers, crushed
1 can condensed milk
½ cup corn syrup

Mix all ingredients together. If not moist enough, add 4 or 5 tablespoons warm water. Put raisins in boiling water. Let set, then drain and dry well. Put in tube pan and store in refrigerator for 2 or 3 days.

BabyLand General™ Hospital

CHESS PIE

4 eggs, beaten
1¾ cups sugar
1 teaspoon vanilla
2 teaspoons vinegar
2 tablespoons corn meal
½ cup margarine
One 9-inch pie shell, unbaked

Combine first six ingredients, beating until well mixed. Pour into pie shell and bake at 350 degrees for 45 to 50 minutes. Yield: 8 servings.

The Wood Shed

SAUTEE INN

In the early 1900's, the Alley House was a well-known summer hotel, where coastal and city residents gathered to escape the heat. That time of "summer in the mountains" ended with the depression years. Now, more than 50 years later, the Alley House, renamed the Sautee Inn Restaurant, serves meals in an atmosphere reminiscent of that earlier, more leisurely, time.

John and Emily Anthony serve food that reflects not only their Southern heritage, but a lifelong interest in good cooking. Everything is prepared by the Anthonys, with homemade biscuits, corn muffins and gingerbread as specialties. Service is buffet, with individual tables in adjoining dining rooms.

The following recipes were taken from the Anthony's cookbook, *Sautee Inn Recipes,* available at the Inn, on Georgia 17, near the Old Sautee Store.

Sautee Inn, GA 17 at GA 255, P.O. Box 28,
Sautee, Georgia, 30571, (404) 878-2940.

BEEF BOURBONNAIS

3 carrots, thickly sliced
2 or 3 stalks celery, cut in large, diagonal pieces
4 medium potatoes, peeled and cut in ½-inch strips
1 medium onion, chopped
1 tablespoon shortening
¼ teaspoon garlic
½ teaspoon salt
¼ teaspoon pepper
1 can tomato soup, undiluted
¾ cup red wine
¼ cup water, more or less
¼ teaspoon basil
¼ teaspoon thyme
1½ to 2 pounds cold roast, cut in 1-inch x ½-inch pieces

Prepare the three vegetables and start them cooking first. Drop each in the boiling water as you finish, in the order given. They will be done about the same time. While the vegetables cook, sauté onions and then add all other items. Add drained vegetables when they are ready, with enough of the liquid to make the gravy to suit your taste. There is plenty of flavor to go around, so add flour and water mixed until it is as thick as you desire. A couple of hours in a double boiler or slow cooker will improve this very, very fine stew.

Emily and John Anthony
Sautee Inn Restaurant

SAUTEE INN SQUASH CASSEROLE

3 cups summer squash, chopped
1 cup onions, sliced or chopped
1 can mushroom soup
1 cup Cheddar cheese, shredded
1 cup bread crumbs
¼ cup butter, melted
¼ cup almonds, finely chopped
Salt and pepper to taste
Paprika

Cook squash and onion together in small amount of water until tender. Drain well. Mix with other ingredients. Place in baking dish and top with additional crumbs and paprika. Bake at 350 degrees until slightly browned, about 45 minutes.

Emily and John Anthony
Sautee Inn Restaurant

OATMEAL CAKE

This cake tastes almost like a German Chocolate Cake.

1½ cups boiling water
1 cup oats
1½ cups flour
1 teaspoon cinnamon
1 teaspoon soda
½ teaspoon salt
1 cup brown sugar
1 cup white sugar
½ cup oil
2 eggs

Pour boiling water over oats. Sift dry ingredients together. Add sugars, oil and eggs to oats and then stir in dry ingredients. Bake at 350 degrees in 9 x 13-inch pan until top springs back when touched lightly, approximately 35 minutes.

Topping:
Mix and bring to rolling boil:
½ cup butter
1 cup brown sugar
½ cup milk
½ cup nuts
1 can coconut

Simmer 15 minutes, stirring occasionally. Remove from heat. Add nuts and coconut. Pour topping over cake, in pan if desired. Cool before cutting.

Emily and John Anthony
Sautee Inn Restaurant

SPANISH OKRA

2 cups onions, chopped
2 cups canned tomatoes, crushed
2 cups okra
⅓ cup sugar
1 teaspoon salt

Cook onions in as little water as possible. Add tomatoes and continue heating until they boil, then add okra and again continue cooking until okra is done, about 10 minutes. Stir with a spoon, vertically, so that onions stay on bottom.

When the okra is done, add sugar and salt and mix thoroughly. Warmed over Spanish Okra is just as good, if not better, than the first time!

Emily and John Anthony
Sautee Inn Restaurant

CHICKEN STROGANOFF ANTHONY

2½ pounds chicken winglets or 2½ to 3-pound fryer, cut up
Flour
Salt
Pepper
Paprika
2 tablespoons oil
1 tablespoon water
Melted butter
Parsley

Preheat oven to 350 degrees. Shake chicken pieces in seasoned flour. Place in one layer in a shallow baking dish in which you have placed 2 tablespoons of oil and 1 tablespoon of water. Brush chicken with melted butter. Bake about 25 minutes for wings and 35 minutes for larger chicken parts. Pour sauce over chicken, sprinkle with parsley and continue baking until bubbly, about 30 minutes.

Sauce:
1 can chicken broth
¼ cup onion flakes
¼ teaspoon pepper
1 teaspoon poultry seasoning or ½ teaspoon sage, or ½ teaspoon basil
1 cup sour cream
8-ounce can mushrooms, drained

Mix first four ingredients and simmer for 5 minutes. Stir in sour cream and mushrooms.

Emily and John Anthony
Sautee Inn Restaurant

BAKED CABBAGE WITH APPLES

1 medium head cabbage, coarsely chopped
2 cups apples, sliced, cooked
⅓ cup sugar
1 cup fine bread crumbs
6 tablespoons butter, melted

Drop chopped cabbage in boiling water and cook 3 to 5 minutes until slightly tender but still crunchy. Drain well. Layer cabbage and apples in a 2-quart casserole, sprinkling sugar and bread crumbs on each layer. Pat top layer flat before adding last crumbs. Pour melted butter over top of casserole. Cover and bake at 350 degrees for 45 minutes until hot throughout. Remove cover during last 15 minutes. Yield: 4 to 6 servings.

Emily and John Anthony
Sautee Inn Restaurant

STOVALL COVERED BRIDGE

Once Nacoochee and Sautee Valley were known for the many covered bridges which dotted this uniquely beautiful area. Until the paving of GA 17, it was still possible to thread your way from Nacoochee Station to Clarkesville along much of the original Unicoi Turnpike built between 1813 and 1816, through what was then part of the Cherokee Nation. Along the way were several covered bridges, including a large one over Sautee Creek. When the highway was paved on GA 255 the bridge over Chickamauga Creek was bypassed and saved. It still stands today on a small state park open to the public. Above the bridge stood the Stovall Mill which was swept away in recent years during a flood. The Stovall bridge has the distinction of being the shortest bridge in Georgia, being only 33 feet long.

HAM BISCUITS

I may be Northeast Georgia's only *emigré* who settled here because of a couple of Ham Biscuits for breakfast. By profession I could have nestled anywhere in the world. But on a travel-writing tour I met a former Miamian, Warren Smyth, who had converted an old Helen residence into a restaurant. He introduced me to Country Ham Biscuits and one thing led to another and before I even digested this most delectable of mountain fare I bought Sautee Valley acreage.

It should be noted that "Ham Biscuits" are not "ham and biscuits" and that the capitalization is deliberate, for these morsels when properly prepared must be accorded utmost reverence and respect. Unfortunately, Mr. Smyth has since moved to greener pastures, masterminding a gourmet restaurant in Gainesville called Rudolph's. Ham Biscuits are not included in his Continental menus but the current lack of that pleasurable dish is compensated by a myriad of other mountain delicacies embodied in this compendium of Northeast Georgia gastronomy. The folks up here know how to cook; the fare is tasty; and portions are usually sufficiently generous to warrant a "doggie bag" for your next day's lunch.

Happily for the calorie counters there is an abundance of anti-obesity activities available in this region. Trodding the Appalachian Trail or canoeing on the Chattahoochee River will quickly burn off excesses. But, personally, I'd rather meander through flea markets or small plots of maples during technicolor autumns, or re-visit such mind-boggling sights as the leaping trout at Mark of the Potter and the museum of ancient Georgia life at the Old Sautee Store—or perhaps marvelling at the glass-enclosed beehive in Betty's Country Store; or just sitting on a rickety bench in front of a gas station listening to old mountain codgers telling tales of moonshine, gingseng, black bears and wildcats.

Fall is festive: a backdrop of spangled hillsides accents sorghum cooking, Indian Summer, smokerise and woodchopping. Then it's Thanksgiving time and the hint of colder days waiting over the gap.

One awakens and listens—and listens; absolute quiet. Stumbling to the window, eyes squinting, there it is, a dreamworld, a white fairyland!

Later the kettle whistles from the hearth. The cat lounges, feigning indifference, 'neath the kitchen table.' This is a time for remembrance, for sharing loving thoughts and tender moments. There is time for casual walks in crunchy leaves, astronomical studies on cold, clear nights, holding hands by firelight.

This is mountain living.

HERB RAU

STOVALL HOUSE

The Stovall House, built in 1837 as a private residence, has recently been renovated by Ham and Kathy Schwartz and opened as a country inn. Based on its prominent location and history in the Sautee Valley, the house is listed in the National Register of Historic Places. The original structure, one of the first residences in the area after the departure of the Cherokee Indians, was built for Moses Harshaw, a colorful character in the history of the area who was reputed to be "the meanest man who ever lived." Although an attorney by profession, he worked the land as a farmer and a gold miner. The Inn is named after the William Stovall family who resided in the house from 1893 until the late 1940's. The Stovalls were also important in the development of the valley and many descendents still live in the area.

One of the finest settings in the Northeast Georgia mountains provides views which can be enjoyed from the restaurant, the five guest rooms or the wrap-around porch. Room rates include breakfast, so please join us.

Stovall House, The, GA 255, Route 1, P.O. Box 103 A,
Sautee, Georgia 30571, (404) 878-3355.

DEEP DISH PEACH PIE

Pastry:

¼ teaspoon salt
¾ cup flour, sifted
2 tablespoons shortening
1½ tablespoons ice cold water

Sift salt with flour and cut in shortening with fork until broken into pieces. Add water in several places. Mix with spoon into ball and roll into flattened ball with hands. Place on floured board and roll out to desired thickness.

4 cups firm ripe peaches, peeled and sliced
1 cup brown sugar
2 tablespoons flour
2 tablespoons butter
1 thick slice of lemon, including rind
¾ cup boiling water

Line sides of well-greased deep pottery baking dish with ½ of the pastry and put in the peeled and sliced peaches. Mix sugar, flour, butter, lemon and boiling water in saucepan. Bring to boil, squeeze and remove lemon and pour liquid over peaches. Roll remaining pastry ¼-inch thick, cut with biscuit cutter, place over peaches with space between rounds for steam to escape. Bake at 375 degrees for 40 minutes until fruit is juicy and crust is golden brown.

Kathy Schwartz
Stovall House

SPINACH DIP

1 package frozen spinach, thawed, chopped
2 cups mayonnaise
2 cups dairy sour cream
1 teaspoon Worcestershire sauce
½ cup onion, finely minced
3 sprigs parsley, finely snipped
½ teaspoon celery salt
½ teaspoon garlic salt
1 dash paprika
3 to 4 drops Tabasco

Thaw spinach, squeezing out all moisture. Break compressed spinach with fork. Add remaining ingredients. Mix well, chill 1 hour before serving. Place in compote, hollowed red cabbage head, etc. Place in center of large platter. Arrange fresh asparagus spears, sliced mushrooms, sliced cauliflower buds, sliced broccoli flowerets, sliced zucchini, etc., around dip. Separate vegetables with curly endive. Garnish endive with cherry tomatoes.

Unicoi State Park

UNICOI STATE PARK

LODGING: Unicoi's versatile 100 room lodge serves conference groups, families and individuals.

Guest rooms are located in four adjacent buildings, are cedar paneled, carpeted, with individual temperature controls and telephones. Each cluster has a commons room where comfortable sofas, chairs and a free standing fireplace create a perfect atmosphere for informal gatherings.

COTTAGES: Twenty of the cottages at Unicoi were designed so that trees and plants would not have to be bulldozed away for construction sites. Five other cottages are of conventional design. All cottages are completely furnished and equipped with cooking utentils, silverware, stove, refrigerator, fireplace, electric heat, hot water, linens and blankets.

Cottages are rented for a minimum period of one week from June through August; and are rented for two nights minimum, with a maximum of two weeks during the remainder of the year.

CONFERENCE: Unicoi houses Georgia's only state-operated Lodge/ Conference Center and will accommodate 10 convening for a seminar or up to 350 gathering for a national meeting. Unicoi Lodge was designed and built primarily as a Conference Center; the exceptional recreational facilities and tranquil environment enhance this primary function.

Meeting facilities include fully equipped seminar and conference rooms; commons rooms, verandas and amphitheaters for more casual sessions. Unicoi offers the latest audio-visual equipment, such as a built-in sound system and projection booth in our main conference room.

A professional conference staff provides assistance to your group in planning and program presentation.

Programs and meals can be tailored to meet your group's special needs.

RESTAURANT: The specialty at Unicoi's restaurant is mountain trout. Delicious buffets are often served where one price buys all you can eat, including salad, dessert and drink.

Unicoi is famous for its breakfast buffet and Sunday dinner.

The fireplace and peaceful view of the surrounding mountains complement the good food.

Picnics, cookouts and banquets may be arranged for groups. The restaurant is open year round to the public and park guests.

CRAFT SHOP: Appalachian culture is the core of Unicoi's Craftshop. Handcrafts representative of the mountain area convey to the public the folkways and the life of the Southern Appalachians. Featuring mountain toys, dolls, pottery and one of the largest quilt displays in the Southeast, the Unicoi Craftshop benefits not only local craftsmen but the public by presenting a living educational experience.

CAMPING: Secluded campsites, surrounded by woods, provide full benefits to campers with minimal impact on the land. The 96 campsites include 50 recreational vehicle sites, 30 tent sites and 16 hillside platforms called squirrels' nests.

Each site has a picnic table and grill and nearby comfort stations are equipped with hot showers and flush toilets. All campsites have water and the R.V. sites have electricity. A Trading Post in the campground sells camping supplies.

The park offers a variety of outdoor recreational activities including scheduled programs concerning natural resources, folk culture and the history of the north Georgia mountains.

Unicoi State Park, GA 356, P.O. Box 256,
Helen, Georgia 30545, (404) 878-2201.

SWISS CHARD SOUFFLÉ

2 cups bread
1 cup water
2 eggs, separated
1½ cups Swiss chard, cooked, chopped
Salt and pepper to taste

Soak loosely packed bread in water; squeeze out excess water and chop until fine. Combine 2 egg yolks with bread and add seasoning to taste. Fold together the bread mixture and the chard. Beat 2 egg whites and a pinch of salt until stiff and fold into the Swiss chard-bread mixture. Grease a quart soufflé dish and fill with mixture. Set into pan of hot water. Bake at 325 degrees for 25 to 30 minutes.

Amalie Graves
Unicoi State Park

LIVERWURST PÂTÉ

One 8-ounce package Braunschweiger liverwurst
3 tablespoons butter or margarine
6 slices bacon, cooked crisp, drained and crumbled fine
1 spring onion, including tops, finely minced
1 teaspoon caraway seeds (optional)
Dash dill weed

Mash liverwurst with fork. Blend with butter or margarine until smooth. Add other ingredients; blend well until smooth. Pack into crock, cover and chill. Serve with your favorite cracker.

Unicoi State Park
Sam Sosebee

MEXICAN SHRIMP DIP

½ cup onion, chopped
Vegetable oil for sautéing
One #303 can green chili salsa
1 pound American cheese in ½-inch cubes
5 ounces tiny cocktail shrimp, peeled and cooked
Dash cayenne pepper
Tortilla chips

In medium saucepan, sauté onions in oil until translucent. Stir in green chili salsa. Heat to steaming. Add cheese and cook on low heat until melted. Stir in shrimp and pepper. Transfer to small chafing dish or fondue pot. Keep warm; serve with tortilla chips.

Unicoi State Park

ANGELS ON HORSEBACK

8 slices bacon
16 oysters, shucked
Seasoned salt
4 slices white bread
2 tablespoons butter
1 lemon

Cut bacon in half. Partially cook; drain on paper towel. Wrap each oyster with one piece of bacon, securing with wooden pick; sprinkle seasoned salt on each. Place in shallow, ungreased baking pan. Bake in 450-degree preheated oven approximately 10 minutes or until bacon is crisp. Toast bread; spread with butter. Cut bread diagonally into 4 triangles; place an oyster on each triangle. Serve immediately with lemon wedge. Yield: 16.

Unicoi State Park

NACHOS SUPREME

2 pounds ground beef
2¼ ounces taco seasoning mix
1¼ cups water
1½ pounds tortilla chips
1½ cups taco sauce
1 pound Cheddar cheese, shredded

Brown ground beef and drain. Stir in seasoning mix and water. Heat to boiling. Reduce heat; simmer 20 minutes uncovered until liquid is reduced. Place tortilla chips on an ovenproof plate. Top each with one tablespoon of ground beef mixture and 1 teaspoon taco sauce. Sprinkle with cheese. Bake at 400 degrees for 3 minutes until cheese is melted. Serve immediately.

Unicoi State Park

RUMAKI

1 pound sliced bacon
½ cup soy sauce
2 tablespoons sugar
¼ teaspoon ground ginger
1 pound chicken livers
1 #303 can water chestnuts

Cut bacon slices in half; place in shallow baking pan. Partially cook bacon in oven at 375 degrees. Combine soy sauce, sugar and ginger for a marinade. Halve chicken livers and water chestnuts; place these items and the bacon in marinade for 20 to 25 minutes. Then wrap 1 piece of liver and 1 slice of water chestnut with half-slice bacon. Secure with wooden pick. Pour off excess fat from baking pan used for bacon. Place wrapped livers in pan and bake at 450 degrees until bacon is crisp, approximately 10 to 12 minutes. Yield: 36.

Unicoi State Park

APPLE COBBLER

Filling:

5 cups tart apples, peeled, sliced
¾ cup sugar
2 tablespoons flour
½ teaspoon cinnamon
¼ teaspoon salt
1 teaspoon vanilla extract
¼ cup water
1 tablespoon margarine, softened

Batter:

½ cup plain flour, sifted
½ cup sugar
½ teaspoon baking powder
¼ teaspoon salt
2 tablespoons soft margarine
1 egg, slightly beaten

In medium bowl, combine apples, sugar, flour, salt, cinnamon, vanilla and water. Turn into a 9-inch square pan. Dot apples with margarine. Combine all batter ingredients. Beat with wooden spoon until smooth. Drop batter in 9 portions on apples, spacing evenly. Batter will spread during baking. Bake 35 to 40 minutes at 375 degrees or until apples are fork tender, and crust is golden brown. Serve warm with cream. Yield: 6 to 8 servings.

Glen LaRowe
Country House

VEGETABLE SOUP MIX

2 cups butter beans
16 ears corn, cut off cob
1½ cups okra, fried
1 cup sugar
1 quart water
2 gallons tomatoes, quartered
4 onions, chopped
2 hot peppers, cut up
1 cup vinegar
1 pound ground beef, scrambled and browned
2 cups potatoes, boiled and cubed

Cook beans and corn until almost done. Fry okra; combine with all other ingredients and boil for 30 minutes. Seal or freeze after putting into jars or containers. If canning, add 1 teaspoon salt to each quart. If freezing, leave off salt. Before serving add ground beef and potatoes. (The more you add the better the soup.)

Standard Telephone Company, "Kitchen Directory"

STATE PARKS

Unicoi State Park: Located approximately two miles northeast of Helen on Georgia 356; has year-round activities on its unique 1023 acres. Known for its restaurant, conference facilities and cottages shaped like barrels, Unicoi also offers scenic trails through forests and fields. Boating, swimming, fishing and camping are offered, plus courses in folk art, music and natural resources. See recipes from Unicoi State Park in this cookbook under list of contributors. Unicoi State Park, GA 356, Box 256, Helen, Georgia 30545 (404) 878-2201.

Anna Ruby Falls: Located off Georgia Highway 356 near Unicoi State Park; has two falls, one dropping 153 feet and the other 50 feet. Surrounded by 1600 acres managed by the United States Forest Service, this beautiful area has picnic areas, restrooms, and a pleasant hike of less than ½ mile from the parking area to the falls, with benches along the path. Unicoi State Park is nearby with various facilities for camping and recreation.

Moccasin Creek State Park: Located 25 miles north of Clarkesville in Rabun County on Georgia 197. The park covers 31 acres at an altitude of 1,850 feet on Lake Burton. Activities include boating, fishing, picnicking, hiking, and water skiing. There are 53 tent/trailer sites. Moccasin Creek State Park is adjacent to the Georgia Department of Natural Resources Fish Hatchery. A brochure is available from Moccasin Creek State Park. Moccasin Creek State Park, GA 197, Route 1, Clarkesville, Georgia 30523 (404) 947-3194.
State Game and Fish Commission, Lake Burton, Route 1, Clarkesville, Georgia 30523 (404) 947-3112.

Amicalola Falls State Park: Located 20 miles west of Dahlonega off Georgia 52; features the state's highest waterfall, the 729-foot Amicalola Falls, which is accessible by car or hiking trail. The 400-acre park is near the southern end of the Appalachian Trail. The trail starts 6.9 miles above the falls at Springer Mountain. There are other well maintained trails within the park, as well as 25 campsites and 15 cottages. A brochure is available. Amicalola Falls State Park, Star Route, Dawsonville, Georgia 30543, (404) 265-2885.

Black Rock Mountain State Park: Located off US 23 & 441 in Mountain City, it is the highest of Georgia's state parks with a maximum elevation of 3,800 feet. Special summer programs include wildlife tours, mountain music, craft demonstrations and historical presentations. There are 53 campsites and 10 cottages. A brochure is available. Black Rock Mountain State Park, Mountain City, Georgia 30562, (404) 746-2141.

Brasstown Bald: The highest mountain in Georgia, it offers three challenging trails to its summit of 4,784 feet. These are moderate to strenuous trails. For those who wish to ride, a shuttle bus carries visitors from the parking area to the top. An observation deck with a spectacular 360 degree view of the mountains, a picnic area and the Brasstown Bald Visitor Information Center provide a delightful excursion. Ten miles north of Helen on Georgia Highway 75, turn west on Georgia 66.

LAKES

Lake Burton: Located in Rabun County off Georgia 197. This lake offers fishing, boating, swimming and other water sports. There are five public recreation facilities including concessions, marinas and launching ramps. A public beach is located south of US·76 on the Charlie Mountain Road.

Lake Rabun: Located in Rabun County off Georgia 197 and old US 23 & 441. The lake offers fishing, boating, swimming and other water sports. There are three public recreation facilities including concessions, marina, launching ramp and camping.

Lake Seed: Located in Rabun County off Georgia 197 and old US 23 & 441. There are no public recreation facilities on this lake.

Other lakes in the region include:

Lake Tallulah: In Rabun County off US 23 & 441.
Lake Tugaloo: In Rabun County off US 23 & 441.
Lake Yonah: In Habersham County off US 23 & 441.
Lake Russell: In Habersham County off US 123, two miles north of Cornelia.

NORTHEAST GEORGIA RIVERS

Amicalola: Located in Dawson County, the "best whitewater creek in the state" is accessible from Georgia 52, 53, 136. Activities include fishing and boating and sections for all levels of canoeing. Scenery is exceptionally beautiful, with sheer rock faces rising several hundred feet from the water's edge. Amicalola Falls State Park brochure gives details.

Chattahoochee: Sections of this beautiful river, which runs from north of Helen to the Gulf of Mexico, are located in Habersham, White and Hall counties (accessible from Georgia 75, 115, 52.) Exciting whitewater canoeing, camping, kayaking, rafting, fishing and floating are popular along the Chattahoochee.

Chattooga: Located in Rabun County, accessible from Georgia 28 and US 76, this is one of the most spectacular Appalachian waterways and one of the longest free-flowing rivers in the southeast. Over fifty miles of the unsurpassed beauty of the Chattooga are included in the prestigious National Wild and Scenic River System. Expert paddlers enjoy this river, which can be quite dangerous in some sections. Other activities include fishing, hiking, rafting and kayaking. Licensed outfitters can be contacted for whitewater excursions.

Soque: A tributary of the Chattahoochee, some areas are Chattahoochee National Forest land and some areas along this river are popular with trout fishermen. Most of the land along the Soque River is private property and is posted so check with the Georgia Game and Fish Department for legal fishing areas. They will also tell you about streams that are open to trout fishermen. The line between Rabun and Habersham Counties runs along the ridge of Goshen Mountain and Hickory Nut Mountain and forms a divide. The water to the southwest of that ridge forms the Soque River watershed. The Soque River joins the Chattahoochee River in White and Habersham Counties and flows into Lake Lanier, on past Atlanta and eventually into the Gulf of Mexico. In Habersham County it runs along or crosses GA 197, 115 and 105.

Tallulah: A small stream of outstanding beauty, the Tallulah has a variety of activities to offer. These include picnic areas, fishing, rafting and floating, and the river is appropriate for beginners to advanced canoeing. The ridge of Goshen Mountain and of Hickory Nut Mountain forms the county line between Rabun County and Habersham County. Northeast of this ridge the water flows into the Tallulah River which helps form the Savannah River. This water forms Hartwell Lake, Clark Hill Lake and flows on into Savannah and the Atlantic Ocean. Located in Townes and Rabun Counties, it is accessible from US 76, 23 & 441.

WATERFALLS

Amicalola Falls: Located in Amicalola Falls State Park in Dawson County northwest of Dawsonville from GA 136, 183 and 52. Amicalola, the highest falls in the state, cascades down 729 feet. Additional information is available in the State Park brochure.

Anna Ruby Falls: Located in Unicoi State Park north of Helen from GA 356. Anna Ruby Falls is actually two falls—one from Curtis Creek which drops 153 feet and the other from York Creek which drops 50 feet. Brochure available from the U.S. Forest Service.

Tallulah Falls: Located on US 23 & 441 at Tallulah Falls, Georgia, in Rabun County. There are five falls in the bottom of Tallulah Gorge. The main water flow has been diverted for the production of electricity.

Minnehaha Falls: Located seven miles west of US 23 & 441 south of Clayton, make a left turn on the dirt road just below the Seed Lake Dam, follow for two miles to the Forest Service sign pointing to falls. Falls drop approximately 50 feet.

Becky Branch Falls: Located three miles east of Clayton off Warwoman Road directly across from Warwoman Dell Recreation Area. Round trip hike from parking area approximately ⅓ of a mile. Very steep.

Holcomb Creek Falls/Ammons Creek Falls: Located thirteen miles east of Clayton off Warwoman Road. Just after Warwoman crosses the Chattooga River is Forest Service road 86. Follow this road for approximately seven miles to sign pointing to falls. The first falls on the trail is Holcomb Creek which drops approximately 200 feet. About ⅓ of a mile beyond on the same trail is Ammons Creek which drops approximately 150 feet. Round trip hike from parking area is approximately three miles.

In addition to the above there are many more exciting and beautiful waterfalls in the region.

HIKING TRAILS

The Northeast Georgia mountain region contains some of the most scenic trails that may be found anywhere in the nation. Several of the shorter hiking trails are to be found in the National Forest Recreation Areas. Almost all of the State Parks have hiking trails. This section is devoted to two of the most beautiful and demanding trails in the Southeastern United States.

THE APPALACHIAN TRAIL

The Appalachian Trail, the longest continuous trail in the east, represents the efforts of thousands of private citizens working toward the common goal of a marked trail along the entire length of the major mountain range known as the Appalachians. The trail traverses over 2,000 miles from Springer Mountain, Georgia, through 14 states, to Mt. Katahdin, Maine. In Georgia, the trail covers 79 miles to Bly Gap on the North Carolina border. There is an eight mile approach trail to Springer Mountain (altitude 3,782 feet) from Amicalola Falls State Park. Many hikers feel that the Georgia portion of the trail is the most scenic along the entire trail. The Appalachian Trail crosses several major state and US highways and may be entered at any of these points.

THE BARTRAM TRAIL

The Bartram Trail is named for the young Quaker naturalist, William Bartram. Bartram journeyed through many miles of the extreme northeastern portions of the region in Rabun County during 1773-1776. An account of his journey stands as a monument to discipline, art and the appreciation of life; it was published in 1791. The Bartram Trail in Rabun County covers 37 miles of rugged, up-and-down hiking. It includes several beautiful waterfalls, wildlife areas, and the observation tower on Rabun Bald Mountain (4,696 feet). Its semicircular path is conveniently bisected by Warwoman Road. Shorter hikes of 18½ miles each may be taken if desired. To reach the northernmost entrance of the trail, turn east off US 441 and travel approximately seven miles on GA/NC 106/246 to the Village Superette store and then turn right on Bald Mountain Road. This paved road becomes gravel after two miles and forks after another ½ mile. Go left at the fork; the Bartram Trail crosses the road after approximately 1½ miles. Warwoman Dell recreation area, which marks the trail's midpoint, is located three miles east of Clayton on Warwoman Road. The end of the trail in Georgia meets GA 28 just a few yards from the Chattooga River's north bank.

FAIRS & FESTIVALS

Northeast Georgia is blessed with some of the most interesting and varied fairs and festivals in the state. A few of the major ones are discussed here. Exact dates of fairs and festivals will be furnished to the Visitor Information Centers in the communities prior to the events.

Mountain Laurel Festival: Held in mid-May each year in Clarkesville, Georgia, at the height of the blooming of the mountain laurel. The three-day festival in Clarkesville is packed with such activities as a beauty pageant, bluegrass music, an army band performance, collectibles sales, home-grown and home-baked foods, parachute jumping, a parade of floats manned entirely by children (for the enjoyment of "children" of all ages), square dancing, clogging, and arts and crafts exhibits. The Mountain Laurel Festival is the culmination of a two week festival of color, a time to enjoy Nature's gift of the rebirth of springtime. Follow any of the roads on the maps in this Cookbook Guide to the Northeast Georgia Mountains; see mile after mile of blooming laurel and experience for yourself the enjoyment of springtime.

Georgia Mountain Fair: Held each year in the first two weeks of August in the Towns County park west of Hiawassee on US 76. Activities include local crafts, country, bluegrass and gospel music by local musicians and major recording artists in each field. General fair rides available.

Fall Festival: Held in Cleveland, Georgia, the middle two weeks of October. As fall in North Georgia begins, one will find the spectacular beauty of the fall leaf colors at their peak. Many fairs and festivals are held at this time of the year in the North Georgia mountains and the one at Cleveland, Georgia is a fine example. Come to the Northeast Georgia mountains in October, and leisurely travel any of the roads found in this Cookbook Guide to enjoy our fall.

Oktoberfest in Helen: Oktoberfest comes to Helen every September and lasts until early October because the harvest season is early, the crops are in and it's time to celebrate! And, an "old country" Bavarian celebration it is with German music by oompah German bands, polka dancing, German singing, leiderhosen, bier, sauerbraten, beer, Wiener Schnitzel, clogging and the list of fun, food and drink goes on. Oktoberfest: Helen, Georgia, every weekend early September to early October every year.

CAMPING

Northeast Georgia is a camping paradise. The areas shown here are all within or just a little over 100 miles of Atlanta. There are thousands of campsites ranging from the most primitive tent sites to sites with full hook-ups large enough to accommodate the longest trailer or motor home. All are scenic; all have easy access to the entire beautiful Northeast Georgia mountains.

CLARKESVILLE:

Tallulah Falls: 12 miles north on US 441 & 23.
Raymond's Campground: 17 miles north of Clarkesville on GA 197, near Lake Burton.
Wagon Wheel Campground: Old Chimney Mountain Road, 12 miles north of Clarkesville just off intersection of GA 255 and GA 197.
Moccasin Creek State Park: 25 miles north of Clarkesville on GA 197.
Terrora Park: at Terrora Visitors Center, 12 miles north of Clarkesville on US 441 & 23.

CLAYTON:

Andy's Trout Farm: 6 miles north on US 441 from Clayton. At Dillard turn west on Betty's Creek Road for 5 miles and follow signs.
Lake Burton Campsites: Tiger Road near Lake Burton.
Rabun Beach and Camping Area: 6½ miles south on US 23 & 441, 1¾ miles south on GA 15, then 4¾ miles west on County 10.
Tallulah River Camping Area: 8 miles southwest on US 76, 4¼ miles north on county road, then 1¼ miles northwest on Forest Service Road 70.
Tate Branch Camping Area: 8 miles southwest on US 76, 4¼ miles north on county road, then 4 miles northwest on Forest Service Road 70.

CLEVELAND:

Desoto Falls Camping Area: 14¾ miles northwest on US 129.
Mountain Shadows: GA 356 north of US 129.

CORNELIA:

Lake Russell Camping Area: ½ mile northeast on US 123, 1 mile southeast on Forest Service Road 63, then 2¾ miles southeast on Forest Service Road 59.

DAHLONEGA:

Woody Gap Public Use Area: 14 miles north on GA 60.
DeSoto Falls Public Use Area: approximately 16 miles north of Dahlonega on US 19.
Dockery Lake Camping Area: 11½ miles north on GA 60, then ¾ mile northeast on Forest Service Road.
Waters Creek Camping Area: 12¼ miles northeast on US 19, then 1 mile northwest on Forest Service Road 34.

DILLARD:

Betty's Creek Recreation Area: 4¼ miles west on Betty's Creek Road, 1½ miles west following signs on dirt road.
Andy's Trout Farm: 5 miles west of Dillard just off of Betty's Creek Road.

HELEN:

Andrews Cove Camping Area: 6 miles north on GA 75.
Unicoi State Park: on GA 356 just east of Robertstown.
Gold Valley Campground: off GA 356 east of Robertstown.

For further information write or call:

Georgia Mountains Travel Association, P.O. Box 9, Tallulah Falls, Georgia 30573

Greater Helen Area Chamber of Commerce, P.O. Box 192, Helen, Georgia 30545 (404) 878-2521

Dahlonega-Lumpkin County Chamber of Commerce, P.O. Box 386, Dahlonega, Georgia 30533 (404) 864-3391.

Habersham County Chamber of Commerce, P.O. Box 366, Cornelia, Georgia 30531 (404) 778-4654.

Rabun County Chamber of Commerce, P.O. Box 761, Clayton, Georgia 30525 (404) 782-4812.

Georgia Department of Industry & Trade, Tourism Division, Box 1776, Atlanta, Georgia 30301, (404) 656-3545. Call or write for a copy of *SPECIAL EVENTS IN GEORGIA.* It is published every 6 months.

Bruce Galphin is editor and publisher of *WINEWS,* a bi-monthly newsletter of wine events and evaluations. He has written about wine for a variety of newspapers and magazines since 1970, and he has traveled extensively in the wine areas of Europe and California. His wine articles are presently published in the Atlanta Weekly section of the Sunday edition of *THE ATLANTA JOURNAL and THE ATLANTA CONSTITUTION,* and in *SOUTHERN ACCENTS.*

For a free copy of *WINEWS* address request to: *WINEWS,* 217 Westminster Dr. N.E., Atlanta, Georgia 30309.

GALPHIN ON WINE

If this book were devoted solely to native product, a wine chapter would be concerned mainly with muscadine. Though that grape with the rhinoseros hide and the sweet, chewy pulp makes delightful jelly, only a few devotees would serve the fermented version with meals.

Wine is a fairly new experience for post-Prohibition Americans. The so-called wine boom is a phenomenon of the Seventies and Eighties. It started in large cities and only gradually rippled into the countryside.

Furthermore, the mountains' distance from wholesale distributing houses makes it difficult for local restaurants and stores to maintain a broad stock. On Georgia mountain dinner tables, you're still more likely to find iced tea, coffee, beer or even harder stuff.

But wine is growing in availability and popularity as diners discover the special pleasures of well-matched food and drink. California labels and a few imports join the New York state wines which have had a small but established following for many years. Wines are available in some grocery stores as well as restaurants. A few mountain area farmers are experimenting with varieties of grapes grown in Europe and California.

It's a good idea to check a restaurant's wine policy. Some have wine, some don't. Some allow patrons to bring their own bottles, whether or not they serve wine; some of these may charge brown-baggers "corkage" fees, while others do not.

Supply problems aside, what wines go with mountain menu specialties?

The process of choosing wine for a given dish is the same no matter what the food's origins. It's true that in some parts of the world where only a few styles of wine are made, the local cuisine fits them beautifully—Burgundy with its rich sauces and bounteous butter, Alsace with its sausages and goose liver patés, etc. Whether the dishes or the wine styles came first is a chicken-and-egg question.

But in America we are blessed with a wide range of wine flavors and styles, both home-grown and imported. Similarly, we have borrowed and adapted cuisines from around the world to add to our own.

We're like a painter whose palette has a full range of colors: We can paint culinary pictures of great subtlety and great precision.

Some wine books offer tables recommending specific wines with specific dishes. Tables generally are all right as far as they go, but they ignore the ifs and the ors. Beware of any list that says "Wine X goes with chicken." Depending on how the chicken is cooked and seasoned, for example, you may want to pour a white wine or a red wine, a wine of simple flavors or a complex one.

Because excellent trout are available fresh from the streams of the mountains, trout is a popular dish in the region. One recipe in this book, trout almondine, has just a few straightforward flavors: trout, butter, parsley and almonds. A California Sauvignon Blanc or white wine from Bordeaux (made in part from Sauvignon Blanc grapes) would match those flavors nicely.

But the recipe for spinach-stuffed trout is a busy blending of many flavors: trout, butter, mushrooms, spinach, tarragon, parsley, orange and lemon. These multiple flavors would overwhelm a mild-flavored wine. A spicy Gewurztraminer (from California or France's Alsace district) could hold its own in that company, though.

A primary consideration in matching wine with food, then, is flavor. Are the flavors of the dish and the wine compatible, or do they clash?

A related consideration is weight or texture. Think of a thick cut of prime rib beef. Think of a dark Cabernet Sauvignon or Bordeaux red, then think of a rosé. Which would match the beef better? Despite occasional advice that "rosé goes with anything," the heavier red wine is the better choice. The rosé would taste watery ("light-bodied") by contrast. Yet that same rosé might be delightful with some cold boiled chicken.

Sweetness is another factor in matching. Wines for main courses—especially meat dishes—should be dry. Truly sweet wines are best saved for dessert. In between, slightly sweet white wines (German Rhines and Mosels, some California Chenin Blancs, etc.) sometimes go well with fowl and other light dishes.

That raises another important factor: color. The rule of thumb is that red wines go with red meat, white wines with white dishes (poultry and fish). The red-with-red has fewer exceptions than white-with-white. True, the thought of red Burgundy with trout sets your teeth on edge. But many preparations of chicken (including the classic *cog au vin)* call for red wine. And believe it or not, red Burgundy can be delicious with lobster, though white Burgundy (Chardonnay) can, too.

The more you get into wine, the more exceptions you encounter. A person truly interested in wine must plunge on and on, sampling different styles and labels, learning both family kinships and individual differences of given grapes. But for a short overview such as this, the general similarities of certain wine types are more important than subtle distinctions. Availability also must be considered.

More than 70 per cent of the wine sold in America is produced in California. And of that about 80 per cent is what is called "generic"—that is, wines blended from different grapes and different growing regions. Generics borrow famous European names: Chablis, Burgundy, Rhine, Chianti. California wines with these names are the ones most likely encountered in grocery stores and short restaurant lists. They can be well made and reasonably priced, but the names do little to define them. Trying to match them with a diverse menu is like a painter's trying to capture a scene with only three or four colors on his palette.

About 20 per cent of California's wines are "varietal"—i.e., named for the principal grape in the wine.

In Europe, the naming system is different: Wines (at least most of those exported to America) are named for the area where they are grown.

Because of strict appellation laws in France, Germany, Italy and increasingly in Spain, if you know the place name, you also can know what grapes are permitted for that label. Here is a brief taste profile of some principal grape types:

WHITES

Chardonnay (sometimes called Pinot Chardonnay; the grape of white Burgundies). Slightly apple-y flavor. Usually given oak-barrel aging and thus a hint of vanilla. Excellent with scale fish, veal or fowl with white sauce, buttery dishes, cheese quiches.

Sauvignon Blanc (often called Fumé Blanc, in France Sancerre, Pouilly-Fumé or, blended with another grape, white Bordeaux). Compared with Chardonnay, rather green in taste, sharper-edged, sometimes grassy. Good with smoked fish or fowl, slightly tart sauces, some omeletes and soufflés.

Johannisberg Riesling (and various Rhines and Mosels). A perfumy wine, typically a little sweet (except in Alsace). Some "late harvest" versions dessert-sweet. Good with shellfish, fresh non-citrus fruit, shrimp, some quiches.

Chenin Blanc (in France, Vouvray). Distinct fruity nose makes it popular in California "Chablis" blends. Made dry, medium sweet, and occasionally quite sweet. Dry version good with scale fish, chicken; sweeter with fresh fruit.

Gewurztraminer. Spicy and fruity. Good in dishes with mixtures of herbs and spices, even Oriental foods.

REDS

Cabernet Sauvignon (the principal grape of most fine red Bordeaux). Distinct berry flavor. Ranges from light to heavy body. Fine with beef in natural gravy, lamb, pork, some game fowl.

Zinfandel. No comparable European wine. A touch of spice along with wild fruit or blackberry flavor. Very versatile red for beef, fowl, game, cheese.

Pinot Noir (the red wines of Burgundy). California version rarely approaches the fruity, rich character of French Burgundies. Good with richly sauced meats, game fowl, cheese, some poultry.

Napa Gamay (in France, Beaujolais) and its cousin Gamay Beaujolais. Fruitier and lighter than Burgundies but good with lighter versions of similar dishes.

Petite sirah (in France, Hermitage, Cotes-du-Rhone, Chateauneuf-du-Pape). Heavy-bodied, dark red wine. Pour with venison and other game, heavily sauced beef.

Bruce Galphin

INDEX

NOTES

discover
the northeast
GEORGIA
MOUNTAINS

JOHN KOLLOCK, a native of Northeast Georgia, began his training in theatre as an actor, scene designer and makeup artist. From there he moved into animated films and free lance commercial art.

His lively pen and ink drawings made him popular as an illustrator of articles and books.

Later he began to combine a lifelong interest in the historic past of his mountain area with his ability to write, and produced a number of articles for *Georgia Magazine.* This led to books of his own including *These Gentle Hills, The Long Afternoon* and *Meg's World.*

John began painting in the early 1960's, and found that watercolor was the perfect medium for him. It gave him the freedom to work loosely and capture the mood of a subject, and still add the calligraphic detail for which he had become known.

In his painting John seeks to express a mood of weather, season, or remembered moments. He feels that a painting must have a life of its own and say something to him before it is finished.

See page 114 for information on the family operated *"Saturday Shop."*

JAY and CATHY BUCEK are the owners of the Mark of the Potter.

Jay's background includes a Masters of Fine Arts from North Texas State University. He has taught pottery at several universities in the South and has been making pottery for a living since 1972.

Cathy received a Bachelor of Fine Arts degree in 1980 from North Texas State University. In addition to making pottery, Cathy is co-owner and manager of Mark of the Potter.

Somethin's Cookin' in the Mountains has sold 50,000 copies and is in its 6th printing.

Please see pages 56 and 98 for information on Mark of the Potter.

COLOR PRINT of the COVER

Please send me a full color print of the cover of SOMETHIN'S COOKIN' in the MOUNTAINS 11 x 15 inches with canvas texture finish suitable for framing for $5.00 including postage and handling. (Georgia residents add 20¢ sales tax).

Name ______________________________

Address ______________________________

City__________________ State__________________ Zip__________

Make check payable to SOQUE PUBLISHERS Route 3, Clarkesville, Georgia 30523

Please send me the following copies of NORTHEAST GEORGIA—1733 at $1.50 each plus 30¢ postage and handling fee.

Non-residents—$1.50 plus 30¢ = $1.80 each __________ copies

Residents of Georgia add sales tax of 8¢ to above
= $1.88 each __________ copies

Name ______________________________

Address ______________________________

City ______________________________

State __________________ Zip__________

Make check payable to *SOQUE PUBLISHERS* Route 3, Clarkesville, Georgia 30523

SOMETHIN'S COOKIN' in the MOUNTAINS will make a perfect gift for any occasion. Complete the order blank below and order one for a friend today. Then, complete the gift card and we will include it with the book when we mail it, or perhaps you may wish to include your own gift card.

TO:

FROM:

SOMETHIN'S
COOKIN'
in the
MOUNTAINS
a COOKBOOK GUIDEBOOK
to NORTHEAST GEORGIA

Reorder Additional Copies

Please send me the following copies of SOMETHIN'S COOKIN' in the MOUNTAINS at $9.95 each plus postage and handling fee.

Non-residents—$9.95 plus $1.25 = $11.20 each __________ copies

Georgia residents add 40¢ sales tax = $11.60 each __________ copies

Name ______________________________

Address ______________________________

City__________ State__________ Zip__________

Make check payable to SOQUE PUBLISHERS Route 3, Clarkesville, Georgia 30523 Hard Back __________ Spiral __________

Please personalize to: ______________________________
Name

Please send me the following copies of SOMETHIN'S COOKIN' in the MOUNTAINS at $9.95 each plus postage and handling fee.

Non-residents—$9.95 plus $1.25 = $11.20 each __________ copies

Georgia residents add 40¢ sales tax = $11.60 each __________ copies

Name ______________________________

Address ______________________________

City__________ State__________ Zip__________

Make check payable to SOQUE PUBLISHERS Route 3, Clarkesville, Georgia 30523 Hard Back __________ Spiral __________

Please personalize to: ______________________________
Name

Please send me the following copies of SOMETHIN'S COOKIN' in the MOUNTAINS at $9.95 each plus postage and handling fee.

Non-residents—$9.95 plus $1.25 = $11.20 each __________ copies

Georgia residents add 40¢ sales tax = $11.60 each __________ copies

Name ______________________________

Address ______________________________

City__________ State__________ Zip__________

Make check payable to SOQUE PUBLISHERS Route 3, Clarkesville, Georgia 30523 Hard Back __________ Spiral __________

Please personalize to: ______________________________
Name

Would you please send us the names of shops in your area that would be interested in selling "SOMETHIN'S COOKIN' IN THE MOUNTAINS."

Would you please send us the names of shops in your area that would be interested in selling "SOMETHIN'S COOKIN' IN THE MOUNTAINS."

Would you please send us the names of shops in your area that would be interested in selling "SOMETHIN'S COOKIN' IN THE MOUNTAINS."

Please send me the following copies of SOMETHIN'S COOKIN' in the MOUNTAINS at $9.95 each plus postage and handling fee.

Non-residents—$9.95 plus $1.25 = $11.20 each ____________ copies

Georgia residents add 40¢ sales tax = $11.60 each ____________ copies

Name ____

Address ____

City____________________ State________________ Zip__________

Make check payable to SOQUE PUBLISHERS Route 3, Clarkesville, Georgia 30523 Hard Back ____________ Spiral ____________

Please personalize to: ______________________________
Name

Please send me the following copies of SOMETHIN'S COOKIN' in the MOUNTAINS at $9.95 each plus postage and handling fee.

Non-residents—$9.95 plus $1.25 = $11.20 each ____________ copies

Georgia residents add 40¢ sales tax = $11.60 each ____________ copies

Name ____

Address ____

City____________________ State________________ Zip__________

Make check payable to SOQUE PUBLISHERS Route 3, Clarkesville, Georgia 30523 Hard Back ____________ Spiral ____________

Please personalize to: ______________________________
Name

Please send me the following copies of SOMETHIN'S COOKIN' in the MOUNTAINS at $9.95 each plus postage and handling fee.

Non-residents—$9.95 plus $1.25 = $11.20 each ____________ copies

Georgia residents add 40¢ sales tax = $11.60 each ____________ copies

Name ____

Address ____

City____________________ State________________ Zip__________

Make check payable to SOQUE PUBLISHERS Route 3, Clarkesville, Georgia 30523 Hard Back ____________ Spiral ____________

Please personalize to: ______________________________
Name

Reorder Additional Copies

Would you please send us the names of shops in your area that would be interested in selling "SOMETHIN'S COOKIN' IN THE MOUNTAINS."

____

____

____

____

Would you please send us the names of shops in your area that would be interested in selling "SOMETHIN'S COOKIN' IN THE MOUNTAINS."

____

____

____

____

Would you please send us the names of shops in your area that would be interested in selling "SOMETHIN'S COOKIN' IN THE MOUNTAINS."

____

____

____

____